Ruthie Deeply

VINCENT PALMIERI

Copyright © 2021 Vincent Palmieri
All rights reserved
First Edition

NEWMAN SPRINGS PUBLISHING
320 Broad Street
Red Bank, NJ 07701

First originally published by Newman Springs Publishing 2021

ISBN 978-1-63692-309-3 (Paperback)
ISBN 978-1-63692-310-9 (Digital)

Printed in the United States of America

To all the New York State foster care system residents,
past and present, whose stories will never be told

Today, again, the whirr of a vacuum cleaner, sounds of cups and saucers clinking in the kitchen sink while being washed, and a feminine figure outside my bedroom door, a broom or mop or dustpan in hand. Thus, I, Vincent Palmieri, begin my lifelong relationship with Ruth Richardson Morgan. Yet, this narrative begins much before my time as we begin to unravel it in September 2014. It begins much more deeply. It begins with Ruthie and Loretta. It begins in 1934, in the throes of the Great Depression. It begins with *Ruthie deeply*.

Prologue

Setting the Stage

The Depression is raging. Massive unemployment, soup kitchens, the Dust Bowl—what else could possibly go wrong? Atrocious, large-scale problems all across the United States. Still, small-scale, very small-scale issues were active but incomprehensible to Ruthie's four-month-old psyche. Small issues compared to those massive problems in the United States but survival-level issues for Ruth and Loretta that would be the driving forces of their lives over the next twenty-five years. Food, water, protection from the elements, medical care, and abandonment. Lack of the prior and the reality of the latter. A stark cold reality looming outside the door, and no one to help them see their way through it. Only a handful of people with biological but minimal emotional attachment to both children existed. Here begins an irresistible human tale that begs to be told and teaches timeless human values. Values pure, illuminating, and perfectly aligned with the human experience. Lessons that will never void as long as mankind travels the face of this beautiful green earth.

They were infants at the mercy of the Oneida County Boarding Home and its employees. Here, Ruthie and Loretta begin their long trying experience, in her own words, "as children at the hands of adults."

Inside Ruth and Loretta's world through birth and the 1940s, she remembers very little. In the world, a tumultuous scenario was unfolding. The Japanese had already invaded and occupied China. They were now in the impressment business with the advent of the "comfort women," those forced into the various purposes of the Imperial Japanese Armed Forces. The military concept of "island hopping" was being formulated by Hirohito and his advisors. The practice would be to move through the Pacific Islands to eventually reach the West Coast of the United States. That concept brought the United States into World War II with the attack on Pearl Harbor. While in America, Japanese Americans were being interned in camps throughout the United States.

The situation in Europe was slowly beginning to inflame. In late 1938, with the Kristallnacht, anti-Semitism burst on to the European stage. Also in 1938, Germany was allowed to annex the Sudetenland soon after they invaded Poland then France. Italy, being part of the Axis powers, invaded East Africa, only to be repelled by the Ethiopians.

Of course all of these happenings were out of Ruth's realm. George Herman "Babe" Ruth Jr. was still a huge factor in America's love affair with baseball. Babe Didrikson also burst on to the scene as one of the first female golf figures. Her golf swing was effortless, and her shots were impeccable. Even the National Football League was loosely organized and playing games. "Escapist movies" took the average American out of the uncertainly and hardship of the day into a world that distracted them from their problems and reinforced their values. In order to calm a quickly evolving business downturn, Franklin Roosevelt responded with his historic "fireside chats" by way of an innovative medium called the radio. The Works Project Administration (WPA) and the Civilian Conservation Corps (CCC) were putting able-bodied Americans of all skills and abilities to work plying their trades and learning new ones. History now views most of the New Deal programs that FDR initiated as worthwhile, but at that time, he was judged by some to be a traitor to his class. People in America were on the move seeking a better life. FDR continued to communicate a sense of calm and focus for America to deal with her problems. Problems Ruthie was wholly unaware of. As Ruthie turned into her teenage years, her awareness was increasing each day.

Far from that national and international stage, there was a local, personal history connected to all of these grand issues that was also beyond Ruth's and Loretta's comprehension. My own grandparents were living on Orchard Street, working very hard to improve their lot in the midst of this massive economic downturn. Surrounded by families like themselves, they supported each other and kept their families safe. My mother—being age ten, living with her mother and father and seven brothers and sisters—has no idea of Ruthie, nor Ruthie of her, but they would meet soon enough. My father's family, living in Herkimer, were much in the same situation—numerous children, and a family working toward the same conditions. On Orchard Street, very small and close, many families had to interact with the others in a positive way in order to maintain security in a new environment far removed from their earlier Southern European roots. My grandmother, Mary Iocovozzi, I understand, would allow young and old often-hopeless men, to sit on the step on the back of the house and give them something to drink and eat but not allow them in her house. Her actions indicated she understood their plight and wanted to help, but her sense of survival was so strong that she knew she had to protect her family and herself first. Knowingly or unknowingly the residents felt no sense of depravation being that most people were in similar situations. A set of values and mores were unknowingly codified with the purpose of advancing everyone's life. The values were based on respect and cooperation. Although those codes were temporarily put on hold early in the 1940s mostly due to World War II, they returned, starting in 1945, continuing through the early 1960s.

As the Depression deepened, a Southern politician named Huey Long, also known as the King Fish, openly denounced the rich, and he called for the Share Our Wealth program. Long was assassinated in 1935, ending a long career, but his ideas gained a large audience and still have some that adhere to this day. His popularity affected millions of Americans. A Roman Catholic priest named Father Coughlan also emerged at first as a huge supporter of FDR and the New Deal. As the years passed, he evolved into a critic of the New Deal. Father Coughlan was the first religious figure to use radio as a medium, copying FDR, for "fireside chats." After being forced off the air in 1939 mostly due to anti-Semitic views, he continued to see conspiracies in banking and money management practices in the United States, practices mostly managed by Jews. Turmoil and outrageous ideas were the "soup of the day" all across America. All that turmoil unknown to Ruth, since her world was in more turmoil, but on a vastly personal level.

The environment on Orchard Street tended to be relatively calm. Yet, at times, the large issues in America showed themselves on Orchard Street. A section of society called hobos would show themselves, as previously mentioned, often in my grandmother's backyard, being that her yard was along a railroad track. They were generally migratory workers or homeless penniless vagabonds that would board freight trains and crisscross the United States, riding until they choose to get off or were thrown off the train. As I think back to the setting myself, when I was six or seven, a man we called John Peach had taken up residence under the milk station at the end of the street by the Drops. I remember, with someone else, looking under the building, which on the low side was sitting on four-foot stilts, and seeing some blankets and some shoes and other personal items. Thinking back, perhaps John Peach was the last of the 1930s hobos. Behind my grandmother's house, running two miles east and back two miles west, was a New York Railroad Central spur that would pick up and deliver grain to Corrado's Feed Mill and fresh-cut trees to the sawmill of the Union Fork and Hoe Co. to be made into rake, shovel, etc. handles. When a train would pick up or deliver and go back east to connect to the engine on the other side of the Mohawk River in Schuyler, some employees would sleep in a caboose in the off-hours. Those employees would come out on the back steps of the caboose and throw us candy, bubble gum, and sweets, which we would joyfully accept. I am guessing, but I would bet that Ruthie was there having as much fun as possible trying to help herself progress.

Seven or eight large families populated Orchard Street. Ruth's Uncle Wally's family being one of them. Most of those families had seven or eight children in each one, living on a block of about 250 yards. There were Carusos, Ruffalos, Kippers, and numerous

Iocovozzis. The built-in code was that they all looked out for each other. Even people that moved into Orchard Street found themselves quickly absorbed into the neighborhood routine. The summers tended to be hot and dry, and the winters didn't seem as severe. We didn't venture far from home because everything needed was within walking distance. In a matter of three blocks, you could walk to pay your utility bills, buy groceries, walk to work or the bus line and to the numerous bars/restaurants located in the area.

I tell Carol a memory that sticks to me this day as if it happened yesterday. I would walk east on Orchard Street with Joe Reina holding my hand to the corner of Railroad and Orchard Streets to Sam Talerico's store to buy three or four pieces of candy that cost half a penny each. I remember most vividly the walk west back to my grandmother's house, looking into the sun with its warmth, its light, and its dryness. I couldn't have been quite five years old. Anytime you step into something new, it can be frightening; but in this case, it wasn't. It was enlightening. I don't think I have ever experienced anything as emboldening in my life again thus far.

This all comes in to mind by way of a friend named Bob Reina. We sat together this past weekend at breakfast, and I started to tell him the status of *Ruthie Deeply*. It's amazing how having those types of discussions opens up all of my memories from fifty-five years ago. The people that keep coming in and out are really the same. Their names change, but their faces and their families stay the same. The Bible records Jesus never traveling more than fifty miles from where he was born. Many of these people, myself included, have not even gone twenty-five. Jesus was two thousand years ago. No matter how much it seems time has changed, equally it shows it has not.

Carol tells me, "Old sayings always ring true, there is nothing new under the sun."

As we are working our way through *Ruthie Deeply*, for perhaps a year at this point, together Ruthie and I keep encountering people and memories that really light up our brains. Our collective memories, especially from early on, become more evident as we talk and write and write and talk and review her New York State foster care history. The same names and families continually pop up over and over again. I tell Ruth that I recently made the connection as to a guy I have known for a few years in terms of how I knew his family my entire life. When I discuss with Ruth how I knew by him by family, Ruthie immediately knows exactly the family I am talking about.

We both get a huge laugh as I tell her a memory I have that must have happened sixty times when I was a child.

In these days, it would not be appropriate, but when I was four or five years old, I was allowed to walk from my aunt's house to the corner of Orchard Street and Railroad Street to a small premodern convenience owned by a family friend. It was at one time a gas station; at that time, it didn't sell gasoline but had newspapers, candy, bread, everyday items we all use and consume quite rapidly. The building still stands, in much disrepair. I drive by it all the time; my daughter and I walk by it sometimes. I get the biggest laugh out of it every time I go by to this day. The ironic part about all this is I remember the same man who ran the store from those days, and he was my parents' age. As the years went by, I was always happy to see him, and he was equally happy to see me. Sometimes he would spot me in a crowd quicker than I would see him. He passed away many years ago, but I can still see him—flowing gray hair, a big smile, and "Hello, Vinny." The irony goes even further. His son Richard was my cousin's friend; they were both about ten years older than me and were friends for many years. He was a teacher, I was a teacher, my cousin, his friend, was a teacher; we worked together at a local country club in the summer when we were both off work. We always had so much fun and even got in some trouble. Rich has also passed away now. I miss them both, and it makes me sad.

As I made my daily trips east on Orchard Street to Sam's store—I do not recollect it even having a name—I would often pass an elderly neighbor named Nick. Recently, by coincidence, I met a grandson of Nick's, which lit up all sorts of brain waves in my head.

The common dialogue would go like this.

Nick, in broken English, would say, "Whatsa u name?"

I'd quickly reply, "Vincent Palmieri."

"Okay," was his comeback.

This went on for years, as long as the weather complied. After many, many trips up and down the street with the same conversation over and over again, I asked my mother, "Why does this guy keep asking me my name?"

She said, "Just keep telling him your name, he is a family friend for many years."

In the long run, it really paid off for me because at times Nick would give me two or three pennies. When you can buy three or four pieces of candy for a penny at Sam's store, you really made a good deal that day. Couple that with the few pennies my mother gave me a day, the ones my grandpa gave me, plus what my aunt would give me, and perhaps even Ruthie did. I thought for sure I was really living. Oddly, when I started doing business with a friend of mine about three years ago, myself and one of his mechanics were meeting for the first time. When he told me his name, I immediately knew who he was. Besides being a hardworking man, a few years older than me, a musician, and an avid hunter, he and I were cut from the same cloth. I also knew his dad, Nick, but literally had no contact with these people for fifty years. Suddenly there he was. Sometimes I think that Jesus didn't even have to go that fifty miles.

Ruthie bets she must have taken some of those walks to Sam's store with me.

Just as quickly as that memory dissipates, I begin to tell Ruthie how I had seen another childhood mutual friend recently.

I tell Ruth I attended a wake for a childhood friend of my mother's, one of the few that were still alive. Often, when I see people my age or younger or older that I don't see very much anymore, it suddenly reopens memories from up to fifty-five or fifty-six years ago. I spoke with an older yet lifelong friend by the name of Alex, and it reconstituted long-ago-filed memories in my brain. Alex, being about five years older than I, was on my radar for as long as I can remember. He was always more advanced than me, at least to adulthood; he was a very strong athlete and probably the most mischievous person I have ever met right up to this day. He still had the look on his face like, "It's still me Alex, and I am still the same." For the past few years, he had moved to Saranac Lake, New York, for his wife's job so that she could finish the remaining time she had working in the New York State Prison system so she could fully retire. Having finished the remainder of her career, she and Alex returned to live in Frankfort. I was as happy to see him as I think he was to see me.

I went directly over to talk to him and said, "Alex, it's good to see you again."

He shook my hand, hugged me, and replied, "Good to see you too. It's guys like you I miss. How is your mother and father?"

"Good," I replied, "I am going to visit them when I leave here."

We did a little more small talk, and I left to see my father and mother. The next day when my father and mother attended her friend's funeral, Alex was there. My mom told me he came right over, hugged her and my father, told them he had seen me the night before, that they were the kind of people he missed and was very happy to see them again alive and well. I gather, almost the same conversation we had the previous night.

Now, the floodgates were really opened. On Orchard Street, as a child, Alex could always ride his bicycle the fastest, right down the middle of the street with complete abandon and no regard for the traffic. He was always the first person to jump from the highest point above the Drops with no consideration of what rocks, points, or sharp edges lay beneath the surface of the water often in view of John Peach, who got the biggest chuckle out of Alex. Alex was the one who tied a rope to a tree above the surface of the Mohawk River, put a loop in the end of the rope, and was thrilled to swing out over the river while I gasped in horror, certain that each swing would be his last. All the while, in the back of my mind, knowing that I was forbidden to be down by the river by my mother but went anyway. Alex had what is now called swagger, and I was fascinated by him and hoped some of him would rub off on me. Fifty years later, looking back, I think at times it did, and it never hurt me one bit. As a matter of fact, it may have helped me. Alex has been married for probably forty years, has two adult sons and at least one grandchild. Like all of us, his life has had its ups and downs, and he certainly did not calm down much during his thirties and forties. To this day, he is still Alex, and I would never want him to not be. He still has the swagger, the mischievous look in his eyes, and is the kind of person I want to be around, just enough to allow some of him to continue to rub off on me. It has been a great experience in my life to know him and to respect him. I just want him to feel the same way about me, and I think he does. My consciousness swoons back to Orchard Street with Alex, John-John, my aunt Josie, Ruthie, an entire niche of good solid people, and me smack-dab in the middle. Wonderful, exhilarating experiences that can never be replicated for both Ruth and I.

Yet, at the same time completely, beyond my knowledge, there were problems and issues for Ruth that were in some ways smaller than the ones she had in the Syracuse State School but in other ways bigger and still swirling around her.

As the 1940s emerged, Ruth was fully engulfed by the New York State foster care system, and the world was in possibly the worst position it had ever been. The Japanese attack on Pearl Harbor in 1941 launched the United States into World War II. The Imperial Japanese military has expanded well across the Pacific, even reaching into the South Pacific, and the threat was felt as far away as Australia. Deadly battles raged in places like Iwo Jima and Guadalcanal. These tiny specs in the Pacific Ocean became huge strategic positions. Meanwhile, the Nazis in Europe had developed the Final Solution, which ended the lives of 6 million Jews. The integrated system of arresting, deporting, and exterminating Jews was happening all over Europe on a daily basis. This scale of mass murder had never been witnessed before in history. Those returning from World War II wanted to get their lives back to normal as quick as possible. Many were marrying, starting families, and opening businesses, attending college under the GI Bill, and some even returning to high school. Industry in America was changing from a wartime production model to a consumer-based production model. Discoveries made, often inadvertently while doing wartime research, were rapidly morphing into consumer products like the soon-to-come transistor radio, a favorite of teenagers. Early business-applicable computers and software were being developed by budding corporations like IBM. The long-term power of computing was as alien to those early software developers as much as the concept of the World being round was to the Europeans in 1492. The classic philosophy sets the age of reason at the onset of puberty, approximately fourteen years old. As all of this swirled around her, Ruthie was unaware of that world, but the awareness of her world saw an equally ugly and dangerous situation up close. Her world now became well-documented in approximately fifty pages of notes, placements, Social Service histories, etc. that are undeniably complete and horrifying. Couple those reports with Ruth's then gathering awareness and her current recollections as we sit and discuss those pages are as vivid to her as they are appalling to me.

Ruth's history that comes into focus in the late forties and early 1950s is more clear. Dates and times are documented and signed off by physicians, nurses, and various workers. Ruth can now sit and recount her version of many well-documented incidents. She tells Carol and I her side of the story passionately—how else could she? It was her. Ruth remembers Eisenhower first. She had at another time mentioned Truman, but Eisenhower and Kennedy were the first presidents she remembers. For all intents and purposes, she is cut off from the outside world by the policies of the New York State foster care system in both Onondaga and Oneida counties. She had been living in the Syracuse State School for approximately eight years, and every day is a trial. Meanwhile, housing was booming; planned communities such as Levittown New York sprang up overnight. In the middle of all this, in 1955, I was born. Churchill, FDR, and Stalin were long-ago memories, and the diplomatic world was now focused on the Korean Peninsula.

Ruth recalls nothing of sports or movies or music. The exposure she has of everyday living in America was closely controlled. She was wet-packed almost on a daily basis. She was in detention regularly often for being in a "highly excited state." Seclusion came day after day. She left the state school for shopping at Chappell's Department Store. Ruth was given some vacation, and opposite of that, she was accused of being involved in an escape attempt. Much of America was abuzz with the music of Elvis Presley and Chuck Berry.

Alan Freed was in New York City spinning 45s. I lived on Orchard Street with my mom and dad, with my sister upstairs from my aunt and uncle, who purchased the house from my grandparents. My great-grandfather Dee lived with my aunt in the downstairs apartment. My father caught the six thirty bus to go to work at John's Market because he could not afford a car. My mother had at the bottom of our stairs a small hallway where she had a dryer, two chairs, and a sink for washing hair.

Ruth and I were in constant contact living across the street from each other. She was in and out of our apartment and my aunt's too all day long.

Ruth said, "There is a story I have to tell you."

"Go ahead," I said.

She proceeded to tell me how my uncle Jim threw her out of his house because he told my aunt that he didn't want her in his house.

I asked her how she felt about that.

She told me while laughing, "I didn't care one bit."

I was shocked to hear that my uncle Jim would do that. As I remember it, though I knew him for a short time, he was a wounded World War II veteran who spent time after the war immobile. He died young, and Ruth got a big kick out of the whole incident.

The constant contact stemmed from the fact that Marge was my neighbor across the street, with her husband, Wally, who was Ruth's biological uncle, that Ruth was living with on Orchard Street. Marge was very flamboyant, a colorful dresser, and always fun to be around. Wally was always quiet, and if my memory serves me correctly, he smoked a lot. In some sense, I feel sorry for young people today because they didn't have an Orchard Street. They grew up with cell phones, cars, and Snapchat instead of playing cards with their brother and sisters. Or how about during the day describing the shapes of the clouds in terms of rabbits and spaceships? The price that they pay with modern devices is not in dollars and cents but rather in attention. That is a unique currency that which all of us have very little of while we are on this earth. Their lack of an Orchard Street makes me know I was better off then and hope these same young people would come to the same conclusion. I often feel we are victims of our own affluence. The fact of the matter is if you don't earn something, you don't fully appreciate it; if someone gives it to you, the lesson is "someone will give you another one, so you can waste this one." Ruth firmly believes you can't waste anything because she earned everything. Clearly even with starting behind the average newborn in America in 1934, she has used her skills and abilities to prosper and lead a happy life even now.

Ruth is a living testament to why all this electronic stuff is in the end meaningless. She didn't have food to eat or a safe place to stay. Even though she survived and in the long run did quite well for herself. Today she's sitting in my kitchen laughing and joking, proving further that what had happened to her over the past eighty-four years, horrible as it often was, didn't mean anything either. Let alone all this modern stuff having some value.

As the 1960s began, my own family moved from Orchard Street to the south side of Frankfort on Fourth Avenue, near Frankfort High School. Ruthie is trying to live in Ilion with her mother, and as usual, it is not working very well. As we discuss that time when she was just released from the Syracuse State School, we both agree that everything seemed to be much easier when we were all living on Orchard Street—again contained in that little world with its self-generated code that worked so well for all of us.

As we reminisce, it again strikes a chord in my memory. In about 1961, when I was approximately six or seven, I decided I wanted to go back to Frankfort. With that decision, I took it upon myself to walk unsupervised from my family's on Fourth Avenue back to Orchard Street. By the grace of God, I got myself across a busy Main Street safely. As I walked to Orchard Street, my great-aunt Josie looked out her kitchen window and saw me walking along Litchfield Street alone. She immediately called my mother—chances are on a black Bell and Howell rotary telephone.

She asked my mother, "Where is your son?"

My mother replied, "Out in the yard playing."

My aunt Josie replied, "You better go look for him because he is at my house with me."

I had truly gone back to the "real" Frankfort. The one that all of us, with Ruth nodding her head in agreement, lived so comfortably in those many years ago. Ruth also agrees it is the most content environment she had ever lived in.

Now times had changed again, and Ruthie was struggling to make a life with her mother. She recalls working at two or three jobs, at least one in a dairy and another at a dry cleaners, trying to get a decent life started. Her relationship with her mother was a very difficult one. Ruthie was working as hard as she could, and her mother expected Ruthie to provide her with income. Naturally, Ruthie was dead set against it. With the emotional turmoil in the works, she is 100 percent certain she could make a successful future for herself.

With her now at least being out of the Syracuse State School, she had something of an idea of what was happening in the world. She knew that John F. Kennedy was the president of the United States. She was aware of the botched Bay of Pigs invasion. Ruth clearly, as most people alive at that time do, vividly remembers that Kennedy was assassinated even though she says she wasn't that shocked, probably because of all the rejection she had personally been exposed to up to that point in her young life. Short of that, she knew nothing of music, movies, etc. As unlikely as it sounds, Ruth expresses that she felt somewhat in contact with the typical American lifestyle of the 1950's. All while living the chaotic life of a resident at the Syracuse State School. Yet, she was still coming to grips with the fact that she really was out of the New York State foster care system. Her recollection is, whether she was in or out, she was still not really connected to what was going on around her.

We discuss what is commonly called culture shock, and she fully agrees that it was probably her case for the first three or four years after her release.

She told Carol and me, "I tried to stay at home a lot with my mom. I saw a lot of Uncle Wally and Marge. Still, for some reason, I was always in trouble."

Another incident, I express to her my vivid recollection of, happened in about 1960. There was a cousin of hers she was living with at the time in her uncle Wally's house on Orchard Street. His name was Tom. Tom was a child of her aunt Marge from a first marriage, prior to Marge marrying Ruth's uncle Wally. Tom was a close friend of my aunt Flora's son Joseph. Joseph, Tom, probably Ronnie, and a few other friends had firecrackers. I being about five or six years old, and the others being sixteen or seventeen, I was awed by associating with the older teenagers, including Ruth, who was not much older than my cousin Joe and his friends. I was sitting with the group by the Mohawk River, which my mother warned me a thousand times not to do. I watched as Tom decided to place a firecracker in his mouth and encouraged someone to light it because he couldn't see the wick. Someone did light it. As I watched the fuse burn, hoping he would spit it out, the firecracker exploded. I can still see Tommy's lips flap open and the red—very red—blood immediately begin to drip then run on his white tee shirt.

Tommy asked with some panic in his voice, "Am I bleeding, am I bleeding?"

He was bleeding.

As I tell Ruthie about the firecracker incident in 2015, her immediate response was, "I must have been babysitting for him at the time. That's when I was living with my uncle and babysitting Sharon, Tommy, Terry, Larry. I don't remember that happening. Tommy must have hidden it really well."

She sprang into a story that jumped back into my memory equally as quick as hers.

"Do you remember what happened to Carmie?" she asked.

"Like it was yesterday," I replied.

Ruth continued, "I was watching Thelma and the rest of the kids. Thelma asked me if she could go down by the river with Debbie and Carmie. I told her that she was not supposed to be there, especially now that the water was frozen over." I was thinking it was the winter after Tommy put the firecracker in his mouth on the Fourth of July because it happened in about 1960. "Without Thelma, Carmie and Debbie proceeded to walk to the river. Apparently Carmie was walking on what she thought was the frozen Mohawk River. Sure enough, the ice broke, she fell into the freezing water, and drowned."

I was aware of that incident of Carmie's but forgot about the others involved, Debbie, and being "involved" myself until Ruth brought the whole situation back to me over fifty-four years later. The story went: while struggling in the freezing water, Carmie wouldn't let Debbie go and almost pulled her into the chilly dark water.

Ruth continued, "Thelma wanted to go exploring with Carmie and Debbie. I was babysitting Thelma at the time and would not let her go because she had to eat lunch. Plus it was too dangerous by that frozen water. As luck would have it, that lunch probably saved Thelma's life."

All of Frankfort was in shock and discussing it.

I started to tell Ruth that I went even further the day poor Carmie drowned.

My parents and my aunt and uncle were in my parents' basement kitchen discussing the accident of that day on a cold winter night. Separating the basement kitchen from the other half of the basement was a quasi-wall of a cabinet, chimney, and hot-water tank. Along the right-hand wall, probably to this day, was a coatrack filled with coats, shirts, and sweaters. I decided I was going to make myself disappear—but certainly not in the same way as Carmie. Being only about five feet tall at the time, I was able to move under the coats and stand with my back against the wall, my feet appearing to be the same as the shoes along that same wall and under the coats. I can remember my parents noticing that I was gone…and starting to search the house for me on the first floor, in the attic, etc. My aunt Grace and uncle Bill eventually joined in the search. All along I remained hidden behind the coatrack, being able to hear everything they said and see a lot of their movements. I must admit they sounded a little panicked looking for me. I must have stayed there for about forty-five minutes trying to control my giggling. With Carmie drowning that same day, I bet my parents were a little worried that some awful tragedy had befallen me also. Eventually I emerged with my mother asking, "Where have you been?"

They were angry but glad to see me, and I couldn't control my own laughter. I still find it hysterical today.

Ruth didn't think it was hysterical.

Now some fifty-five years later and having raised my own children, maybe it isn't so hysterical.

Having now spent the first two months of our expedition to write *Ruthie Deeply*—reconnecting, reminiscing, and getting our collective minds straight after about twenty-five years of no contact—Ruth, Carol, and I agreed our goal now was to follow this long winding road that will, hopefully, in the end be a project that we can all be proud of. None of us at this point have any idea where this is going, but we are determined to see it through. Ruth deserves it.

Part 1

Chapter 1

Survival

The inconsistency of the weather in Upstate New York is legendary. As the locals say, "If you don't like the weather, wait five minutes, and it will change." or "You can experience all four seasons in twenty-four hours." In terms of the weather, December 18, 1934, may have been in the 40s, dry and sunny. It may have been a blizzard with wind gusts of 50 mph and snow accumulating at a rate of two inches an hour. There is no certainty to be found other than it is the day Ruth Laura Raymond was born, the oldest child of Theodore and Elizabeth Richardson Raymond. At some point during the next year, Elizabeth Raymond gave birth to another daughter and named her Loretta, under equally sketchy conditions. A report from October 1, 1946, gleaned by interview or some unknown written record, reads,

> Story of Child
> Ruth
> Left by parents with a lodger in a rooming house. Case referred 4-18-35 to the Dept. P.W. Oneida County by Humane Society. Anemic, dirty, and ill kept. Removed to the House of the Good Shepherd. Parents returned in 5 days. At the age of 6, used "baby talk." No outstanding behavior problems, quite tractable. Health good.

No apparent lameness. First impression of child (10-5-42) is excellent, for she is friendly, shows excellent care, and wears her clothes well. Her speech is very babyish and defective, and the content of her conversation is hardly more than that of a four-year-old.

10-4-42: Carman test C.A., 7-10; M.A., 5-2; I.Q., 66.

For comprehension and memory, generally retarded. Dr. Marion Collins said "Child comes from very poor background, and her mother was a low moron. When child was seen in April 1938, she was about a year and a half retarded. Since then, she has had the advantage of an excellent boarding home so that the environment cannot be blamed for her retardation. She is a mentally defective child with an I.Q. of 66 and a mental age of 5 years 2 mos."

The parents were living wherever they had employment and did not see the children regularly. Man said he has moved 25 times in a short time; he usually rented a partial room. Normal homelife until they were discharged to the parents from the boarding home care. A home was established, and man and wife seemed congenial and cooperated in making a home. The mother had a boyfriend who practically lived in the house, and there was a great deal of marital discord. The mother claimed that when she and her husband quarreled, the children were very frightened. She feels they are partial to her.

The mother brought the children in office during summer. They were extremely well dressed, had new permanents, and the woman said that man was supporting the home and assisting in care of children.

When the mother was taken to the hospital as an emergency, and the boyfriend took them to his home, the children made no protest, nor did they object to leaving the home, was in Mohawk, and coming with the father, knowing they were to go to the House of Good Shepherd.

It appears Betty had her husband and her boyfriend living under the same roof at the same time. Caused marital discord? I would bet. I would bet a lot.

Ruth temporarily was a resident at the House of the Good Shepherd in Utica, New York, at an age of less than six months old, at the request of the Oneida County Public Welfare Department. Approximately two years after that 1946 history was written, Ruth had already been placed in detention and a wet pack applied "on January 5th and 6th for having been insubordinate over a long period. She has periods when she is excitable." Early hospitalizations for Mrs. Raymond for undisclosed illnesses (severe hemorrhaging was often cited), lack adult of supervision, and a severely dysfunctional home-life had already morphed into an almost daily terror for a fifteen-year-old girl.

As we broke into what was our second or third discussion of the loosely organized narrative that sat on my kitchen table, Ruth seemed very comfortable and willing to discuss a situation she obviously could know nothing about. Time is a healer, but in Ruth's case, there was no allowance to heal in that she can know nothing about it. She often repeats that she cannot understand how anyone can give up their child and that she would kill before she could do it. Yet, it is obvious that those statements are not driven by hatred but rather a profound understanding of all that goes wrong in the world, today being no different than the struggle it was for her and her sister in the 1930s. As we discussed the earliest recollections that she has, names and places popped into her head, but most were not being related to the point in her life we were discussing but are certainly real for her. We all wandered off track about the topic at hand, off to the weather, or her dog, Little Foot, or "Would you like more tea, coffee, perhaps more to eat?" It was aimless talk, but it led back to "How many orphanages were there?" "Did anybody know where they were located?" A name popped up. "Dr. Clark, or is it Dr. Clark*e*? I used to play ball with his kids. He oversaw the orphanage at the Masonic Home." Masonic Home with an orphanage? Must consider that. How sketchy can this get? We were all somewhat unfazed by it—the small talk, the tea, etc., but it was vivid to Ruthie. I saw it in the expression on her face.

A large gap existed from four months old to two years, likely in various orphanages in the area she suggested. She pointed out that she was baptized in Grace Church. I just drove by it today, and she suggested that she could pursue more info there, and I agreed that they may have just that. So, we continued to talk and ruminated about all the years that have passed, and the discussion turned to nutrition and food. Several years ago, a friend stopped over to visit in the middle of winter, and our discussion turned to, of course, the Upstate New York weather, the high taxes, the dysfunction of the New York State government—the usual topics of discourse. After a lengthy talk, I posed a question to him.

"So, Steve, explain to me why we live here again?" I queried.

"The food," was his immediate response, and which certainly was a factor to be considered.

On this day with Ruthie, appropriately our discussion turned to food. "Ruthie," I quizzed, "how was the food?"

"Actually, it was pretty good," she replied. "Sunday's dinners were the best, but they were all pretty good. Breakfast was always good. Lunches were light but good."

"How about dessert, soft drinks, etc.?" I wondered.

Ruthie replied, "Not very often, but at times was a treat, and they were good also."

I wanted to know if there was enough to eat. She felt that there was, as long as you behaved.

"How about birthdays, maybe a cake, ice cream?"

Ruthie thought for a second. I could feel some sadness running through her in that she had obviously missed so much as a child and

I bet was sure to not allow the same thing to happen as she raised her own children.

"Not usually, occasionally, if someone in the kitchen knew it was your birthday, they might make a small cake for you, or even if one of the employees knew it was your birthday that might bring you in a cupcake or a candy bar. I would have to be snuck to you or the employee, and I would get in trouble for it. All this came to a quick end whether on a day-to-day basis or a special occasion when you got in trouble."

Ruthie got in a lot of trouble, and she would be the first to admit it.

The sadness was clear now. She had lost so much, and she understood that she could never get it back. Yet, maybe there was a way to get it back, and over the past eight to ten years, she had; in her own low-key, laidback way, she found it. She obviously was a long way from "all set," but she was and has been fighting her way back in for the past fifty-five years.

To quote a famous fight manager, "We was robbed." Ruthie was, but the match was far from over.

>It could end at any time. (Ruthie, June 2015)

We continued to discuss meals and the whole realm of nutrition. It all went quite well until a behavior problem arose and the Syracuse State School had an entire new set of rules that came into effect. A resident could find themselves in a variety of punitive situations such as detention, solitary, "wet pack"—an entire topic in itself; and the worst of all, hunger came into play. The discipline was progressive and more aggressive at each step. Questions arose about detention, and food again dovetailed into the discussion.

"Tell me about food, if you had a discipline issue?" I asked.

Ruth was quick to respond—little or no thought, I was still alive for her. "You could end up in detention for a real reason or just a reason that one of the matrons thought was real. It usually started with detention. If you kept misbehaving, next was solitary, and then wet packs."

I asked, "Were you afraid of the punishments getting worse?"

"Never scared me one bit. I told them, 'Go for it,'" she answered.

I wondered why it didn't frighten her.

"It had happened so many times, I just didn't care."

"How about the pain and loneliness, did that come into having any effect on your behavior?" I quizzed.

"Nope," immediately she answered. "I went up to them. I told them, 'Hit me if you want. Is that what makes you happy?' When it came time to be disciplined, 'Here we go again,' was my usual response."

"Now, let's discuss food while being disciplined." Ruthie jumped on the opportunity to give her recollections of an ugly situation.

"Food, what food? It was two pieces of bread and a bowl of milk—a bowl, like, you would use to eat cereal, three times a day, for however long you were in solitary. If you were good after two or three days, they would start to give you the regular meals everyone else had, but if anyone felt you were still misbehaving, it was right back to bread and milk, nobody really cared." It seemed to hurt her, but then it also seemed she didn't care. After all she's been through, after all these years, her tenacity was still paying huge returns on the strength adversity had installed in her.

I wanted to know if being hungry while in detention made her want to behave or made her more defiant.

"Defiant," she answered quickly. "I am not sure what their problem was. Maybe they had problems at home, and they took them out on us. They were not nice. People in jail were treated better, and they did something wrong. I didn't do anything wrong. Except be born."

So, all the decent meals and what minimal comforts there were "could end at any time."

This story got more complicated each time we met. I thought I knew a lot about it from Ruth's stories. I heard about it when I was young, but I was fully ignorant and didn't even know it. I got the real impression now that we would be at this a long time. Our start was good, but it was only scratching the surface, and it may need to be revised/retold many times to be accurate. This road would be long, but the trip needed to be made because the truth will set you free—all of us, but especially Ruthie.

> They tried to make you crazy. (Ruthie, September 2015)

We met again on Labor Day Weekend. Little Foot came along for the ride. Ruthie told me right away about a name that kept reoccurring to her—that being *Ferguson*. We went back and started reviewing the history from the House of the Good Shepherd, and sure enough, the name *E. H. Ferguson* turns up. Ruthie couldn't remember, when I asked her, if Ferguson was good to her or not. So, we discussed the workers that she could remember that were good to her and those that were not.

"Have any specific names that treated you well?" I asked.

The answer was immediate. "Mary Christine LaGraff. I would have done anything for her. I went so far as to name my daughter after her. When I was out living in a private home, Mary would remember my birthday and come over with a cake. She would bring me soap, shampoo, all kinds of treats, candy, etc. that I would really look forward to whenever she visited."

Carol suggested that Mary provided Ruthie with all treats and necessities that she would provide to her own children and family if she had them. Opportunities that were being denied by Ruthie's own family but were provided to her by someone else, a stranger. The depth of the attachment to someone she did not even know, over fifty years later, was made clear. She proceeded to explain how even when she was released at twenty-five years old, when she went to the New York State Fair in Syracuse on a few occasions, she would stay at Mary's house. Ruthie stayed in touch with Mary for many years. Mary is probably dead now, yet the impression she made on Ruthie was and is powerful. This aspect of Ruth's story was generally discouraging, but here was a real bright spot that still was having an emotional effect on Ruth. It made her smile and laugh. Through all these years and all the hurt, the good that Mary did was still evident. Ruth truly appreciated it to this day.

"She was my best friend, that Mary LaGraff, and I would have done anything for her." Ruthie truly meant it. Under the circumstances, I couldn't agree with her more. "All you need is love," the Beatles sang; that love right from day one would have saved Ruth a lot of needless pain and suffering "as children at the hands of adults."

At one point, Ruthie went to live with a Dr. Farchione, who treated her at the Syracuse State School, mostly to do housecleaning and maintain the house while he and his wife, a nurse, worked. She readily admitted that they treated her well, but having just been released from the state school, she was not the best person to be babysitting or living in a family setting.

"When the children didn't behave, what was I going to do, give them the sick needle?" she asked.

I was dumbfounded by that question. After all these years, my heart broke for her. After all the research and in-depth discussion of this tragic part of her life, after all the years I have known her, I was completely shocked by that question. My heart sank to the floor.

While she lived at Dr. Farchione's house, during the day, the family hired a babysitter, who Ruthie made nervous mostly because she worked too hard. She was paid $8.05 per week and $2.05 for personal effects.

"When I left the state school, I didn't know how to treat people. I only knew how to fight, push back, protect myself—because I had no one to protect or help me. It was all that I ever knew. It took a while, but I realized there was another way. That way was based on kindness, love, respect, and being good to each other."

I must admit, again, how impressed I was with the resolve she showed. When Ruth first came today, she had photos of her grandson's graduation from high school, family photos of her two daughters and her son. From all the turmoil, good has come. Ruth deserves all of it. She has paid a big price. Now she was getting a payback—and a just payback at that. She obviously missed all that as a child but was now certainly getting it back full force. It struck me as a lot of karma and dharma at play over the last twenty-five years.

> Vinny: Where were you the first four months from birth to April 16, 1935?
> Ruthie: What the hell do I know.
> (September 2015)

A six-word quote certainly reveals the whole story of Ruth Raymond's life for the first eight or nine years. No consistent records, no for-certain memory from such a young child. Sporadic, inconsistent notes and observations. If Ruth fell into thus morass so easily, how many thousands—possibly millions—of other children in the most advanced country in the world did the same? And bigger question: what happened to them? Did they make something out of themselves like Ruthie did, or perhaps even bigger? Did they spend their whole life institutionalized and die that way? Did they end up homeless and die a pitiful death on the mean streets of America? I have a strong feeling all the previous and many even far more tragic stories are out there.

Several years ago, my family and I visited the New York State Museum in Albany, New York. There were numerous striking displays from the September 11, 1991, World Trade Center attack in New York City. After viewing those displays, we continued to peruse other displays and found one equally as striking called "Suitcases from a State Hospital Attic." The display contained clothes, pictures, golf clubs, and numerous effects left by people that were surrendered to various New York State mental institutions and often abandoned there. As the years passed, many died, and it was no longer financially feasible for New York State to keep these institutions open. Most of these people came with only the clothes they had on and a suitcase. The suitcases were stored in an attic and not opened until those mental health sites closed. The artifacts left by these people—many of those people buried in an Ovid, New York, cemetery—were eventually made into a display and placed in the NYS Museum. Ruthie lived through her experience and has a story to tell. Those whose property are now part of the displays, their histories could never now be told, but Ruthie's can. Ruth was practically forced to believe she was insane and she could not cope in the world. She never bought it. Ruth fought, pushed back, never gave up. What else could she do? End up like those people whose property was left in the attic? Not her, not then, not now, not ever. The human will to survive is very strong, and Ruthie is living proof of that.

Having come into this world on December 18, 1934, and not having been admitted to the House of the Good Shepherd until April 16, 1935, a four-month gap exists in terms of her location. An early history has both Ruth and Loretta "taken in by a friend in Mohawk." A friend? No name? Who is this friend? A second record indicates that her mother is in the hospital, and she is referred to the HGS (Home of the Good Shepherd) at the request of Mrs. Cline of Oneida County Welfare. When did she take her home? No questions, no penalty, no protection for newborn Ruthie? The wheels were coming off already. All in a four-month period, with overlapping records? Which record is the truth? Unreal set of incomprehensible circumstances for a newborn, and it was only going to get much worse long before it got any better. With a written history of over fifty pages in hand, it was still nearly impossible to paint an accurate picture of the first ten years of Ruth's life. Only when she reached her preteen years and she became more conscious of her surroundings did she somewhat have an accurate picture of her life by way of recollecting images. Yet, to ask an eighty-year-old woman to remember back to a period sixty to seventy years ago, living in such a tumultuous environment, is at best an iffy proposition. Only Ruth could tell the story. Only Ruth could survive. Only Ruth could make it better, and she would, and she does. Clearly evidenced by the fact she is alive and well, sitting in my kitchen again on this beautiful October morning.

Fall was quickly waning and turning into one of those legendary Upstate New York winters. Ruthie came today with her granddaughter Faith and, of course her faithful dog, Little Foot. She had spent the Thanksgiving weekend with her daughter Colleen in Albany and was very happy and content as always.

I asked her if she had a good Thanksgiving, and she emphatically replied, "Yes." Amazingly happy for all she has gone through.

We discussed a car repair bill she recently got for over $900. She told me how she never "approved all of the repairs" and how she will have to pay overtime in that she doesn't have the money to pay all of that money at once. Still struggling but still happy—again, amazing. Ruth was planning a dinner for someone she knows, and she was happy to do it and proud of the fact that the women asked her for her help.

I suggested to Ruth she get a boyfriend. She laughed and said, "No way."

I asked Faith, "Should we get your grandmother a boyfriend?"

An instant smile and reply of "Yes." Faith is so cute and looks like Ruthie.

I asked Faith, "Should this boyfriend be white, black, Asian—what do you prefer?"

"She would prefer Asian."

We all laughed.

I was reading the local paper this morning. A woman named Helen, a Holocaust survivor that made it her life's work to tell people her story, passed away yesterday at ninety-five. I am struck by the similarities between Ruthie's story and Helen's. I was there hearing Helen speak at school one morning, and the school I worked at was in a city school district where many students had behavioral issues. I remember an auditorium with approximately three hundred students in it, and not one making a sound when Helen spoke. The silence was deafening. I remember Helen telling the students, "You are the last generation that will be able to hear what the Holocaust was from a person who lived through it."

Although Ruthie's story is different in that she was not persecuted for her faith or nationality, she still suffered through—obviously a less-intense state-sponsored version, but still intense enough and still a state-sponsored form of terror. The same connection can be made with the relocation to the two reservations of Native Americans, to slavery in the South; and in the modern world, many would agree to abortion. A more genial American version of the

Holocaust but certainly plenty of horror for many from birth right through to adulthood. In the case of abortion, even before birth. All with the same common perpetrator: white European Christians. I now find myself in the same situation as those teenagers in school. We are the last generation that can hear the true story right from Ruthie's or any victim's mouth. In that she is in much the same situation as Helen, and so are we. Few, if any, of the perhaps one hundred thousand young people across the United States that were foster home residents or in situations exactly like or similar to Ruth's can still be alive and in good health today, and I suspect the numbers are dwindling fast. Much the same as Holocaust survivors or World War II veterans. Very sad but all true. This is the same timeless story that needs to be told by Ruth. Those that were in the same situation as Ruth are Holocaust survivors, World War II veterans, all veterans; and indeed all living humans have a story to tell. Names change, faces change, locations change, but the lack of values that drove all the tragedies in the long pedigree of mankind are the same. Ruthie's story is certainly different or no less timeless.

> Ruth: Guess who called me?
> Vinny: Who?
> Ruth: Betty
> (December 2015)

Later after our last session, Ruth called my house in a very good mood with two good pieces of news. First is that her grandson had qualified to compete in a divisional swimming competition. I explained what I know of those sorts of competitions, that usually the top three qualifiers continue further, eventually to a national competition, and the top six or seven qualifiers make the Olympic team. She was ecstatic. The second bit of news thrilled her even more. After she left my house and got home, there was a message from the granddaughter of a woman Ruth was with at the Syracuse State School. Her name is Betty, and she is alive, a resident of a nursing home in Albany. At some point in the past, Ruth had been in touch with her; but over the last three or four years, she had lost contact. She was happy to know Betty was still alive and could corroborate many of Ruthie's experiences and had suffered through similar protocols.

I asked, "Was she worse than you, Ruth?"

"No," she replied, "but she got in a lot of trouble too. Betty was the one I helped go over the wall by boosting her up. We both got in a lot of trouble for that. At the time, I wasn't going to go over, but probably would have too. I also think that Betty never got the sheets, but she was the one whose head got dunked under water."

"What do you know of Betty's life after her release?" I asked.

Ruth told me, "Not very good…married a number of times, alcohol and drugs—pretty bad. Now she is in a nursing facility and can't walk. I told her, 'I would get out of that bed and walk. Nothing would stop me.'"

"You fought through it, didn't you?"

"Damn right I did!" she immediately replied.

A perfect example of the "gunslinger attitude" that has allowed her to survive, thrive, and give back right up to this second—at its best. You gotta love it and her.

We began to go back to and research a topic that we had touched on earlier but now wanted to reconsider it in depth. Conversations would now center on Ruth's relationship with her mother and father, although she believes that individual was not her biological father. There were situations that her mother and father simply abandoned her. Situations like a hospital stay for the mother that found Ruth and her sister taken in by a friend in Mohawk, New York. She had been under the care of Oneida County since 1935. She was a resident of the House of the Good Shepherd for two weeks in mid-April 1935. She then returned to the House of the Good Shepherd again in 1937 for approximately three years until March 1940. As a resident from about four months old in April of 1935 to May of 1937 obvious question is, why is there no record of Ruth, at least sporadically being at the House of Good Shephard. That two-year period is striking. She and her family lived somewhere. Were they homeless? Did they live with a relative? To see the whole picture, you have to understand that the period of time you have to consider is with two infants in hand. If that wasn't striking enough, in 1940, she was placed in a boarding home, apparently by the New York State, then she was discharged in December 1942 "to her parents under supervision." From 1942 to 1946, she again was apparently with her parents, but there is no record to corroborate that time. Oneida County Children's Division considered discharging Ruth from care, but before that could happen, there was a "marital riff" in the family due to a "friend of the family's interest in Mrs. Raymond." She was admitted to local hospitals, possibly St. Elizabeth's, and the children returned to the House of the Good Shepherd. There is a quite a bit of history while she was at the House of the Good Shepherd from 1937 through 1940. The writer of the placement record describes Ruth as "well-built, is not what might be called an attractive child. However, she is an affectionate youngster who wants to do what is right if only she knew how." The statement "worldly knowledge as well as her language is far advanced for her years" is now usually associated with sexual abuse, neglect, and abuse in general. These records were from the House of the Good Shepherd, and it is hard to tell when they were written, and must have been when Ruth was very young—at best guess, probably around 1935. It seems that this report was written as an intake protocol. The group she was assigned to live amongst does not appear to like her but were adjusting and bringing to understand Ruth and "accept her for what she is." How old could she have been, two or three years old? The history continues to illustrate health concerns. Wassermann proved negative, but "at 4 months old appeared to be pale and thin and weighed only 10 lbs and 3 ounces" and with vaginal smears. From a report from 1938, she was found to have chronic gonorrhea and was sent to Oneida County Hospital for treatment. From some prior record, a statement exists: "information taken from a mental hygiene report found in our old records states she does not talk as well as she should for her age. Seems to have difficulty learning to talk. Walk. Other habits seem normal." Same report dated April 15, 1938; the typewriter, probably made in Utica, got into the act with some of the strangest quotation marks I have ever seen. It all looked like someone hand-penned in every set of quotation marks. It didn't seem likely, but it was strange.

Ruth came back on a still nice day in late December just before Christmas. Of course, she brought Little Foot and immediately started to tell me about her recent contacts with Betty.

I asked, "Who was worse-behaved, Betty or you?"

A quick reply: "Me by far." We all laughed. Even Little Foot seemed to get a kick out of it.

The next question that begged to be asked: "Were you the worst-behaved person in the place?"

"I think I was, at least the top five," she answered with a big broad smile.

There was that attitude—all survival, at its best. No fear, nothing holding her back. She was actually proud of her history, and in light of the situation she was in and the terrifying experiences she had been exposed to at such an early age, I must say that I saw her point. I saw her attitude, and she has a right to be proud of herself, even in light of the fact that, in her own words, she wasn't very nice.

"So what?" was my reply to that notion, even if it is hers.

An educational report indicated that Ruth was in first grade at the age of seven and showed "poor coordination between brain and hand." She was attending at various times the Bleecker Street school and the James Street Kemble School. Ms. Buckley, principal of James Street Kemble School, reported that after discussing the situation, it was the consensus that Ruth would benefit from special class training and was enrolled in such a class. She was examined in Utica at the Child Guidance Clinic on April 15, 1938, at approximately three and a half years old, and demonstrated a mental age of twenty-three months, half of the chronological age. "She was considered one year retarded. Probable causes: no suitable home."

What an outlandish statement! Was there any home at all? Was she ever in it enough to make a difference? Nature or nurture? Lack of either? No real relationship with her mother or assumed father? How quickly they pigeonholed this innocent child.

Report from the Oneida County Welfare is as follows:

> At age of 6, used baby talk. No outstanding behavior problems, quite tractable. First impres-

sion of child (10/5/42) is excellent for she is friendly child, shows excellent care and wears her clothes well. Speech very babyish and defective. Content of conversation hardly more than that of 4 years old. Clinical report of 10/4/42: CA 7-10; MA 5-2; IQ 66. Psychiatrist commented "Child comes from very poor background and mother low moron."

The ghost of Elizabeth Raymond, Ruth's mother, fills the room even in December 2015. She is "tractable"? We are struck by the word "tractable." *Tractable* is defined as "easy to control or deal with." Ruth Morgan? The Ruth Morgan I have known my whole life? Who always had been that way with my family and me but not at the Syracuse State School? If nothing else was certain, she got in a lot of trouble in Syracuse. Wet packs on a daily basis, detention, isolation bread and water, etc. Was this report writer interviewing the same child as everyone else? Ruth "wears her clothes well." The same report earlier specified, "Has very little clothes sense and seems to like queer color combinations." Did two different children walk into two different offices? "Her worldly knowledge as well as her language is far advanced for her years," but then, "Speech is babyish and defective. Content of the conversation hardly more than that of a 4-year-old." These people were all over the board. The statements told more about the writers than they did about Ruth and her family. There must have been some good going on with her mother and her family that enabled her to display "a good side" at times.

We started discussing her relationship with her mother, Elizabeth, and her alleged father, Ted. Most of these early years were spent at the House of the Good Shepherd, but when Ruth and Loretta were allowed to return to her family, she vaguely remembers an apartment on Washington Street in Mohawk.

I asked, "What was the shape of the apartment—destroyed, neat? How would you describe it?"

She told me, "It was fair, I had my own room. My mother tried to keep it neat, but she didn't have any help."

I wondered aloud about Loretta's status at that time.

Ruth told me, "They used my sister to get me to behave. If I was good, they would let Loretta come home too. So, I wanted to be good for her sake. It is hard to remember, it was so long ago."

Yet, I could tell by her tone of voice it hurt her to this day.

The first evidence of the status of Ruth's relationship with her mother showed up in that 1946 placement record that was apparently constructed from earlier reports, which we do not have, and was drafted by someone at the HGS. Again, that report in 1946 did not indicate where the intake information came from, but it did contain a great deal of history in terms of health, education, etc.

The record states, "Ruth seems to be fond of both of her parents but not overly so. She is not particularly demonstrative when they call. She has seen a great deal and overheard a great deal relevant to her parents' marital difficulties and might be considered worldly wise for a child her age.

"Her housemother reports that she observes well, can learn and wants to do things correctly. The housemother feels that she has been handicapped because 'of her mentality and the things she has seen and heard in her own home despite the excellent boarding home care she had previously had.'"

I asked Ruth if she would agree with "excellent boarding home care."

She explained, "I can't remember the boarding homes, but the HGS was pretty good. Until I was placed with older girls. They would bully me."

Ruth recollected how on three or four occasions, the older girls would strip off her clothes, stand her in front of the housemother's door, knock on it, and run off leaving Ruthie standing there naked. "When the housemother saw this a few times, she would get the idea that I was crazy."

Ruth's opinion that incidents such as this—when coupled with her mother's mental state, lifestyle, and an obviously dysfunctional family life—were in the end what got her placed in the Syracuse State School. The specter of her mother and family haunted her even when she cannot exactly remember what happened to her.

The various incidents at the HGS, in her opinion, did not directly affect when and if she could see her mom, as she recalls, but they certainly got her pushed further into the New York State foster care abyss, in the form of the Syracuse State School.

After Saturday morning with Ruth, prewinter ball gathering then a hockey game. We decided to make Sunday an easy day. We would have breakfast, take a shower, and prepare for the upcoming holiday. At about 8:30 p.m., I got a twinge of ambition and decided to check my e-mail and phone calls etc. On Saturday when Ruth was here, we discussed her recent telephone call from Betty and the possibility of traveling to Albany to visit her. When I opened up my e-mail, I found three messages from Colleen. For the sake of security, the general practice is not to open an e-mail from anyone unless you know who it's from. I decided to take a chance and open one, and as it downloaded on my screen, at first, I didn't recognize any of the people in the photo; by the time I opened up the last e-mail, the phone rang. It was Ruth.

"Did you get the pictures?" she asked.

I replied, "I just opened them."

She said, "I have notes too. My friend took them. They might be a little confusing but told him you could get them right. She signed it, we put the date on it, and she said a lot of the same things I do."

She had taken it upon herself on Sunday morning—managed to get to Albany, even though she had some knowledge of Albany because her daughter lives in the area—to locate Betty in the nursing home. I had given her a basic Google map on Saturday, and she apparently used that and her instincts to find the facility. Self-motivation is blatantly evident if this woman has interest in it. On December 21, I had promised to meet her at local not-for-profit holiday party. She wanted me to meet some of the people that have known her over the last ten to fifteen years. She was proud of the fact that she was part of this community-based agency. Ruth had been served by it, and she has served it. I was glad to go. I drove into the parking lot the same time she did. Ruth got out of the car of a friend who also did work for this agency. There were hors d'oeuvre, tea, coffee, wine, desserts, and candy. I knew three people at the party; one was the mother of a former student that I knew worked there, another was a member of the board of education where I was employed. When I retired at a moving-up ceremony for my school, I was introduced as a retiring teacher; she was there to represent the board of education.

She shook my hand and then told me that I was too young to retire.

I thanked her and told her, "I am not."

On the walk into the party, Ruth handed me a bag with some sheets of paper inside that were "the notes from Betty."

In an attempt to stay on the topic of family, I asked Ruth what she knew of Betty's release from the Syracuse State School. Ruth has the impression that Betty's life turned out more difficult than hers. It was her understanding that Betty had three marriages, and she didn't know if Betty had any children She understands that Betty had trouble with alcohol and that her life was largely a struggle. I asked Ruth if she knew of anyone else in Betty's family. As she recollects, Betty had a brother, and they had been placed in the New York State foster care system due to the death of their parents. She had no knowledge of whether Betty's family before the parents' death had been one with a strong family structure or a completely dysfunctional structure.

I asked her if it made any difference.

She quickly replied, "None at all. She was in it just like I was. It didn't matter who you were before you got there. We were all treated the same. If you did what they wanted, they left you alone. If you didn't do what they wanted, there was all kinds of punishments."

I asked her, "Did Betty follow the rules?"

She told me, "More than I did, but she got in a lot of trouble too."

I asked her for the hundredth time, "Who was the worst behaved in the place?"

Emphatically, she answered, "Me. I was a bitch."

In a second attempt to stay on the topic of family, I wanted to know if she knew anything else about Betty's family; she said she did not. But what she did have was a two-page handwritten statement from Betty that corroborates all the documentation—everything we have discussed and more, including but not limited to the "sick needle."

My reaction was swift. "These people are nuts. What do they think gave them the right?"

We had to stop there. Immediately.

We started up again a few days after New Year's Day. Ruth filled in Carol and I about her Christmas. Her daughter had come to visit from Virginia. Ruth told us it went pretty well with her but could have been better and that she left possibly angry. When her daughter left without saying goodbye, Ruth felt bad and decided to drive by her daughter's girlfriend's house to see if she was there. She wasn't.

I think Ruth felt bad, but she wouldn't let us know that. Her mother's ghost comes back into the room and has a bad effect on her relationship with her own child? The wheel just keeps on spinning some seventy years later.

We made plans to go visit Betty in a couple of weeks. Ruth, Carol, and I would drive to Albany to see Betty, taking time to hear more of Betty's story. Then we'd go to Cross Gates Mall for lunch and to meet Ruth's daughter Colleen.

Obviously, Ruth's family situation is of maximum effect on her life and Loretta's. The notes are vague on her mother and father, but they are there. Trying to piece those notes together was much harder than trying to piece Ruth's together. At least Ruth has some history in writing, and verbally, she always has a lot of information to convey.

We continued to research the notes about Ruth's mother, who "was admitted to the Rome State School at the age of 12 and discharged to her father at 16." The report continues, "The mother had died during that year and the father, who was anxious to do all he could for the child, was unable to give her the supervision she needed. There were four brothers and sisters in the home, from two to fourteen years of age. On admission, Elizabeth was a restless, active child with a mental age of seven years, two months and I.Q. of 56. Later tests gave practically the same results." Elizabeth was receiving training at the institute in elementary domestic work, music, story work, and physical training. The reports from teachers said that she was cheerful and neat about her work, but she was troubled by dreams that frightened her, which she talked about to the children, often frightening them. She was transferred to a colony to have advantage of the schoolwork given there. She was a good student in academic work and did light domestic work well. She was paroled to her brother, Mr. Wallace Richardson, 19 Elm, Ilion, New York.

Oneida County DPW was informed that in November 1934, Betty Raymond was attending Utica Mental Clinic because of her overwhelming fear of confinement.

Note: at this time, the Visiting Nurse Association was working with the mother. They reported:

> March 31, 1937—came to prenatal clinic. She was extremely nervous and poorly nourished. ****For although Mrs. Raymond had at times tried to follow instructions and give the proper care to the children, she seemed to realize that she was not capable of this responsibility, and she seemed anxious to have the children cared for in an institution. It has been our impression that although Mrs. Raymond cannot be counted upon for bearing much responsibility because of her mental condition, yet she might be encouraged to do better if she were not under the influence of Mr. Raymond. But we are convinced that as long as they are together, they are absolutely incapable of having the responsibility of the children.

In 1942, the children were both released to the parents and showed some improvement. But the situation deteriorated rapidly in a six-month period. When a Harry C. came into the picture and paid a great deal of attention to Elizabeth.

> The husband contends that there are excessive sex activities that have undermined her health, and Mr. C. has assumed all medical

expenses. He visits her at the General Hospital often, and Betty wears a ring he gave her and says it is an engagement ring, and she plans to marry him. They both seem to disregard the fact that the man has a wife in the State Hospital but dismissed that by Betty saying, "She won't live long." Worker having known Betty over a period of years believe she has both mentally and physically, and has talked with Dr. DeLalla to get his co-operation in continued clinic attendance for recommendations in the matter. She is so childish that she will become a victim of unscrupulous people.

Ruth's "father" is even more of a confusing situation than that of her mother. It was even harder to piece together than the history of Ruth and her mother. Which at times seemed impossible.

We haven't even touched on the history that was documented of the man who Ruth believes is not her biological father but her mother, Elizabeth, always portrayed as her father. The effect of both parents on the children generally seemed to be negative. When Harry C. was factored in, the effect was devastating for both the adults involved relationship and even to a great extent for the children's daily care. How can any nurturing relationship have developed between Ruth and her mother in such a tumultuous environment? This all occurred years after Ruth had been flatly abandoned by her mother and father in a boarding house at approximately four months old. The picture certainly wasn't getting any prettier and would surely get much worse before it got any better. Years later when it did turn around and get better, it was only because Ruth was determined to make it that way for herself and her children. There was no time in this long pedigree that Ruth got any breaks other than the ones she made herself. All this happened under the umbrella of childhood and a dysfunctional family. It was hard for Ruth, Carol, and I to see how any good could come of this, but sure as the day was long, it did. We were all in awe, Ruth included, that this played out in the long term as well as it did.

Yet, it did, and we were equally impressed as we were completely confused.

The man Ruth "understood" as her father was born in Rochester, New York, in the winter of 1915. He was also known as Theodore Williams, but Ruth knew him as Theodore Raymond. He moved to Utica in 1921. The record indicates his parents were divorced, and his stepfather deserted him. "He attained 8th grade at age of 15 years, attended part time school until 16 and has been self-supporting since then. He claims many jobs, watch making, papering, body and fender work and is now in the roofing and painting business." He first came in contact with Oneida County DPW in 1935, after he and his wife deserted an infant, leaving it in a rooming house. He soon after that had a second child and was ready to place him/her out for adoption. Almost immediately he was looking for someone to claim responsibility for Ruth and Loretta. He did not visit his children at Christmastime nor did he and his wife send presents. He was paying $1 towards their maintenance but changed jobs and residences so frequently that he did not pay it. There were reports of heavy drinking, bad temper, and was often interested in other women. Nothing in his history indicates any verification of these rumors. He was given a psychiatric and psychometric examination to determine his mental capacity to care for his children, and we gained some understanding of his reactions to everyday life situations. He expressed a lot of interest in other women, but nothing had ever been proven.

> This thirty-four-year-old married man, except for evidences of instability and increased tension, showed no signs of actual mental disease. On the other hand, he is of borderline intelligence and his personality is much that he may be properly classified in the group: simple adult maladjustment. His feebleminded wife, who has been a patient at this clinic, further, contributes to his maladjustment. His glib promises, evasion

and general unreliability are characteristic, and at his age little improvement can be expected.

Confounding this psychiatric and psychometric exam dated April 14, 1939, it quickly jumped to 1945–1946, when Ruth was now in the Syracuse State School, that he had established a home and was caring for his family. He was in dire financial condition, and a local attorney was assisting in paying his bills and keeping his records for him. All money that Mr. Raymond earned was deposited by this attorney, and he was urging him to have his children released from the boarding home to the family. Again, the marriage was in shambles. Mr. Culver was in the picture frequently, and Raymond didn't seem to complain since he had known Culver since childhood. He reported that Culver had been helpful in getting his children back and was childish in his request that the record be changed that the family had not been broken up because of his neglect. Again, "the unusually sexual activity between Culver and Betty has contributed to her illness." The entire situation was making Theodore very anxious.

The history has just jumped through ten years with literally no information in between. From the other mishmash of records, some information could be pieced together in that ten-year period. Sometimes the writers of these reports were more confused about the family history than the family was. Almost 75 percent of these records crisscrossed, contradicted, and repeated what was probably erroneous information to start with. Raymond and Elizabeth struggled with their daily existence due to documented mental inconsistences—are what the people trying to convey as their history to the report writers. Seems to me they were no more aware of their true circumstances, past and present, than the writers of the reports were. It could all be completely fictionalized in 1936 or 1946 or 2016. None of us know really for sure what was happening, and there was no way to verify any of it except for these random reports, which are turned upside down constantly with information provided by man "with simple adult maladjustment" and his "feeble minded wife."

The couple was married on June 4, 1934. The woman was pregnant at the time of the marriage, and Mr. Raymond stated he was not the father. He has known Betty for years that she had been in the Rome State School. "He would give the child his name and that she was capable of keeping a home clean."

"The Dept. of Public Welfare of Oneida County first knew this case April 15, 1935 when both parents had left the city, address unknown, and Ruth, then four months old, was left with people in a rooming house. At this time the parents' whereabouts were unknown for 5 days. The child was taken to the House of the Good Shepherd," the record clearly states.

Also, "The marriage was never secure, the man was most unsteady emotionally, went from one job to another to better himself and as he was a weak personality, with no moral support from his wife, this couple drifted into a very unsatisfactory marital status. The couple was on relief at times. They resided in furnished rooms, moving from one place to another." Again, from the records.

From about 1942 through 1946, the marital situation improved. It wasn't until Harry Culver came into the picture. It was believed that Raymond had a business of his own, and the couple would get along. Harry Culver has Ruth's mother and father believing that he can be helpful in getting the children back to them. Raymond was almost childish in his request that the break in the family life not be attributed to him. He stated he worked long hours and was doing his best but was concerned that publicity will hurt his business. Raymond said he was anxious about unusual sex activity between Culver and Betty that contributed to her illness.

Apparently on Saturday, September 28, 1937(?), a neighbor called the police reporting that Mrs. Raymond had gone to the hospital for severe hemorrhaging, and Mr. Culver was allowed by Mr. Raymond to take the children to his sister's home in Mohawk. The author of the report asked Mr. Raymond if he didn't contact the Children's Welfare Division about the situation. He responded that it was only a temporary thing, that he has been very careful not to antagonize the rest of the Culver family, whom he said were very nice people, and he knew that the children would not become frightened if they went there. "The two families have known each other for years, have visited in each other's homes, and the children have gone with the parents many times to eat there. Also, he said that he did not want us to think that at the first opportunity he wants to place the children. He would have allowed the children to remain there permanently had worker thought it advisable. Permission was given to the man to leave them there until Monday, when a plan could be made for them, and we knew more about his wife's condition. (See record for visit to the woman at the hospital September 28.) On Monday, September 30, Mr. Raymond removed the children from Mohawk, New York, and took them to the House of the Good Shepherd. He was very insistent in his statement that we must not think that at the first opportunity he got rid of the children."

A period of nine years from 1937 (?) to 1946, there is no record currently in our hands. Today being February 27, 2016, Ruth came this morning with Little Foot, with a letter she recently sent to Rome, New York, DDSOCNY, concerning the release of her mother's and her sister's records. Ruth's mother being dead, and her sister having signed off on the release request, our hope was that the new records will shed light on numerous large gaps in the records Ruth already possessed.

As in a previous situation, suddenly, "In June 1946, the man came in the office… At the present time, Raymond has no plans to continue living with his wife after her release from the General Hospital. He wanted his children released from supervision in their own home, and said that he was earning enough to support his family. His wife was doing very well and was an exceptionally good housekeeper. The woman came in a few days later, confirmed her husband's statement, and from her appearance, it was believed that they were getting along well. The children were dressed in identical dresses of different colors; they had had permanents and seemed happy, healthy youngsters. The woman told how well the man provided for them and their plans for the future. Soon after this, the man came in the office, said that he had not told the exact truth; that his wife had disappeared from the home with the two children, and he did not know where they were. This was of short duration.

The children came back after the man looked for them, and the situation cleared. It was after this that Harry Culver came to visit and persisted in his attentions to the wife. Raymond knew that they were intimate, felt that Culver was in the home much of the time that he, the husband, was absent. When the woman was taken to the hospital for hemorrhaging, Mr. Raymond placed the entire blame on Culver. At the present time, Mr. Raymond, through his attorney, William Ribyat, plans to divorce her. The woman told worker (Cline) that she intended to marry Harry Culver. He gave her a ring, which she wears on her engagement finger, and is very childish about her affection for the man. He has a wife in the Utica State Hospital. At the present time, Raymond has made no plans to continue living with his wife after her release from the General Hospital."

The notes never clearly delineate who is "the man that came into the office." Then, "the woman" comes into the same office and validates all "the man" had told them a few days before. It all seems so staged, so planned to give certain impressions to the people that have the authority to make decisions about Ruth and Loretta. But, nobody knows, including Ruth, Carol, or I, exactly what was happening to Ruth and her sister. Ironically, Mr. Ribyat, who was handling all the money Ted was able to generate, also owns a boarding home. The question that begs to be asked, was he the owner of the boarding homes that Ruth and Loretta were bouncing back and forth to? Seems to me that Ribyat was keeping the entire set of circumstances under his control—I would guess for some type of monetary reward.

Suddenly, Ruth raises the possibility that Mr. Raymond was married to two women at the same time. There is no record of Mr. Raymond's first wife's name but there are notes that a paternal divorce was granted at some point. A marriage license was then granted to Mr. Raymond and Elizabeth on June 4, 1943 by the Reverend Albert G. Judge. Two wives at the same time? Unclear but possible.

There are a number of relatives in the area: Mrs. Raz Johnson in Frankfort; Wallace Richardson was believed to have been living in Ilion at the time; and his wife, Betty (?), had died ten years before.

Continuing, there were two sisters mentioned in the record, Harriet and Ellen (?) Richardson, and it was noted that they had had police records or at least were known to be unstable people. There is a sister, Mrs. Gillian, who worked at the Marcy State Hospital. Ruth is named after her aunt Ruth Gillian. I have to wonder if her aunt was ever a party to the isolation, wet packs, detention that her niece was exposed to in her position at the Marcy State Hospital? It would be a huge irony if she were ever party to such mistreatment—knowing what was happening to these people, she never did anything to aid her niece's plight. If true, what planet do these people live on? Denial is a powerful tool and seems to be at play here.

The report by M. B. Cline, date and initialed "10/1-2/46-car" ends with, "An attempt was made to clear the relatives, but Mr. Raymond had four men in his employment and several jobs, which he is supervising and was unable to give us the necessary time to make arrangements for committing the children. The mother at the hospital became too hysterical, talked in too loud a voice and appeared to be very nervous even with ordinary conversation."

Ruth had a good relationship with her sister and didn't seem to mind that they were in different groups, and she saw her on the playground and going to school. Mr. and Mrs. Raymond visited the girls on two occasions, and the father was allowed to take them out for a short ride with the approval of Oneida County Welfare. When the girls returned, they seemed to have had fun and were not upset. However, the mother's visits were causing problems.

The records states, "The mother's visits have been most disturbing to the children. Being a mental defective, the mother's talk has been such that the children became very much excited, cried, and was somewhat disturbed when returned to their departments. Because of the mother's mentality, it is difficult to make her see how such conversations disturb the children and interfere with their placement. She has been very insistent that she be allowed to take them out. Upon the recommendation of the Oneida County Welfare, this request has been denied."

Under a category named Special Needs and Problems, it states that Ruth was in need of supervision and guidance that the House of the Good Shepherd had to offer. She was labeled in the "mental defective bracket; with controlled living and supervision, she may improve. She should be given at least six months to a year of this training before any changes of plan should be considered." Ruth continued to reside at the House of the Good Shepherd in December of 1946. In May of 1944, Ruth had an IQ of 67 and was in a special class at the James Kemble School. At a conference of the principals of the James Kemble and Bleecker Street schools, she was placed at James Kemble School because of "poor coordination of the brain and the hand."

Ruth does have some recollection of early school attendance while at the House of the Good Shepherd and attending the Utica City Schools. Once she was placed in the Syracuse State School, there is little indication of any public school attendance, and Ruth does not clearly remember any. There are indications that Ruth and others walked back and forth to some type of school probably in the Syracuse City Schools, but there is no mention of a specific school.

Meanwhile, Ruth is reported to be very energetic and can complete tasks after being shown.

> She likes to be neat, she likes the limelight and has a happy disposition. She has been accepted into a group, and they seem to understand her.
>
> She has an attraction to the opposite sex, is not doing well in special class. Teacher feels she talks too much and complains about her liking boys. Recently had a tonsillectomy and was quite sick. Seemed to suffer a great deal of pain for several days after. Seems to be a child who "if she is ill, it goes hard with."

I asked Carol, "What does that mean?"
She shrugged her shoulders and said, "I don't know." Seems that if she has some type of sickness, it was harder for her to recover.

In March of 1940, both children were placed in a boarding home. They stayed in the boarding home until they were discharged in December of 1942. While with the parents, supervision was coordinated by the Oneida County Children's Division. Both children were returned to the House of the Good Shepherd because of "home condition." About a year after that, they were discharged to the placing agency with an intention of a more permanent placement in the Syracuse State School. Ironically Ruth was reported to be sweet and affectionate but was not able to keep up with normal activities. She was considered to be an excellent candidate for the Syracuse State School, and the school would be able to help her because she would be going at such a young age. She got along with her sister, and it was the report writer's opinion that the two should be kept together. Ruth demonstrated a great deal of loyalty to her mother, and she had a hard a time leaving the House of the Good Shepherd's because of a fear that she may be returned to her father.

Ruth commented, "You can kill me, but I will never go back to live with him because of the way he treated my mother."

Ironically the next statement in the report was that Ruth was baptized in the fall of 1946 and attended Sunday school at Grace Episcopal Church while at the House of the Good Shepherd. The contrast between those two entries drips with irony. That same ironic drip jumped at me again when we visited Betty, an entire topic that we have yet to discuss. Ruth's health was not that good; she had a physical in September of 1946 and again in December of 1946, while she was recovering from a tonsillectomy performed by a doctor at St. Luke's Hospital.

I asked, "What do you remember about these physicals and vagina smears that go back to 1935 and 1936?"

Ruth replied, "Nothing."

Again, I asked, "Were they medical, or were they perverted?"

"I don't remember, but I think they were medical. There was one that I remember as perverted, but I am not sure if it had anything to do with medicine."

Her eyes reddened and sunk in a little bit. Sadness and cluelessness leapt across the table at Carol and I. She chuckled about something she was reading. We continued to plod along.

I must confess there were times when I was moved to tears. They usually happened when those "dead" words of written reports, interviews, etc. from Ruth's history came "alive" by way of her recollection of specific incidents duly recorded in those same notes and interviews. The wet packs literally for days, the isolation, sick needles, Betty, and so on and so on. Ruth would not weep, so neither would I. I would only when she does. I hope it never happens to either of us.

A school history dated September 1946:

> Grade 4-1. Loretta. More vivacious, brighter than Ruth. Poor comprehension and memory. Generally retarded.

Dr. M. is quoted as saying, "Child comes from poor background, and mother is a low moron." Dr. M. continued, "Since then she has had the advantage of an excellent boarding home, so the environment cannot be blamed for her retarding. She is a mentally defective child with an IQ of 56 and a mental age of 5 years and 2 months."

I said to Carol, "That is weird-looking. Do you see how they release themselves from their responsibility that far back in the history? The date of the report is was 1946, like other reports that place Ruth at the age of 12 in the Syracuse State School. That's just about the time the wet packs, solitary etc., began."

I said to Carol, "What astonishes me the most is how loose the agencies are with these two children. They place them in boarding homes, no address. They release them to individuals who they have some kind of relationship with. Everything is so vague. Who knows what living conditions they are in? Who knows the adults in charge? Who knows if there were other children there? They play such a losing game that I am amazed that they are able to survive. If these two did survive, how many did not? If Ruth and Loretta lived to a great degree in the norms of society, I wonder how many never got anywhere near the degree of survival."

With Ruth coming this Saturday, it seemed like a good place to stop. Of course we will have to see how the weather was this weekend. We were almost through our second winter with *Ruthie Deeply*, and we continued to make slow and steady progress because slow and steady win the race.

The focus of the conversation came back to the medical records. From 1937 to 1939, Ruth was given chicken pox, measles, and whooping cough vaccinations. She was given a chest X-ray, blood Wasserman test, and another vaginal smear. The blood Wasserman and vaginal smears continued into the mid-1940s. The records show from January of 1939 through September of 1946, she was growing taller, gaining weight, was well-nourished; heart, lungs, and other organs were normal along with normal reflexes and extremities. The inconsistencies of the medical records were stunning. From 1936 through 1939, records show whooping cough, chicken pox, measles, gastro upsets, and a temperature 102.8 in August of 1938. It is difficult to determine on one hand that she was growing normally, and on the other hand, she had numerous childhood illnesses. The truth was buried under layers of anomalies. Being so young, Ruth has no recollection of any of this.

I wondered out loud, "Who was keeping these records? I am not even certain that you can call these records. They are snapshots. There is no continual record. It jumps from issue to issue, examination to examination, sickness to sickness—all the while suggesting that is growing normally. Obviously young children get sick a lot, but this seems to be an inordinate amount. Can you picture all these sick children infecting each other back and forth for months on end? Although the medical care seems sufficient, I have to wonder if it was through or just another cover to give the appearance of propriety. Better yet, maybe a money machine so everyone sends a bill."

I asked, "Ruth, was the medical care decent, or was it superficial—that we examined this child and send a bill."

Ruth told me," It was just so they could send a bill and cover the bases."

I wondered aloud again about all these vaginal smears; it all seemed a little weird to me for such a young girl.

Carol suggested, "They're looking for something."

I was guessing maternally passed syphilis, gonorrhea, or even sexual abuse. I asked her if she has ever been tested for any such diseases.

She replied, "No."

Goodness gracious, I'm sure hoping Ruth was clear of any such illnesses at eighty-one years old!

For the first time in early 1947, the Syracuse State School was mentioned and that she should be transferred for vocational training. A report was drafted from an examination at the Child's Guidance Clinic in the House of the Good Shepherd on August 8, 1947. The report discusses, "She is developed and nourished, her teeth are good, she has a normal hair, tonsils are out, and no secondary sex characterizes. From a psychiatric viewpoint, she is clean, neat, cooperative, and talkative. She shows infantile speech and is cheerful and pleasant." It is reported that "she is accepted at the House of the Good Shepherd, everyone is good to her, likes to draw and sew. Ruth used to like to fight with her sister but doesn't anymore. Now, Loretta likes to fight with her." The summary states she scored about three to four years off in chronological age. "Therefore, she is considered retarded and placed in a special class. She is quiet and friendly during the testing." On September 24, 1947, at the recommendation of Child Guidance Clinic, on January 8, 1947, Ruth was discharged from the Oneida County Welfare and placed in the Syracuse State School. Mrs. Marjorie C. of the Oneida County Welfare Division took her to Syracuse. There the real horror stories began with Ruth, and Betty remembering them clearly. The horrors being so powerful, some fifty to sixty years later, they are still causing nightmares and phobias. For both of them.

Each time we restated this process, it began the same way—with a cup of coffee, some small talk, and a clear kitchen table to work on. By the time we were finished, that clear kitchen table ended up covered with papers, notes, pens, pencils, and newspapers. What caught my eye the most was the constant revelations that sprung up and only tended to muddy the water even more. We continued to sift and file and reread constantly. One new discovery led to another, and they all continued to lead us down this confounding trail.

Ruth's story so far, both from the New York State foster care system's "official" history and Ruth's markedly different "personal" history, we all agree, is going to need some strong collaboration.

As fate would have it, we readily found it. In the form of two living individuals: Ruth's longtime friend from the Syracuse State School, one Betty Cable, still alive in the Guilderland Center Nursing Home in Guilderland, New York; and Ruth's younger sister, Loretta Hall, that ironically lives about a mile from Ruth's house.

Chapter 2

Betty: Collaborating Ruth's Story

In late January 2016, Carol, Ruthie, and I decided we had to go to see Betty in the nursing home that she has been residing. Ruth has been saying the last two months that we better go see Betty because she didn't sound well on the phone and was not in the best medical condition. On December 20, 1915, Ruth had visited Betty at the Guilderland Center Nursing Home. On that date, she brought along with her a friend, Paul, to take notes, ask questions, and take pictures. Paul had Betty sign that she was making the statement. Betty was in the New York State foster system from ages ten to twenty. She was admitted in 1945 or '46 and then "age of 20 when she got herself free." She had clear knowledge of wet packs and sick needles. She saw no stress on education and most time worked in the laundry room or in the canning facility. Betty's memory is clear about the bath. A tub was filled up, and patient was placed in a straitjacket. The attendants would then have to hold the patient in the water for about fifteen seconds. The purpose was to make the patient agree to be good or "get a controlled response."

I asked Carol, "Who used the words *controlled response*? Was it Betty? Was it Paul taking the notes?"

Back at our start when Ruthie made mention of these baths, I asked her if she knew what that was called. "She said no.

I told her, "It was called waterboarding, and it was a form of torture. It is about from the fourteenth century, and it gives you a sensation of drowning."

She plainly stated, "It is torture."

To this day, Betty does not take a bath, only a sponge bath. She is not fond of water. Looking back from visiting Betty and seeing these notes, now I can see how the women suffered immensely. She was in the same exact situation as Ruth and can corroborate everything Ruth says. I must think that if these two are still alive, there must be others; I am guessing maybe a thousand.

Betty was also subjected to the wet packs. Paul's notes from Betty's description are as follows:

> Put your arms to your side and legs together and wet wrap you up similar to a mummy (to the neck), ice pack you to the back of your head and neck. Unwrapping process took approximately 2 ½ hours to 3 hours. Patient has red sore areas. Very uncomfortable (blisters) when finished. Then place you next to hot radiator to dry out fast. You are also covered in heavy army blankets—occasionally tie you to the bed. Wet packs could be up to 3 days consistently done by staff. Sometimes causing patient to pass out.

Even the first discussion that Betty, Paul, and Ruth had verifies almost to the letter everything Ruth describes as her experience with the wet packs. It seems that from both Betty's and Ruth's perspectives that all of the punishments were random. They depended on the opinion of the individual employee of the Syracuse State School, the seriousness of the infraction in the observation of the employee, and the degree to which the employee liked or disliked the individual. These reports were forwarded to the doctor in charge, and the doctor prescribed the punishment that was then administered by the same individual that made the report. Obviously personal opinions and biases played a big part in the type of punishment administered.

There was one worker in particular that Ruth does not speak fondly of who looked for reasons to aggravate Ruth, which didn't take much, so there could be prolonged periods of punishment.

I asked Ruth, "How long did it take to get the sheets on and off and the punishment time in between? What was the total amount of time the whole ordeal took?"

Ruth recalled, "Between four to five hours, closer to five."

In Betty's opinion, the process was two and a half to three hours. Either way, it was a terrible ordeal for a teenager or an adult of twenty-five years old to endure. A teenager might have been able to easily dismiss it and move on, but for an adult, it must have been unfathomable.

I asked Ruth, as I have asked numerous times, "Was it torture?"

Ruth quickly replied, "Absolutely, nothing nice."

I asked, "Was it painful?"

"Of course, it was very painful. How would you like it?" she replied.

I said, "I probably would have killed somebody in there."

Ruth said, "I have scars from it. Look it."

And she showed me. Again.

Ruth said, "When the wet sheets dry, because they were so tight, it pinched your skin, and when they removed the sheets, it pulled the skin and left scars in random spots. When you get out of the sheets, you are so weak you almost pass out."

Again, almost verifying word for word the notes Paul took while interviewing Betty, which is cited above. Two people independently relating the same story is irrefutable proof that it was a common occurrence. All the documentation aside, the living history from Betty and Ruth are two primary sources that can't be denied.

The notes from Paul on December 20, 2015, have a vivid description of the detention process:

> Detention—called solitary confinement, scrub your cell, average time 3 days with break and milk. On the 6th day, good behavior, a full course meal. Back to your room when they

decide. A wing of detention cells, (10) solitary confinement, 2 cells.

Back to ward—Could be one week to 3 months after you have been given sick needle. Have a reaction of vomit or diarrhea, asked to clean this up rudely. By staff workers—Doctors or this method. (Dr. M. Naples-Sarno and Dr. Briscoe). Still being as so called detention (cell or cage). Allowed 3 bathrooms visits a day. A cot or floor to sleep on be in. A ticket dress you would be placed while there. This would identify and segregate patients in the system of detention.

Out of detention: out of ward, given a task of pulling threads from old rags apart. Then to a so-called class: In classroom, allowed to play with other patients of same age or older. All girls/boys were in another area of home (institution).

Out of detention—to the ward—allowed to be taken by staff to a hill to "the playground." All fenced-in areas to hide and possibly try to jump fence and get away.

On occasions tried—clothing got caught trying to jump another patient. Ruth assisted in a climb over fence. Allowing Betty to be free of this home/institution. Never to return. Found help from others at a bus stop in Syracuse. (The City.)

As Carol and I were reading through Paul's notes with Ruth, Ruth was nodding her head in agreement and verifying it all—right down to the number of cells in the detention wing and the solitary confinement.

Ruth said, "In solitary confinement, there is one black door, one window with bars, one light bulb in the ceiling, and one radiator. They only let you use the bathroom three times a day, eight a.m., with two people watching you and locking the door as they go out. At one o'clock in the afternoon, with two people to watch, and again at six p.m., same routine. Then they would take you back to solitary confinement and lock you in for the night."

I asked Ruth, "Were there any minorities—black, Hispanic, etc.?"

"Mostly white children never saw any other minorities, one hundred percent white kids," she replied.

It made me wonder, if Ruth only saw Caucasian kids, then where were all the minorities? With the living and family conditions of many minority youths in 2016, what was happening to them in 1940s and 1950s that Ruth would have no contact with any of them almost seventy years ago. That is a topic that begs to be researched as much as Ruth's early history does.

Little Foot decided that he had to go to the bathroom, so we decided to stop there for now.

It stood right out to me as we heard about Ruth's story—abandonment, lack of health care, food, and an unstable family life—how Ruth in the long term was able to prosper. I think of my own parents, grandparents, in-laws with the Great Depression and WWII, they faced denial also in the sense of food, health care, etc. That generation survived, and they were certainly able to build strong family ties and lives. In 2016, you often hear even more so with the media exposure the same stories of abandonment, lack of family life, and so on; but the people of this era now often turn to violence, drugs, etc., and many live almost their entire adult life in prison or at least as long as they can survive wherever. What allows one group, actually two out of three groups, move through their situation and prosper right up to this minute are mostly in their eighties and nineties. Yet, current eighteen- or nineteen-year-olds often find themselves imprisoned, with drug/alcohol problems and so on. What are the circumstances that funnel one group into one path and the other group into a different path?

Carol and I discussed it a little more, and I suggested, is it because of low expectations? Unfortunately, it seems young people see no future for themselves, certainly no better futures for themselves than they think so they turn to drugs, violence, alcohol, etc.

I asked Carol, "Do you think it's because of low expectations?"

She replied, "I do, because of the exposure they have to a bleak future with not a lot of opportunities for decent family life, housing, etc."

I said, "I think it's the results of low expectations for themselves, in their families and in their neighborhoods. If you see no way out, there is no way out. Ruth saw a glimpse of an opportunity to improve, and she pursued it, and that effort put her in the situation she is in today. The modern situation is one that low expectations hang so heavy over their heads that they can't see past it. Education is by far the key that pushes everything ahead, and the people don't see it and thus don't see the opportunities."

Carol said, "They do have opportunities, but many aren't willing to put forth the effort and do the work it takes to move forward and take advantage of the programs that are available."

I told Carol, "I am just interested in why two out of three groups prosper, but the modern group is stuck on the path of destruction? An entire adult life spent in a full-scale penal system is a crime for the prisoner as much as it is for the victim. Two lives are literally destroyed, plus the spin-off damage."

A few days went by, and I raised with my father the discussion of low expectations becoming "a self-fulfilling prophecy." My father's dad died at a very young age, and his mother was in a wheelchair with MS by the time she was fifty years old. My dad had six brothers and one sister from ages three though fifteen at the time of my grandfather's death. Obviously with that many children, my grandmother was a stay-at-home mom, as most women were at that time. My grandfather worked for an insurance company but died so young there was little or no money in the family. Yet, they were still able to make a decent life for themselves. Those that were old enough got jobs, like my father did in a grocery store at age seven. The family raised chickens in their backyard, had a garden, and did whatever they could to make ends meet. Each child in the family also had a job at home. Again, my grandmother was wheelchair bound. So, one child had to wash the clothes, one child had to cook, another would have to take care of the chickens and the garden and so on.

Even though being a widowed woman, my grandmother was always home and always working to keep the household running. It seemed the overall attitude of the house was "we can handle this, we will handle this." No one gave up, no one set low expectations for themselves. At times they did things they shouldn't have done, like picking up coal from the railroad companies' tracks that had fallen off the train to keep their only source of heat in the house running.

So, I asked my father, "What do you think allowed your brothers and sister to lead decent lives up to this day without falling into terrible lives like so many young people do today? You didn't have a living father, you didn't have a lot of money, you didn't have a lot of education, what made the difference that pushed you ahead that young people today don't have that pushes them ahead? What kept you from falling into drugs, alcohol, spousal abuse, etc. that is not there to push young people away from drugs, alcohol, etc.?"

He thought about it for a split second and replied, "Most importantly I think it is because we had a mother in the home all the time. She kept us working together, she kept us organized, taught us to respect each other, respect other people, the value of work, she helped us to see the only way that we would survive was through cooperation. Nobody was any better or any worse than us. Remember this was all happening in the midst of the Great Depression. No one had much of anything but each other, and we were all struggling. All we had to do was hang on to each other, and we did it. People today don't have that. They never learned a connection to their parents, brothers, or sisters. They never learned to be proud of who they were and where they came from. They seem to have something missing. They have a void that they can't fill in any other way, so they turn to drugs, alcohol, adultery, abandonment, and so on. They have no idea where they came from, so they have no idea where they belong. So they find self-destructive ways to create an identity and create a place where they belong. It really is very sad, but it is a fact of life now."

I can tell by the sound of his voice and the look in his eyes that through it all, he really does understand how sad it is. As we sat there talking, I was astounded by the idea that the struggles that my father and his family had were similar but much smaller than those Ruth and Loretta were having, it seemed that Ruth's and Loretta's struggles were even then a result of alcohol, sexual promiscuity, no parental guidance from anyone and abandonment by her mother and father. The same issues that caused Ruth's and Loretta's problems are causing the same problems today but on a much larger scale and on a lot more people. Throughout the history of mankind, there has always been an underbelly of society that just couldn't make it. Now it seems that the underbelly is no longer the underbelly; it is the driving factor over the past twenty-five years. Ruth experienced it to a lesser degree, my father experienced, but it still was a struggle. They were both able to pull through it, but many even in their youth couldn't. Startling as it may seem, the number that can't pull through today is multiplied twenty times. Ruth's family structure hardly existed, my father's family structure was strong, but opportunity, education, and finances were lacking. Sometimes it seems, in life, you find situations where you have to tell the world that you are coming for it. To a degree, my father, his brothers, and sisters, and Ruth were able to do that. Even at that time, many people were not able to do it, and it appears, sadly, that perhaps in 2016, 50 percent of the world—for political, social, economic, health, etc. reasons—cannot do it.

In the end, I think my father is absolutely right. It all revolves around family, parents, and connection. Without that glue, society falls apart, whether it be on a grand scale of a nation or the diminutive scale of Ruth and Loretta; the effect is the same. With no family structure, the deductive and inductive situation is the same. In 2016, that effect is in many parts of the world destroying large segments of mankind—its history and its future.

*****

Betty has equally as-vivid memories of the wet packs, sick needles, and the color of the solution in the syringe, being put next to a radiator to dry off quicker, and being released from the detention and back to the ward. I knew then that we would have to go see Betty again after Ruth and Paul did so set a date. There was plenty more information in these first set of notes that were taken by Paul, and I would be even more dismayed at the notes I take when Carol, Ruth, and I go visit Betty, approximately one month later.

Ruth told us, "In seclusion, the doors were black steel with small peepholes in them. In the cells, there were no cots, pillows, or blankets etc. While you were in seclusion, you could scrub the floor of your cell, which was about ten by ten. You were let out three times a day to use the bathroom. The regular cells, you have more freedom—you could open and close doors, but they were supposed to stay closed. You could go in and out to use the bathrooms anytime without supervision. They would bring in a cot at eight p.m. and fold them back up at seven a.m. each day. Once the cots were removed for the day, you had to scrub the floor in your cell. During the seclusion, they would give you random-size pieces of cloth, and you spent the day taking it apart thread by thread. It was something to keep you busy instead of teaching you to read or write, something that might be educational. When other girls had piles of threads, I would reach over and grab some of theirs to make it look like I was doing something. This way, when the doctors or nurses came around, they would think I was doing something. It was just something to filling up time to keep you from being sassy. In the seclusion cells, there was no cot, and they might give you a blanket, depending on the guard on duty. It was usually warm, and the radiator was high up on the wall, probably so you didn't get hurt or damage it. I don't remember the color of the cell, but the pipes were gray. Since they only took you to the bathroom three times a day, I kept the bowl from the milk, and if I had to go to the bathroom, I would use that same bowl and then pour the urine down the small space around the pipe going up to the radiator. We had two little rhymes that went with dumping the urine down the small space surrounding the radiator pipe. The other rhyme was, 'Walls got ears, pipes got holes, back to Jackson, everything goes.' When they brought a new girl into detention, and while they were scrubbing the floors, I lay down on the floor and tried talking to them under the door. I would ask who it was, what they did that got them in detention. Most times it was Betty or Beverly. There were not too many bold ones, maybe ten or more most times. A lot of them that were in the Girls Building, but when they got there, they wouldn't keep acting out. They would behave better and go back to the Main Building. At the most, there were thirty to forty in the Girls Building most of the time. The other half of the Girls Building was the epilepsy ward."

Ruth telling me that the epilepsy ward was the other half of the Girls Building was a clear confirmation, I realize later, that Betty, when we visited her on February 23, 2016, was telling the truth about her experience. With epileptic residents being used as a punishment for Betty's misbehavior. That experience was one Ruth refused to participate in and a situation we discuss with Betty in February and will dig deeper into later in this narrative.

All of this information came from the first time Paul and Ruth visited in December 2015. When we went back to see Betty in February of 2016, she reiterated the same stories to Carol and I as she did to Ruth and Paul. During the second visit, the recollections became even more vivid, with Ruth there adding greater detail. It all seemed to come back to both of them as they reviewed together all those negative experiences from almost sixty years ago.

I asked Ruth if there was anything else from when she went to visit Betty in December of 2015.

Ruth replied, "I believe everything Betty said is true, that I helped her get free. When her coat got caught on the fence, I had to help her get free, but I knew that if I went over, they would come looking for us. It was time to go back in the building, and they would know if I was missing. Where Betty was quieter and would blend in, I was bolder. I did hear the whistle go off when someone was missing. I remember yelling to her, 'Go!' By her getting out, she was able to get married and have children. In about 1961, I went to New Jersey to see Betty. She had her husband and two children. She had a nice home, and she was doing well for herself."

I told Ruth, "It started when I saw your picture on the front page of our newspaper for winning an award for Volunteer of the Year for Community Action. When I saw it, I called you and told you that I have forgotten about you. I told you I would invite you to my son's high school graduation in a few weeks. We started writing in the fall of that same year, had to be September 2014. So it has been almost two years, and the book is still a work in progress."

Ruth remembered Betty talking about the "dunking." How Betty was fearful of taking a bath; even showers frightened her, and never would she go swimming. She was completely traumatized by water from those terrifying experiences early in her life. For her entire life, she took mostly what Carol called "truck driver showers" or commonly known as sponge baths. The veracity of all of this, unknown to me at this time, was fully reconfirmed when we visited Betty for the second time in February of 2016. Two people separately telling the same story certainly reconfirmed it all as the truth. Ruth lost track of Betty three years prior to that December 2015 meeting when Betty went in to the nursing home. For the two of them to collude and make the same story is nearly impossible.

As it says in the Bible, "The truth will set you free."

Clearly these two are telling the truth. With the written documentation that Ruth has accessed from New York State and with the collaboration of the documentation by Ruth and Betty, it stands in and of itself as true. Ironically, about ten years ago, Ruth and Betty went to the Syracuse State School to obtain their records. They both got their records; Ruth kept hers. A fire at a house she was renting destroyed Betty's. Even with that fire, even with her advanced age, when we met, Betty's memories about what befell her and Ruth were as vivid as the day they happened. Pain, depravation, and loneliness are stern teachers that do not allow the person to forget the lessons they were taught. Betty and Ruth got those lessons in no uncertain terms, and they are not about to forget. Not today. Not tomorrow. Not ever.

Again, as it says in the Bible, "The truth will set you free."

I doubt either will ever be set free from those early life experiences. Not in this world anyway. They will see each other again, but not for a while. Then, maybe the truth will set them both free. Permanently.

Both Ruth and Betty were always going to be underestimated. There were both women, they were both short and cute, both from dysfunctional homes. There were classified by the system as idiots and morons. The most appropriate use of all their disadvantages was to use them as a fuel to propel themselves forward.

I asked Carol, "Which of the two do you think did better or worse or the same, knowing what you know about Ruth's life and be assured that Betty's life was very similar?"

Carol replied, "I would have to say Ruth, because it seems that even though they both struggled, Ruth seemed to keep trudging forward, wanting from no one or waiting for anyone."

That is probably a fair assessment due to the situation that Betty was in when we went to visit her and Ruth's current situation. Both women used to be underestimated to their advantage. They are both human beings with the same imperfection as any other human being. Their early histories wrought with real-life survival issues. After knowing Ruth for many years and Betty only a few hours, all of their imperfections, the same imperfections we all have, should play into their lives tenfold, but really they didn't. In fact, for them, it seemed to make them strong, even give them a greater understanding of all other human beings' imperfections. Ruth accepts things for what they are; she does delve deeply into issues but rather attacks them straightforward, almost passing them out of the way because she sees another goal and another objective. For both of their lives, they have fallen off the back of a truck every day. In Ruth's case, through all these years, it has happened in some cases, to my knowledge, falling off a cliff. Ruth always pulled herself up with a smile, brushed herself off, and proceeded forward with a smile. Both women quickly admit they were agitators every day; both of them defied the rules, crossed every line they could, and in Ruth's case, she did it with impunity, as she will tell you. I think Ruth more than Betty.

Once, I asked Betty, "Who was the worst behaved in the Syracuse State School?"

Immediately Betty pointed at Ruth and said, "Ruth."

Throughout history, isn't it true the people that defy convention are the ones that allow the world to move forward? Think in terms of Copernicus, who was excommunicated from the Catholic Church for his theory of the earth revolving around the sun. What at first seems unreasonable seems to end up being the truth. The unreasonable wants to change the world to fit them. The reasonable falls into the same mold, same doldrums, adjusts, plods ahead. For Ruth and Betty, plodding along was enough, but it seems that Ruth, being at times unreasonable is what pushed her further ahead. Betty may have been more reasonable, but over the course of a lifetime, it put her in a less conducive position than Ruth. Betty's reasonableness may have hurt her, and Ruth's unreasonableness hurt her over the course of a lifetime. You just don't give up. What you are going to do is win more. What you're going to do is go harder. Don't stop, only keep going up. Never surrender. I swear she lives the same right up to this moment. As Carol and I sat here in the kitchen on a Spring evening trying to look at this story from all angles, Ruth was moving forward. Ruth will never surrender.

It often strikes Carol and I as funny that even though Ruth is the story, often she did not put herself into the story. She often described it as an outsider looking in. At other times she was quoting people that she interacted with, but mostly she did not inject her story a lot. For Ruth to be able to live through all those cold experiences, she was able to see through them and understand that her life was happening, but she was in the wrong place to make the kind of life she wanted to have. She pushed herself through it for literally twenty-five years to get someplace on the other side. She was certainly at the wrong place at the wrong time. Did she make it because she got all the breaks? Obviously not. Did she make it because she didn't get any breaks? Possibly yes. At almost eighty-two years old, it doesn't make any difference anyway. She is a perfect example of the adage, "It doesn't make a difference where you start, only where you finish." At specific points in time, she almost pulled Loretta along with her, probably without even knowing it. Through that scattered lifestyle, the rejection and the loneliness, they still managed to find each other and live their entire adult life about five blocks apart.

My son is a big fan of English football. I understand that for the first time in 125 years, the Leicester FC won the EUFA championship. I started watching it at times even though it was early in the morning because the fans were really enjoying themselves with their team's championship run. On two or three occasions, I saw television reports from a pub that was a favorite of the Leicester fans. I'm not sure if it was possible, but the same four or five people were sitting at two or three tables behind the reporter. Maybe they were put there as actors, or actresses; maybe they were officials of the league, or team owners. Maybe they—being there at the same time every day—knew there was going to be a report. What I remember is two or three women sitting at those tables had T-shirts on that said, "Forever fearless." Is that a perfect two-word summation of Ruth Morgan? How else could you sum up her whole life?

I asked Carol, "Should we change the name of this book to *Forever Fearless*?"

Carol responded, "I still like *Ruthie Deeply*."

I asked her, "Why?"

Carol said, "Because the title of the book has her name in it."

Seemed like a joke fits in here.

I asked Carol, "Do you know what people say when you show them a picture of Mickey Mouse?"

Carol said, "Mickey Mouse."

I asked, "What do people say when you show them a picture of Abraham Lincoln?"

Carol didn't know.

I said, "Show me another picture of Mickey Mouse."

On that note, Carol and I made an executive decision to end our writing, revising, typing, and retyping for tonight. We will click File, save two or more times just to be certain that we have saved our efforts for today, Memorial Day weekend 2016.

Next, we needed to interview Betty and take notes from the visit that we planned for February 23, 2016. Ruth felt Betty may not live much longer so it was imperative that we get to see her quickly. My father had been in the hospital for about a week with an abdominal illness. On the way to pick up Ruth, we stopped at my sister's house to drop off some financial information that she needed to use in order to make sure his bills were paid. Carol and I left home about eight thirty on an overcast but otherwise dry day. That in itself was a rarity in Upstate New York in February.

On the way to my sister's house, Carol told me about the Beekman Brother starting a company in Sharon Springs, New York, that started producing a specific high-quality tomato. The business has morphed into a whole family of products all driven by being all-natural foods. The business has been on QVC and partnered with Target stores to distribute additional local-produce products from other small businesses. The whole area of Upstate New York was settled by colonists in the 1790s. It is very rich farmland surrounded by small picturesque communities like Richfield Springs, Cooperstown, and Duanesburg. It became famous in the late 1800s for rich people from the New York City area to bathe in the natural warm sulfur springs that flow out of the ground. Much the same as Saratoga Springs, New York, but on a much smaller scale. During the Great Depression, the hotels and spas that were built went bankrupt and fell into disrepair. After about one hundred years, people became interested in the old hotels and spas, with the resurgence of nostalgia for natural products and previously famous locales. We decide to stop on the way back from visiting Betty to browse through Sharon Springs and maybe come back in September when they have a harvest festival. As we were driving along en route US 20, the US highways, being the precursor to the modern interstates, they run through villages and cities big and small all across the United States. If a traveler really wanted to tour the real landscape of America, the US highways are the only way to do it. Those highways are populated with diners, farms, and mom-and-pop stores and motels that many have been there over a hundred years.

When we picked up Ruth about nine thirty, she was ready to go. We put Ruth and Little Foot in the car with his plaid blanket on the back seat so he can be warm and comfortable; after all, it is February in Upstate New York, although by the looks of it, you wouldn't know it and drive away along route 5S east to Mohawk and take route 28 south to Richfield Springs and then US 20 east and drive through Cherry Valley, Sharon Springs, and Duanesburg and so on. Ruth points out the Duanesburg Diner that she and her daughter went to many times for food. We decided to stop there on our way back home for lunch after visiting Betty. We continued driving looking for Route 7 to Guilderland Center and Guilderland Center Nursing Home where Betty was residing at the time. When we did find the nursing home; the front was under construction to the point Carol thought it was vacant. We followed the very unprofessional-looking signs to enter from the back of the building because there was construction in the main entrance. When we walked in, a young woman at a desk greeted us, and we informed her that we had come to visit Betty. She told us that she was happy that someone and come to visit her because Betty rarely had anyone visit her.

Ruth told us, "Betty wanted to see Diane, her daughter, so bad, but Diane's husband prevented her from visiting her mother. Apparently, Betty had another daughter that didn't survive, and her name was Diane also."

When we started walking down the hall to Betty's room, it was crowded with wheelchairs, patients, medicine carts, nurses, and a lot of other staff. The entire building smelled pretty bad; the hallway was well lit. We entered Betty's room. It was dark and crowded, very close quarters, old, and not very clean. Betty had a roommate on the other side of the curtain who we never saw but we heard. I felt bad for the other woman because she expressed to the nurse how she felt that no one paid any attention to her; she was always alone, had no visitors, and felt even the staff didn't pay any attention to her. It was like she wasn't even there. It didn't seem that Betty wasn't in that much of a better situation, but at least we showed up on this Saturday in February.

RUTHIE DEEPLY

We started with introductions and questions. Betty was born in 1933; her father was James Elmer Rhoades (?). All she really knew about him was that he was in the military and that he died in a VA hospital in Virginia. Her mom, Dorothy Groven Berg (?), died when she was three years old, and Betty never even knew her. From her birth through age eleven, Betty doesn't remember much other than she was born in Albany and was in a New York State school at age eleven. At age eleven she thought she was in many foster homes because there was no place for her to go. So eventually she ended in the New York State schools. Betty also had a brother that was in a reform school whose name was Jimmy. She met her brother by chance at a foster home. The chances that they would meet and be able to piece together their relationship was astronomical. To the best of Betty's knowledge, she had a sister named Charlotte that she never met. Her sister could have been living next door to them, and she wouldn't even have known it.

Betty told us, "Any information that I got about my family came from employees of the state school system. I never received any information from my own family. I'm not sure how I got from Albany to Syracuse, and I think I was raised in Gloversville."

She also mentioned some of the same people Ruth mentioned, like Mary LaGraff and a Mrs. Holmcress. Ruth named her oldest daughter after Mrs. LaGraff. Ruth remembered Mrs. Holmcress as the supervisor of the laundry room. Betty, as in Ruth's case, said that there was no education; all you did was work, and anything you learned, you learned on your own. Betty remembered something that Ruth did not: all the patients in the Syracuse State School wore a sign of some sort indicating they were residents of the Syracuse State School.

"Ruth," I asked, "do you remember anything about having to wear a sign?"

Ruth answered, "I don't remember, but I wouldn't be surprised. I probably never had to wear one because I was in detention or solitary confinement much of the time."

It struck me how demeaning it was to force people to wear signs that identified them as a particular group or religion or ethnic background. Much like the Jews during the Nazi years in Europe were forced to sew a Star of David on their clothes. The whole purpose was to ostracize that group from the mainstream of society. If Betty's memory about having to wear a sign is accurate, again I feel the sole purpose was to separate the residents of the Syracuse State School from the population in the surrounding area. If someone such as Betty or Ruth were to escape, they could easily be identified. Same as prisoners in orange jumpsuits. The difference was that the Jews, Betty, and Ruth didn't do anything wrong. They were purely victims of circumstances beyond their control.

Betty told us, "There was a sign on the building that said: Anybody Admitted to This Institution Is Retarded."

Ruth said right away, "I wonder if that is the sign that Betty was talking about?"

For the first time, there was memory that Betty had that Ruth didn't. Unless I was confused when Betty was telling me that the sign went on their clothes. Ruth remembered the sign on the building about everyone in the building being retarded but nothing about the sign on their clothes.

Ruth suggested, "Maybe Betty was confused, because past pictures of people that were at the Syracuse State School did not have any labels on their clothes."

We tended to think that Ruth was correct based on the evidence we had seen. Even though the evidence was scant, we still saw no indication of labels on the residents' clothes. Betty also brought up other names of people she remembered, names such as Luther, Jackson, McCann, Woody the Cook, and Dr. Bisgrove, who was at that time the director of the Syracuse State School.

When the name *Jackson* came up, Ruth had the same reaction.

"Jackson slapped me in the face on both sides until it was black-and-blue and then put me in solitary confinement so no one could see the bruises. Then when my mother came on the weekend to visit me, they refused to let me see her because they knew they would get in trouble. Even the other employees couldn't believe it." Ruth made the exact same statement every time Jackson's name came up.

Betty continued when I asked her about dunking, "They would put you in a straitjacket and force your head under cold water until they wanted to bring you up. You could be under the water for a few seconds or even up to a minute. When they pulled me out of the water, I was usually screaming or crying, and on a few occasions, I vomited, and later they made me clean up. I was usually kept separate from Ruth, but when I sassed back, I got strong punishment too. There was one dorm for sensible people and another dorm for all the others. I was rarely in the sensible dorm, and Ruth was there even less. To this day, I get frightened taking showers and baths. I'm terrified anytime I am near water. Even though it only happened two or three times, that was enough. We had to wear ticking dresses, which the fabric was striped and then went to your ankles and you wore every day. Three times a day you got to use the bathrooms when you were in seclusion. If you were put in a cell, there was no chair, bed, mattress, blankets, or sheets. If someone felt like it, they might bring you a mattress or a blanket to use for the night. If not, you just slept on the floor. After the seclusion, you would go to the detention ward for a week or more. You would work scrubbing floors, polishing and waxing floors with twenty-five-pound polishers, which you would do all day long for hours. We worked in about groups of ten girls. We didn't let anyone take advantage of us. We gave it right back to the workers, and they in turn put us back in detention and punishment. There was no medication in the state school, only the sick needle used for punishment. When you got the sleep needle, you would fall asleep in a few minutes, and they gave it to you whenever they felt you were not behaving. Sometimes I would sleep in a closet for up to two hours, on the floor with no blankets or pillow or witnesses, all by yourself until it wore off. It was all done randomly. Whenever the staff felt you needed to be disciplined, they would administer the drug with a doctor's approval."

Ruth's take on the whole situation was pretty much the same.

Ruth said, "I would rather have the sleeping needle rather than the sick needle for obvious reasons. If you got the sick needle, they put you in the cell, and you upchuck until you finish vomiting, by then you are so sick you can't even remember how many times you threw up. Then the next morning when you woke up, you had to clean it up, it's worse than jail."

As we have discussed this part of the notes from our visit with Betty, Ruth has almost had the same recollections as Betty.

Ruth said, "That was our schooling. We never went to school, we just scrubbed and polished. Even Betty laughed about the idea of education. It was constant—scrubbing floors, working in the canning factory, working in laundry room, and they considered that an education. I know they had classes for other kids, but Betty or I never went. In the Girls Building, there were over one hundred girls that did not go to any classes. In my opinion, they should have had a teacher in the detention area instead of putting us in cells and spend day after day scrubbing floors, and the girls may have behaved better if they had a teacher to teach us rather than keeping us in detention, scrubbing floors, in the kitchen canning, and doing laundry. We were not learning anything."

I asked Ruth, "Was it a way to suppress you, control you and all the other girls?"

Ruth replied, "The purpose was to keep us quiet or busy so we wouldn't get in trouble, but we still got in trouble, especially me. If you didn't behave, you just went back to confinement. When you had to tease the rags apart by pulling the threads out, I refused to do it. When they let me out of the bathroom, I would grab handfuls of the other girls' threads. Sometimes the girls would give the threads and let them think that I teased out the threads in my pile. Everyone in the cells would have to do them—Betty, Beverly, me, everyone. I have no idea what they did with the threads later. I think they wanted us to stay out of trouble, but it never worked with me. When they had me, they had their hands full. Some of the girls were stupid enough to leave their full boxes of threads under the table in the detention ward, and I would grab handfuls and put them in the box in my cell so they thought I was doing it. But I never did. Some of the girls were so afraid of the workers, but I wasn't afraid of them. They could have killed me, but I wouldn't care."

Carol and I discussed how it is so discouraging that young people were put in a situation that led them to near despondency to the degree that they didn't care if they lived or died. Ironically, they had committed no crime; they had no offense against society other than the situations they were born into, which was beyond their control, and still they were punished daily for infractions most of them probably didn't understand and, with some guidance, may not have committed.

I told Carol and Ruth, "It reminds me of the scene in the movie *Guess Who's Coming to Dinner*, when Sydney Poitier tells his father that he chooses to have a son, and because of that choice, it didn't make any difference if he carried the mailbag a million miles. He made the choice to have a family, and he was responsible for that family. Betty and Beverly and Ruth and the hundreds of other girls that passed through this system for probably a century did not make the choice like Sydney Poitier's father, yet they had to bear the responsibility for the terrible choices made by Ruth's mother and the man that she feels was not her father."

I suggested we talk about "the big breakout of 1954" by using both Ruth's and Betty's recollection of the incident.

Ruth remembered it like it was yesterday.

She said, "We went for a walk up to the playground, while the girls were running around and the matrons chasing them. Betty and I walked down the hill, and I asked Betty if she wanted to go over the fence. She said yes. That's all she had to say. I told her to jump on my shoulder and hold on to the fence and jump over. As she jumped over, her coat got caught on the fence. I unhooked it and pushed her over before anyone came looking for us. I couldn't go over because they would miss two of us, and I was trying to cover for Betty. There was no one there that I could trust to help me get over. There was no one that we could trust that would not go back and tell the matrons. If the matrons came and asked me where Betty was, I would tell them that she went in the other direction and wasn't sure where she was. If I went missing, they would know I was gone because I was always in some type of trouble all the time. I could distract them from Betty being missing because she would behave some of the time, and her missing was not as obvious. If I were missing, it would be obvious because I kept the matrons busy all day. There were about thirty or forty girls on the playground. By the time they lined us all up, counted us, checked to see who was missing, and walked down back into the Girls Building, Betty was long gone. It was probably about half an hour before the matrons realized that Betty was gone. By that time, she was free. I can't tell you the rest of the story, but Betty did when we went to see her."

At the time we were talking to Betty, she seemed at times weak and confused. She saw cats on the shelf, sitting on the sink, and so on. On the other hand, she specially remembered what happened sixty-two years ago when she was twenty and went over the fence. Her statements were clear and lucid. Those memories were tattooed onto her brain as if they had happened the day before. Ruth didn't know what happened to Betty when she got over the fence, but Betty knew exactly.

Betty painted the picture, "Once I got over the fence, I got to downtown Syracuse and roamed the streets for a while. I met someone downtown that I had met through the fence while I was in the state school. This guy had been coming around for over a year talking to me through the fence. Ruth and I had been planning to escape for about a year also. The guy's name was Gene, and I had planned to meet him in downtown Syracuse if I got out. Sure enough, once I was out, I bumped into him. I went to live with him and his wife for about a week. Then we drove to New Jersey so I could meet his brother Morris. While in New Jersey, I worked in kitchens, laundries, and I worked for a number of doctors and lawyers ironing to make money. People told me that it would be cheaper to live in New Jersey than Syracuse, so when I got there, I made money any way I could. About two years after I went to New Jersey, I married Gene's brother Morris. Morris and I had two children, Gloria and Arnold. Morris died, and I moved back to Albany. I met Bill, and we had two more kids, Diane and Chrissie. While in New Jersey, I worked for Delmont in Swedesboro. I worked at Watson's Turkey Farm in Blackwood, New Jersey, near the Delaware Memorial Bridge. I was very pretty back then. I looked like Brooke Shields. I moved back to Albany, but there was no work for me there. Many years later, I found out that Dr. Bisgrove and some of the staff were arrested. They should have gotten arrested for what they did in the state school. Things like three days in the sheets for three hours at a time, with isolation in between. Then sheets and isolation the next day again. Two pieces of bread and a bowl of milk when you got out of the sheets. It was terrible. Ruth was the worst one in our gang. I also knew Ruth's sister, Loretta. When I got out of the sheets, I was so weak I would fall to the floor and then have to go right in to a room or isolation. They would make us watch other kids having seizures as a punishment if they even thought we were going to misbehave. At times, if you misbehaved enough, your punishment was to spend the night in bed with kids who had seizures. You would stay in bed with them, and it would scare me to death. The kids would foam at the mouth, twitch, thrash around in the bed all night long. They even had other kids wring out the sheets and give them to the matrons to put on the misbehaving kids. If they didn't do it right, they would be punished. I describe it as being shell-shocked."

Ruth said, "That's the way it was—no ifs, ands, or buts. They treated us horribly, worse than prison. People in prison are treated better than we were, and we were kids, not criminals. We really didn't do anything wrong. We never went to church or did anything normal kids do. We certainly never did anything criminal, but we were treated like criminals. You can't choose the family or circumstances you are born into, but in my case and Betty's, we spent over twenty years paying for the circumstances we were born into. How fair was that? Granted, once we got there we made many of our own problems, but we were not the reason we got there. There was still no reason to treat us like they did. We were children forced into a situation we certainly did not choose. At least thirteen years was a long time to be abused, and even after that, I was still under their control. I don't remember a lot about the House of the Good Shepherd other than it was pretty good. I did get to go to school. But, the Syracuse State School was a nightmare. Even if we did behave, it seems they always found a reason to punish us. The system failed me. I think I could have gotten a good education and made more of myself. Although, in the end, I didn't do bad, they always felt I could never live on my own and would have to be supervised my entire life. How did I own my own home, raise my kids for the most part by myself? I always seemed to do okay? No one helped me, I had to help myself, and I did. George never provided any money or support, never even sent his own kids a Christmas card with $5 in it. I would get my kids

Christmas gifts and sign them 'From Dad' and both sets of grandparents just to make them feel they had family that cared about them. That is what I think broke the chain. My kids certainly didn't have a life like it did when I was young. Thank God for that. It was all a result of hard work and trying to keep my family together. I had no car, I walked to the store. My kids helped me push a filled grocery cart home with my daughter Colleen in it. Colleen was in a coma at the time, and no doctor could ever diagnose what was wrong with her. I would hate myself if my kids ever had to go the same way as me. I wouldn't let it happen, I would just work harder."

Sometimes you just have to close ranks and fight. Ruth undoubtedly did that her entire life, and it served her well.

Ruth agreed 100 percent that every word Betty told us was the truth, and it was terrible.

Betty and Ruth have strong ties from their time in the state school. While we were there, they connected well, made small talk, like all those years and not passed by. They reminisced like the two schoolgirls that they were when they were first placed in the Syracuse State School. After Betty went to New Jersey, Ruth was still in the Syracuse State School, also known as the Colony. Ruth left the Colony and worked in a private home as part of her probation for a year to prove herself ready to leave and return home. During that time period while Ruth was in the Colony and working in Dr. Farchione's house, she still kept in touch with Betty by phone and during her weekly free time on Sundays when Betty would meet her in downtown Syracuse. By that time, Betty had moved back to Albany along with her two children after her husband died. After Ruth left the Colony, she went home to Ilion to live with her mother on a probationary basis. During the time with her mother, Ruth had to go back to Syracuse for probation appointments probably once a month. She got a lawyer in Herkimer to file for permanent release at the age of twenty-five. While living with her mother, Ruth still kept in touch with Betty by phone. In the meantime, Ruth got married and had three children. Betty had two more children in another relationship plus the two from her marriage. On occasions, Betty and her family would go to Ruth's, and Ruth at times with her family would go to Betty's house.

Ruth remembered, "Betty's son Arnold and my son used to walk up to Russell Park at times while they visited. Betty's daughter Christine would take my daughter's bike and wasn't able to ride the bike by the big hill near my house. I told her not to, but she did anyway. She ended up falling and going to the hospital for stitches to repair a cut and ended up staying overnight for observation. Betty and I lost contact for about three years. Betty's granddaughter found me on social media and contacted me to let me know that Betty was in a nursing home. That's when I went with Paul in December of 2015, and we went again in February of 2016. So, from 2012 to 2015, I had no contact with her."

As Ruth, Carol, and I talked more about "the big breakout of 1954," Ruth told us that she heard the alarm that someone was missing about a half hour after Betty was gone. She remembered that a Syracuse police officer came to get a statement from the staff, but by then, Betty was long gone. Ruth didn't think they even looked for her. Betty told us when we visited her the second time that she remembered being stopped by a Syracuse police officer, but the officer never made the connection that she was the escapee from the Syracuse State School. She got so nervous that she almost "crapped her pants." Ruth wondered if they ever even looked for her. Ruth also wondered if they ever contacted any relatives or the foster care system in New Jersey. Carol thinks that because of Betty's age at the time of her escape, they never even looked for her in that she was in her late teens or early twenties.

Betty stopped talking and paused for a minute, and her mind jumped back to the Syracuse State School. The cats are under the sink again. My heart breaks because the woman in the other bed tells the nurse that came in to check on her that she feels left out, she feels like she doesn't exist. That no one ever comes to see her and that she is all by herself. What a pity. Betty is not in as bad a situation as her roommate in that at times Betty's granddaughter would come to see her with some consistency, but adult children came infrequently. The daughter that Betty really missed was Diane. She had previously mentioned she wished she could see her, but she rarely came due to what appeared to be an abusive relationship and denying Diane an opportunity to see her mother. Clearly, it was breaking her heart in that she brought it up again.

Betty started to tell us about an even more obscene punishment she was subjected to, but Ruth was not. There was a ward dedicated to housing children with severe epilepsy. As punishment, people in Ruth's ward were sent to epileptic ward to supervise the patients there. They were supposed to be supervising the epileptic patients, but Ruth and many others refused. In that they refused, their punishment was the sheets, detention, and possible dunking or even the sick needle. As Betty told us, a further punishment as far as her case was to sleep in the same bed as the patients who had seizures, shaking, frothing at the mouth, and twitching. Full-blown grand mal seizures.

To quote Betty, "It scared the hell out of me all night long. Just watching what happened to these kids was terrifying in itself. But to sleep with them alone in that dark ward with probably thirty other kids in different degrees of illness was horrifying, and I will never forget it as long as I live."

It was hard to tell Betty being so "buried" in all the sheets and blankets on her bed, but she certainly appeared to be shaking remembering about the whole situation some seventy years ago. Sad and depressing for her and me, but still amazing that she is on this earth still telling us about it.

As in the case of Ruth, Betty taught herself to read and write. The few good things she got out of life were her kids. There was a time in her life that she was happy raising her kids. She remembered putting rubber pads under her kids' beds during a thunderstorm so they wouldn't get shocked if lightning hit their house. She remembered her son's bright-red hair and his first steps; he was still her baby. She had Arnold's first lock of hair, his first shoes and hospital gown, but they were all destroyed in a fire when her house was destroyed on Livingston Avenue in Albany. Betty enjoyed taking her kids outside, going for walks out in the woods, and playing catch with them. Through it all, she would be the first to tell you she got some good out of life. She kept herself clean; she didn't get involved in drugs or alcohol. The only really health issue up to when we met her in Guilderland was migraine headaches.

"Hey, Ruth, did you ever get the dunking?" I asked.

A quick reply from Ruth: "No, I would have pushed them in the water and see how they would like it. I would have tripped them over the tub and probably killed one of those bastards. I maybe would have ended up dead."

These two corroborated the same story over seventy years later. It's hard to argue against the factualness of all this when two people tell the same story almost to the word and then have it all documented in the form of the reports that Ruth received from the Central New York Developmental Services Office in Syracuse, New York. The truth calls us back from all the people that suffered in a system that meant to deny them opportunities that should be made available to all of us. Ruth in the end has the last laugh because she is alive; she survived and lived to tell about it. Betty on the other hand survived and lived to tell about it, but unfortunately her life ended in dismal circumstances and certainly not to the same degree that Ruth flourished throughout her life. Betty's spirit and Ruth's temperament both will not let this whole lifelong drama be in vain. Ruth and Betty both do great justice in implicating the harm that was done to them. They are both valid examples of the old maxim "whatever doesn't kill you only makes you stronger." These two women had clearly both suffered through very difficult childhoods in their home lives, while bouncing from place to place when they were too young to even remember, certainly in the documented notes from the Syracuse State School, in our interviews with Betty, and from the many recollections and memories Ruth has told me throughout my life. They both had much pain. Yet, that pain begat perseverance, and that perseverance begat character. That character led to a life of hope for both of them. Betty's hope ended when her life ended in February 2016. Ruth's hope is alive, just like she is on Labor Day Weekend 2016. I searched through the various Albany newspapers that I could find while working at my part-time job at the Utica Public Library for an obituary for Betty. I must have looked for two weeks and could not find even a death notice. It seems that Betty died in the same way she was born. There was no certainty, even from Betty's mouth while she was alive, where she was born, how she got into the state school, where she lived her early years etc. Her death happened the same way, at least from our perspective—no public notification, no funeral, and probably a simple burial. Betty was born and died in the same fashion. A cipher.

We left Betty when they started to bring lunches to the rooms. We started back home on US 20 and stopped at the Duanesburg Diner for lunch. The diner is a small typical place that you would find on any of the old US highways as they crisscrossed America. It had an extensive menu from appetizers to breakfast to sandwiches, gyros, steak, full-dinner entrees, and whole board of homemade desserts. The diner was full, and as soon as people left, someone else filled their spot. There were locals, there were people traveling just like us on US 20. There were older retired professional types, young people with families, and those that look like they were on a date. There smelled like home-cooked meals waiting to be eaten. I ordered a Greek gyro sandwich, Ruth ordered chicken and biscuits, and Carol ordered french toast. The waitress was happy and polite as she waited on almost the entire diner. After such a good lunch, Carol spotted the list of desserts. I was too full for any dessert, but Ruth and Carol ordered apple crisp. They both rated it as very good. Our check came to a reasonable $42.16 for a very good lunch with large portions. On the way out, I had to use the men's room. It was an experience from fifty years ago to find it. I had to walk down a narrow hallway, then down a winding set of stairs, up a small step to the bathroom that I could barely turn around in. It was clean and neat, and on top of the paper towel dispenser was an American flag air freshener. Places like the Duanesburg Diner were made famous in television programs like Route 66 and movies like *Diner*. There is no better restaurant than those type of diners that so typify America in both food and small-town lifestyle. I hope they never disappear. I hope my children have a chance to experience such good food and atmosphere.

We pulled out of the parking lot and back on US 20, driving west, and stopped in another small town named Sharon Springs, New

York. Sharon Springs developed in the 1890s in much the same way as Warm Springs, Georgia, did. The natural springs flowing from the ground were considered to have medicinal value. Trains ran from the New York City Metropolitan area to Upstate New York often three or four a day. Hotels, restaurants, and diners sprang up overnight. Some of the hotels were pretty large with up to three hundred rooms. Usually somewhere behind the hotel were the springhouses where the water fed into pools and people immersed themselves into them in order to relieve joint pains, muscle pains, and bruises. As years went by and people were able to purchase their own cars, many of these old hotels and spas fell in to disrepair. People had now moved from the cities to the suburbs, and with their own cars, they can now go to many more places other than the trains could take them. Sometime after 2000, a resurgence of these former hotels and surrounding locations became popular again. We didn't get out of the car but did drive up and down Main Street, and we decided to come back in September when a fall festival is scheduled. We proceeded to bring Ruth home but ran out of time to go in her house to visit. It had been a long week, with my father being in the hospital for the second time in two months. So, Carol and I proceeded home to meet our children and go to church. The day seemed so extreme, so random—with Ruth and Betty reminiscing like two schoolgirls about a normal childhood they obviously did not have, Betty seeing cats that were not there, turning the clock back fifty years in the Duanesburg Diner, going to church with my family like any other Saturday night, and getting my dad released from the hospital, and so on. Truly, a roller-coaster ride of a day. Approximately three weeks later, Betty was dead, but Carol, Ruth, and I were determined to carry on with *Ruthie Deeply*.

When we started our next session, after our visit with Betty, my son came home from his day at college. He looked nice with a black shirt on and khaki shorts.

I said to him, "Those shorts have stains on them."

His reply was, "They didn't have stains on them when I went to school. The stains are from working at Papa's house after class."

Ruth said, "Leave him alone. When I was at the state school, we had to wear those same tick dresses all the time. We had no choice. When we took a bath or shower once a week, we were given a clean tick dress and wore it all week until the next shower, when we got another clean tick dress. Betty said the same exact thing."

That should put it in perspective for my son, but I doubt it will. I bet tomorrow he has the same khaki shorts on. We ended here for dinner and a cocktail on Labor Day Weekend 2016. We had talked about in the past that modern psychologists use wet wraps for behavioral therapy. She told us that it can't be true, why would anyone want to use such a punishing discipline technique? I told Ruth how I just read that it has become more popular in the last ten years. Ruth was shocked, she couldn't believe it.

Quickly she changed the topic to rhymes and ditties that the residents sang and hummed amongst themselves.

"Pipes got holes, walls got ears, back to the owner, everything goes. Oh my goodness, oh my soul, there goes shit down the hole," Ruth quickly rattled off.

I got the impression that both rhymes covered the same topic. Sure enough, Ruth confirmed it, both were a description of flushing items into the sewer.

Ruth quickly stated, "Over your head, under your pillow." I didn't have any idea what that one meant, but Ruth certainly did. She usually laughed whenever she recited any of these verses from her youth while residing at the Syracuse State School.

William James, the twentieth-century philosopher, said, "The deepest principle in human nature is the craving to be appreciated."

We all discussed how Ruth has most times not been appreciated. People took her for granted and approached her like she didn't exist. We all agree that it is hard to imagine your home being the most dangerous place for you to live. Neither Carol nor I had any personal experience with the same situation, so for both of us, it's not real. For Ruth, it was the norm, the only world she knew. I personally find it unimaginable. Being as fortunate as I have been my whole life, to be in Ruth's world, it is an alternate existence. The ability to plan for most human beings is just not in our nature. We all tend to live day by day hopefully by choice. Ruth had no planning, nor did she have a choice. She was thrust into a very difficult situation, not of her doing, and is still paying the price for it in terms of earning power, poverty, and a daily struggle with most issues. Overall suicide rates tend to increase with wealth. I can never see that happening in Ruth's case because she has no wealth, never had a real opportunity to create wealth, and is still subject to poverty. She has endeavored her whole life to break the mold. Her method to break the mold was and is a strong work ethic that no one can take from her and is the only real way to succeed. Ruth Morgan or Bill Gates both work on the same principles, just at different levels. Carol and I both wonder, with better opportunities in her young life, what Ruth's story would be now in 2016. That same question holds true for all of us. The next Michael Phelps may be six or five years old or not even born yet.

It has been my experience that human beings respond much better to stories and anecdotes than they do to statistics. Data tends to get people's attention, but they respond better when that data connects to real-life situations. Unfortunately, in the computer age, we are bombarded with data on every topic imaginable. I once read about something called Rule 34; it seems the rule is as follows: if it exists, there is pornography of it. The computer age has thrust the world into much the same situation. If it exists, there is data about it. It became evident to me recently that from Ruth's written history in the foster care system, there is little hard data, obviously because there were no computers in 1934, and they were just beginning to develop as she grew up through the late 1950s and into the early 1960s, when she was released. I bet now there are reams of data about the foster care system stored all over the United States. I wonder what Ruth's history would look like now, in the computer age, especially in light of the fact that the history she has in hand is generally anecdotal. Having said, in my experience, people respond better to humanized stories rather than data, Ruth's history often elicits a strong visceral response from Michael, Carol, Alaina, and I. To the point we are often shocked. Now, I wonder if that isn't the endgame of this entire project? By shining a light on this woman's early experience, what at first glance is a tragedy then becomes a victory. When we first began this effort, I had a friend, with a PhD in psychology, make a quick read of the info Ruth obtained from the foster care system. His observation was fully appropriate. I quote, "The reports tell more about the writer than they do about the resident." He was extremely accurate even way back then. The writers had their take, not Ruth's. They had no data to back anything they wrote up. All the information they provided was subjective, not objective, to the tiniest degree. If printouts were available about what was happening with Ruth over, say, a three-year period was all formalized and printed in a concise form, would the approach the Syracuse State School took as to her life while a resident have been any different? Might it have been kinder? Might it have been harsher? Those questions now belong to history. Conversely, those should be asked every day in 2016 in order to make foster care the most effective and benevolent it can be. I am not certain there will ever be an answer as to how foster care should ideally exist for the maximum benefit of the residents, but Ruth shows every day that there has to be a better protocol than what she was subjected to at such a young age. It is up to us all to find it, if the system is ever to improve. It is human nature to protect children. Did you ever witness a child fall off a playground swing and start to cry? First thing everyone does is look for the child's parents. If they are not immediately located, five adults quickly run over to the child in order to determine if they are hurt. That is the true human experience. In Ruth's case, when she "fell off the swing," there was no one there to pick her up. Rather, she was surrounded mostly by emotional terrorists that were ready to push her "off the swing" again. Then go home with a clear conscience to have dinner with their families. How they could do it is beyond me. Yet, they did it on a daily basis to Ruth, and only goodness knows to how many others for many years right up to 9:09 a.m. on September 24, 2016. Heaven help us all.

    We haven't restarted our project in about three weeks. Yesterday and today, Ruth called with information she uncovered about Betty's children. I am not certain how she got access to this information other than the World Wide Web. Apparently, she had access to an Internet connection, probably at the day care where she works, and she was able to—or someone helped her—search names and found a home and cell number for Betty's son Arnold. Carol answered both phone calls.

When Carol answered the phone, Ruth said, "Carol, guess what? I found Betty's son Arnold's telephone number, and I talked to him."

Carol said to Ruth, "How did you find that out?"

Ruth said, "On the computer. I called him, and he gave me his cell phone number also. I explained to him that we are writing a book and we were looking for more information about Betty. I asked him if Vinny could call him, and he said it's okay. He also told me when to call because he works nights, and he would ask his sisters if they wanted to give us their phone number to call. Carol, didn't I do good?"

Carol replied, "You're a regular detective, Ruth. You're a cook, baker, volunteer, and now a full-fledged detective."

While Carol was on the phone with Ruth, she suddenly told her that her bathtub water was running. She takes a bath every day. Only this day, she was so excited that she found the information that she left the bathwater running and ran to call to tell us what she had discovered. Ruth takes nothing for granted. She wanted Carol to make sure that she told me so I can pursue it. Ruth was very careful to get the person's permission before going any further.

The next day, October 11, 2016, Ruth called around the same time as yesterday to inform us that she spoke with Betty's youngest daughter, Christine, and now has her phone number also. She was excited, and she reminisced with Christine about coming to her house in Ilion when she was a child with her mother, brother, and sisters. She asked Christine if she remembered falling off a bike and ending up at the emergency room, when Ruth told her not to ride a bike on the hill that was Ruth's street.

Christine told Ruth, "That I later ended up at St. Joseph's Hospital for plastic surgery from the injuries that I received that day when I fell off the bike. I do remember you telling me not to ride the bike down that hill because I wasn't familiar with the bike or the big hill."

It is incredible that with all the turmoil Ruth had experienced in her life from birth right through her early forties, she was able to still build a life and have some type of relationships with people that were in the same situation as her from their birth right up through their forties and even their fifties. These people are the embodiment of good luck being mostly a result of hard work. They make no other purpose than to help themselves go further. Throughout their lives, with obviously some help from various public and private agencies, they could raise children, have some level of permanent residence, and as evidenced by the fact that at least from what we know, their children seem to be doing reasonably well. It's the sort of situation that, as the rappers say, "bless up." In those two words, that's exactly what Ruth, Betty, and many others, I know, could do. It was nothing but hard work and using your head to always try to push yourself forward. All people, especially professional sports teams, need to get in for one purpose only, to win. Ruth always tried to put in a situation where she would end up moving forward, in effect a win. She was determined to win more and more each time. There are probably just as many women that were in the same situation as Ruth and Betty, especially in those early years that ended with short disastrous lives. That can never be said about Ruth right up to this moment, and it appears about Betty mostly the same situation. You must have a good understanding of time and see the whole picture over the course of eighty-some odd years to fully appreciate how far she has come even from when I knew her as a child.

Saint Augustine felt he was sure what time was until someone asked him to explain it. He then drew a blank. How Ruth and Betty always found a way to bounce back is something they knew how to do until someone asked them how to explain it. Very accurate, very prophetic, very Ruth, very Betty.

Having at length spoken to Betty twice—once in person, once by proxy with Ruth and her neighbor Paul—we now turn to our next collaborator, Ruth's sister, Loretta.

Another hapless victim of the New York State foster care system. A system, that in my opinion, is still looking for and locating its next hapless victim.

Chapter 3

Loretta: More Collaboration

On October 1, 1936, Ted and Betty Raymond had their second child and named her Loretta Jean. Early records indicate that Loretta and Ruth were under the care of Oneida County since 1935. Being that Loretta was born in 1936, it is unclear that both could have been under Oneida County's care in 1935. It seems that Ruth was already under Oneida County's supervision; the county automatically took dominion of Loretta. At these young ages, both were placed under the care of the House of the Good Shepherd.

Early records indicate, "While the girls seem to be fond of each other, they are not especially demonstrative and don't seem to mind at all about being in separate groups as they see each other on the playground and back and forth to school."

Under the heading Visitors: "Both Mr. and Mrs. Raymond have visited the children on at least two occasions. The father has been allowed to take them out for a short ride with the approval of the Oneida Co. Welfare. As a whole, the children seemed to have a good time, they were not upset upon return. However, the mother's visits have been most disturbing to the children. Being a mental defective, the mother's talk has been such that the children became very much excited, cried, and were somewhat disturbed when returned to their departments. Because of the mother's mentality, it is difficult to make her see how such conversations disturb the children and interfere with their placement. She has been very insistent that she be allowed to take them out. Upon the recommendation of the Oneida Co. Welfare, this request has been denied."

On March 1, 1940, Ruth and her sister were placed in a boarding home for two years and were discharged on December 22, 1942, to their parents. Both children were returned to the House of the Good Shepherd on September 30, 1946, because of "home conditions." Both were referred to a placement agency for transfer to the Syracuse State School on September 24, 1947.

Early records again indicate, "Ruth and Loretta seem to be very fond of each other. It is our feeling that they should be kept together. Ruth is very fond of and loyal to her mother. She had a rather sad time when she left us because she felt that she would be returned to her father. Her comment was 'You can kill me, but I'll never go back to live with him again because of the way he treated my mother.'"

When I asked Ruth if she had any recollection of her sister not wanting to return to their mother and father, she told me she had no idea; she couldn't remember anything specific. It seemed that Ruth would go home reluctantly, but Loretta just went right along with the idea. Having been born on October 1, 1936, she was placed in the House of the Good Shepherd on November 21, 1936, at an age of seven weeks old. On April 2, 1940, she was discharged to a boarding home and then to her parents on December 22, 1942.

In a period of six years, she was placed in the House of the Good Shepherd, a boarding home, to her parents, and then to the Syracuse State School. The undocumented conclusion is that Ruth was following the same path. The turmoil in the first six to eight years, because they both turned out reasonably well, is indicative of the fortitude that both individuals possess.

> Story of Child
>
> Loretta Jean Raymond was committed to the House of the Good Shepherd November 21, 1936, less than two months old. Mother was not giving the child proper care, and father was a transient worker, family living in inadequate quarters. It is noted in the record that the couple, on December 3, 1936, considered placing her out for adoption.
>
> February 8, 1937, she was x-rayed because of very persistent cough. X-ray negative.
>
> At age of 18 months was taken to C.G. Clinic Mehlman test and had M.A. 12 month. She was returned 10-5-42. Terman test: C.A. 8-0, M.A. 4-10, I.Q. 81.
>
> At times she is moody and disagreeable, had temper tantrums, and talked baby talk. She was more of a behavior problem in school than her sister and reacted poorly to discipline. Health good.
>
> September 1946, same grade as Ruth, Grade 4-1.
>
> The children have not been questioned about conditions in the home now. They have seen and heard many things that they should

have not. The mother said they were increasingly hard to discipline.

School History
Ruth:
    1st grade, at 7 years. Repeated. "Poor coordination between brain and head."
    September 1946, Grade 4-1.
Loretta:
    "Brighter than Ruth, more vivacious."
    Sept. 1946, Grade 4-1.

Exact words recorded from the earliest notes we have available. Already things seemed to be going favorably for Loretta and less so for Ruth. The trend continued from this early start right through both children's release from the Syracuse State School. As we will explore further on later, the same patterns and labels continue through their midtwenties. Those labels affected Ruth and Loretta up to this day. Ruth more so than Loretta, at least in a societal way but not in a practical way.

As we talked about both Ruth's and Loretta's experiences in the Syracuse State School, Loretta felt that she got little or no attention, whereas Ruth got a lot of attention. Most of the attention Ruth received was bad, but in a way, it was better than the no attention she got. Loretta was aware of Ruth often getting the sheets and the sick needles only by way of watching the employees going back and forth between the buildings.

I asked her about taking care of the epileptic residents in the school. It was nothing she had been exposed to, but she did hear rumors about it happening.

She also felt, "Ruth was always in trouble."

Ruth laughed.

I told her, "Ruth, everyone says the same thing."

She laughed even harder. Loretta said she knew that Betty was constantly in trouble, often getting the sheets and the sick needles too.

Again, Loretta felt, "Ruth was the worst."

Loretta was never exposed to the sheets, sick needles, or sleep needles. Yet she had heard about all of those protocols being used. Loretta spent most of her time cooking, crocheting, and knitting to keep herself busy. She felt that the employees aggravated Ruth and made her mean. They never really tried to help her, they just made her worse. The "safe kids" were kept in her building, of which there were about three hundred. In the Girls Building, where Ruth was housed, there were about one hundred girls.

While working toward her full release, Loretta worked for the Cook family in Syracuse and then the Murtaughs in Frankfort.

Loretta's opinion was, "The whole thing was an inch short of slave labor, but it was better than being in the state school."

By way of what Loretta told us, her experience in the New York State foster system was nowhere as horrible as Ruth's, but it was still pretty bad. She did know by word of mouth and what she observed happening as employees moved to one building to the next that there was a lot of bad situations occurring in the Girls Building. Loretta knew of those situations often involving Ruth, and many times Betty too. Word traveled fast in that small environment, and it was usually highly accurate.

Ruth and Loretta never had an opportunity to make their own way. They both had enough ingenuity and still do to find ways to survive. Ruth tended to have better skills in one direction where Betty had better skills in completely other directions. We wondered if it wasn't the typical "left hemisphere, right hemisphere" situation. Ruth being the right hemisphere rational side and Betty being the left hemisphere creative side. Carol felt the opposite. In that, Ruth challenged everyone and every situation that she came across, even to this day.

My daughter Lana suggests, "Ruth is more left sided and would not think about how her actions affected her before she did it. Loretta is right sided, she would think about her actions would affect her and just do what she was told. She would follow directions where Ruth went in the opposite of the directions."

Ruth was stuck with thinking small, which made it harder on her day by day. Loretta excluded the chatter and just went straight ahead doing what she was told all the way. Loretta was thinking larger than Ruth even though she didn't even know she was doing it at the time. Ruth made it complicated for herself, and it kept her excluded. She was housed in the more restricted environment; there were more punishments, were longer and more severe. Loretta tended to make it simpler for herself, which made her more included. More freedom, minimal punishments, and an overall safer situation. In Ruth's environment, fear was weaponized; it was used solely to keep Ruth in line and under control. Loretta, not so much; she was safer, with more opportunities, and although it didn't make any difference in the end— in that Loretta was released after Ruth. Ruth's release was considered a test to determine if Loretta could be released. Ruth was released at age twenty-four, and Loretta was twenty-two. Ruth stayed out of the state schools for two years before they released Loretta, which would make Loretta twenty-four and Ruth twenty-six. Collectively they had spent fifty years in the foster care system in the New York State. When they were finally released in approximately fifty human years, they were released with no sustainable skills or education, and yet they were still able to survive. Felons, when released back into society, many after very long jail sentences, struggle to this day, maybe more so than ever in 2016. There are many services available to these newly released felons, but still they struggle to blend back into society at large. Betty, Ruth, and Loretta had nothing, no services, no educational opportunities, and only bleak employment choices. They were lucky in the sense that expenses in the mid-1950s were much less than the expenses in the mid-two thousand and -teens. Although they didn't make a lot of money, their expenses were also very low. With a decent manufacturing job, an individual could earn steady money and live well. Loretta had that opportunity. Ruth never did to the degree that Loretta did. Ruth had to constantly reassess and work to improve her day-to-day life, and Loretta—in at least an economic sense—would follow directions and get well-paid, just as she learned to follow directions in the Syracuse State School. At least at this point, in reality, not one thing has changed since the 1940s.

Loretta is doing the same thing, and Ruth is doing the same thing, just like they have both been doing since day one.

Loretta's collaboration of Ruth's story proves not as strong as Betty's, mostly because she lived in the Main Building. She did hear the terrible stories about Ruth, Betty, and the entire Girls Building, and that is enough verification for us.

Ruth has contact with Loretta usually every week or so. Their relationship remains intact, not as strong as one would hope, but still there.

Chapter 4

Continuing to Survive

It had to be about 7:30 p.m. in the beginning of November 2016. It has been dark since about 5:30 p.m., and we haven't even moved the clocks from daylight savings time. That happened on November 6, and then it will be dark at 4:30 p.m. Thinking back, this project was a little over two years old; we certainly worked at it at our own pace. Yet we still worked at it consistently, and in the long run, we will finish it. There was no other choice now. Like the life histories of Betty, Ruth, and Loretta, who never gave up and never considered giving up as an option. Even at 7:30 p.m. at the beginning of November 2016, and we haven't even moved the clocks from daylight savings time yet.

Recent events have unfortunately pulled us all away from *Ruthie Deeply*. Yet, as of now, we may be able to get back on track. Approximately three weeks ago, while walking after dinner on a cold, clear moonlit night, I suffered a heart attack, had a stent put in my heart, and spent four days in the hospital. Much of the entire experience was still fuzzy to me, but I was recovering; and with no further complications, I would be soon returned to full strength. Ironically while in St. Elizabeth's Hospital, room 411, my next-door neighbor in room 412 was Ruth with a very high heart rate that doctors couldn't seem to bring down to a normal level. I spoke to a few of the nurses on the floor if it was common to see one patient walk to the room next door to visit another patient. They all agreed

generally it was not. Leave it to Ruth and I to upset precedent. Also, in true Ruth Morgan style, while she was in the hospital under doctor's order not to shower, she took it upon herself to do it anyway. When her care nurse for the night found out that Ruth had showered, she was livid. The point that Ruth missed was that if she had fallen while in the shower, her nurse for the night would have been held responsible, and there would have certainly been repercussions. The poor woman could have possibly lost her livelihood. In true Ruth fashion, she probably would have never made the connection until it was too late and then would have felt terrible. A powerful indicator of her will to survive that has always served her well but oftentimes got her in trouble. Without that will, she probably would have never made it to eighty-two years old or the hospital. She was also released after six days and was back home recovering. Carol, Michael, Alaina, and I visited this past Saturday to check on her. We also delivered a draft of the first fifty pages of *Ruthie Deeply*, which my neighbor Alaine had made copies of for Ruthie, others, and I to read and critique. She looked good and was in good spirits but still was experiencing rapid heartbeat at times. No doctor had called yet to set a date for a follow-up appointment. We all expressed to her the need to contact her own doctor for an appointment and set up a follow-up with a cardiologist. I had a follow-up cardiology appointment scheduled for December 14 and hoped to be cleared, as much as possible, along with organizing a long-term cardiology plan. I did mean long term and hoped Ruth could do the same. It all had set us back but will not deter us from reaching our end goal of documenting the truly convoluted life Ruth has led. Most of it not of her making.

Now finding myself with extra time on my hands in that I have not been doing my part-time job with the Utica City Schools, I decided to contact Betty Cable's children by way of telephone numbers Ruth had provided me with. Even before my health situation on November 6, I contacted Arnold at his home. I explained to a man that told me his name was Fred when he answered the phone who I was, how I got this number, and that it was my understanding that Arnold had expressed a willingness to talk to me about what he knew about his mother's years in New York State foster care. Fred proceeded to tell me he was Arnold's brother as he listened intently. When I told him I was unaware there was another brother, I thought only two other sisters, he quickly explained that he was not really Arnold's brother. They just always called each other that. All completely possible. So, I proceeded to give him my contact info and would he please give the message to Arnold so that, if he wished, Arnold could contact me back. Arnold never did. When I filled Ruth in as to what had transpired, she told me to not even bother to call back. But, on November 25 at 10:30 a.m., I called Arnold back on a cell phone number Ruth had also provided me with. I left a detailed message that the second call was about the same topic as the first and, if he was interested in talking, to call me back when he could. As of tonight, December 5, 2016, at 8:02 p.m., I have not heard anything back. As I sat here typing, it had become evident to me that the Fred I spoke to on my first call was most likely Arnold. I was not certain what the fellow that answered was driving at, but I would certainly not put any more time into it. Human nature being what it is, it would have been easier for "Fred "to just state he was not interested, didn't know anything, and did not want to talk. So be it.

In order to further pursue the whole picture, I then contacted on November 25 at 4:22 p.m. Gloria by way of a number from Ruth. She is one of Betty's two daughters. I spoke with her for approximately five minutes, in which time she conveyed to me that she was presently sick, but when she felt better, she would be glad to speak with me. Someone, other than Gloria, that originally answered the telephone seemed pretty shaky when it spoke to her. Seemingly, the entire situation was at best shaky. I conveyed to Gloria that I had contacted her brother Arnold twice to no avail and probably would not call him again. She expressed no opinion. I mentioned that I would also contact her sister Christine. Gloria told me not to bother in that Christine may have substance abuse problems. I told her I would wait a few weeks for her to get better and then call her again. She agreed that it would be fine although she didn't have much information since it had all burned in a fire years ago, exactly as Betty had stated. I then proceeded to call Christine and left a message with someone, also sounding quite shaky, for Christine to call me back. Again, on December 5, at now 8:35 p.m., no callback. This story now appeared more convoluted than Ruth's and, like Ruth's to this day, constantly in flux. Right straight through to Betty's family—or what has become of it.

Sunday night, December 18, and winter has really settled in. Temperatures have been in the high teens and low twenties since the middle of November. There was about a foot of snow on the ground, and it was still coming down right now. Today also happened to be Ruth' s eighty-second birthday. It is amazing she has survived all these years. Carol and I spoke to her yesterday thinking that was her birthday, but it was today. She was in good spirits and had been shoveling snow, which she probably should not be doing with her heart circumstance. Carol had been shopping for a warm pair of mittens for her when she went out to walk Little Foot or shovel snow, but she had not found anything suitable yet. Ruth's driveway was not very long or wide, perhaps twelve feet by nine feet, but the Upstate New York winters are legendary; and with the snowplows, the snow piles up fast. Ruth is like one of those big snowplows and plows right through everything, like she has done for eighty-two years. Right up to today.

In light of all the bad things that have happened in Ruth's long life, which I feel she was really not to blame for 75 percent or more of them. She was thrust into horrible situations for which she was not at fault and fought to survive. When she prevented bad things from happening, which wasn't very often, especially when she was a teen and young adult, she had no chance to take credit like most people would; and only over the last ten years has she had a chance to get any credit for all the good things she had done. No fairness exists for her in that line of occurrences. Little if any fairness has ever made its way into most of Ruth's life other than what she has generated for herself and her children. Carol, Alaina, and Michael and I have been fortunate enough to witness much of that good. With all the atrocities that have been visited on her right from birth, some of which I have known on a superficial level my entire life, and with more details coming to light through our time together working through this project, her story is powerful and truly enlightening with large/small lessons all should heed. In my opinion, as I sat here, an important lesson solidified that lit up my brain like a Christmas tree: all people that live or have lived on this beautiful green earth through the ages should get the chance to take a full bow when they prevented something bad from happening or the same full bow when they enabled something good to happen. If that were the case, with all the politics and disdain removed, humanity would be able to make huge bounds forward probably like never seen before in human history. Larger than fire, the wheel, the Enlightenment, the computer, the movable press, and many other milestones in this long prodigious human march through time. That is a Christmas wish for all of us to buy into. If for no other reason than to save ourselves. So simple but so incredibly complex. So easy but so incredibly hard.

Ruth's bad behavior—probably not in the eyes of any of the Syracuse State School employees, but in my opinion—may largely have been a result of egotism and difficulty to understand speech. To this day, and I have known her my entire life, she is often difficult for me to understand. Her ego gave her defiance, and it often gives her charm. When you couple that with poor speech, some degree of vulgarity, and poor syntax, I bet much of the difficulty she encountered in her youth was a result of being misunderstood not only in a psychological sense but also in a communicative sense. Often did she "have the name" so to speak in that the employees heard what they wanted to hear but dismissed what she was really saying due again to garbled speech, bad syntax, etc.? The history does suggest many times a speech issue for Ruthie, and I wonder if that was not a big part of her issue. Mix in that healthy dose of ego, speech, and possibly hearing problems, as chefs say, "fold in" poor syntax, soon enough explosions occur both on Ruthie's part and on the employees' part. Could much of this have been avoided with the hiring of a few speech therapists if they existed at that time? If they didn't, some genuine person listening on a physical and emotional level coupled with a lot of patience might have worked just as well. In any case, Ruth again paid the price for the possible shortcomings of others. Ruth has mentioned many times Mary LaGraff, who was kind to her, and she went as far as to name her daughter after Mary. Even when Ruth was released from the state school, she would travel to Syracuse to visit Mary, stay at her house, and attend the New York State Fair. So, Ruth did come in contact with some people that were sincere and kind, but they were few and far between. Most times Ruth did not help the situation, but the workers involved usually did not either. I have explained many times to Ruth—from my career as a special education teacher, with teacher's aides in my classes, sometimes three at a time—often problematic aides are a result of lack of motivation. If the student behaves, can learn quite well, and doesn't generate issues, there is not much for the aide to do in connection to that particular student. Yet, if the student generates behavioral concerns or needs a lot of academic support, then there is work for the aide to do; and many times they are not motivated enough to do it and would rather just sit and waste time. Sometimes, for years, I would instruct aide to connect to a student either for academics or behavior, and as soon as I turned around, the aide would be over to their own desk doing nothing. I would direct them back again; and again, no sooner than I looked up from the Smart Board or helping another student, the aide would again be back at their own desk wasting time. Ruth is a perfect example of the adage "You have to go along to get along," and she would not "go along." That fact created work for the employees, and I bet many of them didn't like the idea since Ruth's attitude created work for them. Betty was in the same situation and also experienced all kinds of issues similar and completely different from Ruthie's. Loretta, on the other hand, would "go along;" thus, she did not have the punitive experiences that Ruth and Betty did. I wonder if when any of these employees—that were so hard on Ruth in both a formal and informal sense, in a conventional documented sense, and in an unconventional undocumented sense—went home from work, did they ever wonder if what they did that day in respect to Ruth, Betty, or others was appropriate, fair, mean, degrading, or if it even crossed their minds at all. I have said to Ruth many times, "What is documented with time/date, signed off by the doctors and nurses, must have been accepted protocol. Otherwise, they would not have recorded it with their names attached." But, there is no record of what both Ruth and Betty confirmed as "sick needles" or "sleep needles." No mention of solitary sleeping on the floor in a closet-size room in the middle of winter without a blanket or pillow. No mention that occasionally someone might come along and, out of a sense of guilt or even kindness, throw maybe a pillow or, goodness, a blanket. No protocol for any such actions—be the actions good or horrible. The rejection and loneliness must have filled that closet with more thoroughness than the air. A teenager exposed to such conditions might have considered death a blessing. I never asked Ruth if she ever considered suicide as an option at the lowest points of her life, but I predicted her answer would be a resounding *no* because then her opinion would be "they would win," and she was not going to let anyone win anything from her.

    Ruth, Carol, and I again discussed a local woman that had passed away and was a World War II concentration camp survivor. Her name was Helen, and after all she had endured, she took it upon herself, as many survivors have done over the last eighty years, to tell the world her story in an effort to never allow it to happen again. I have heard her at school, and she was riveting. With an auditorium full of approximately four hundred unruly seventh and eighth graders, you could hear a pin drop when she spoke. Helen always pointed out that the students there were fortunate to hear the story from her in that those students would be the last generation to hear it from an actual survivor since most of them were dead now. The same could be said of World War II veterans, Great Depression survivors, etc. Part of Helen's story would be how she was beaten senseless by a Nazi guard for a reason she did not know. As it played out, she was put in the hospital; and after she recovered, one of the guards—she thought, perhaps out of some sense of remorse—came to see her. Helen was only fifteen or sixteen years old at the time, and her opinion was that maybe the guard had a daughter her age and realized the mistake he had made, at least in that particular situation. As the story went, he brought an apple and put it on the table by her bed. Although she was starving, she would not eat the apple because by doing so, he would win. He would have exerted some degree of control over her, and she would have none of it. Helen would rather starve than give him—maybe he thought—some sense of redemption. It was not going to happen for any reason on any level. Helen would not allow it. I will bet a hundred to one that even though Ruth was not in as-severe situation as Helen, she would feel the same way. Personally, when I experience conflict or find myself in situations I wish I had handled better, after the fact, I try to learn from the experience so that if I ever find myself in the same exact or a very similar situation, I wouldn't make the same mistakes again. Did that ever happen to the state school employees or the guard in Helen's concentration camp? I hope it did, but in probably a little less than half of the cases, it did not.

One of the most horrifying pictures of 2016 was of a later-identified three-year-old boy face down in the sand on a beach, I believe in Greece, having drowned in the Mediterranean Sea while he and his family were trying to escape from a seven-year civil war in Syria. There he was is his black pants and red sweater with his little fanny up in the air like infants often sleep. Even after that picture spread across the world, the carnage in Syria continued, as did the thousands drowning while trying to escape. Wasn't Helen's experience horrible enough? Wasn't that three-year-old's photo horrible enough. Although nowhere near as life-threating, wasn't Ruthie's horrible enough? What about the billions from the first of mankind through the Mesopotamians, the Greeks, the Dark Ages, the age of slavery, the thousands of abortions performed throughout the world daily, and the situations that drove the parents to make that choice whose stories are lost in the eons? Does Marlon Brando as Colonel Kurtz in *Apocalypse Now* make the perfect statement, "The horror, the horror"?

Elena Ferrante said, "Books, once they are written, have no need of their author."

I question where is the rest of Elena's statement, "What happens if they are never written?"

It was the middle of January 2017 now, and Ruth, along with Little Foot, was on her way for the first time in approximately two months. It was a clear cold day but dry. We were both two months away from our recent heart issues, and we both felt fine. What a blessing. Soon after our concurrent health issues, the weather took a turn for the worse. Snow came for about a month straight almost every day with temperatures hovering in the middle teens. So, with the health issues and weather not cooperating, we didn't have Ruth over. But she was back again along with Little Foot, and we were happy to see her healthy again.

People all over the world discuss whether global warming is real or a hoax. I can attest from personal experience that the weather in Upstate New York has changed. When I was young, once winter set in, usually the beginning of December, it stayed right through the first of April. Then, it seemed for the next five or six years, winter didn't start until the middle of January, but once it did, it wouldn't stop right through April. Now it seems winter starts early, lasts for about six weeks, then dies out; it may come roaring back at some point, but after the first arrival, it slowly dies out. In all my life, I have never seen it come and go like it does now. We usually get about one hundred inches of snow a year, but last year, it was about thirty. Thus far we have gotten about that total for this year. Between Wednesday of last week and Monday of this week, there was about two feet of snow in my yard and about three-foot snowbanks from plows. Where I shoveled snow at the end of my driveway, the pile was about four feet high. On Tuesday, the temperature rose into the high forties. On Wednesday, into the 50s; and by Thursday, all the snow was gone. If you look in my backyard now and couldn't see the little bit of snow in the shadows on my deck or my frozen pool, you would think it was the middle of November or even middle of April. I have never seen the winter come and go like this or not come at all. On the hoax side, I recently read in the local history section of the newspaper that in 1928, farmers were plowing their fields with a temperature of sixty-eight degrees. Maybe things have changed, maybe they haven't. I did see one person raking his lawn yesterday and another trimming his trees. Completely new situations for me, but the newspaper article indicates "not new historically."

Ruth, Carol, and I tried to locate our starting point again after a two-month hiatus. So here we went again. We had been working on this project since September of 2014 for a total of about two and a half years. We still haven't started the real story—all that Ruth experienced and remembers from the Syracuse State School. The experiences and memories that Loretta and Betty verified. Although Betty's experiences were like Ruth's, Loretta's were completely different. About nine months ago, on April 9, Carol, Ruth and I visited Loretta on a Saturday morning at her home in Ilion. She resided with her beau, Bo. The house that she owned was not a pretty picture. The neighborhood was run-down and probably was one of the oldest neighborhoods in the village of Ilion. The apartment was cluttered, very disheveled, and no function at all to its layout. There were two other apartments in the house that Loretta was the landlord. Loretta and her husband, Roger, bought the house around 1969. It's not clear whether when Loretta's husband, Roger, died, they were still married.

We decided to visit Loretta again on July 2, since our first visit, on April 9, of Loretta's house. We knocked on the door, and Loretta told us to come in. Ruth had told her previously that we were coming. Ruth brought her doughnuts, which she knew she would like. She was sitting in the chair, with her dog on her lap watching TV. Bo was in the kitchen cooking breakfast, which I thought smelled good. After some introductions and reminiscing, we began to talk.

The first thing Loretta said was that she never got into any trouble. She didn't spend much time thinking about the past because it was very sad for her. She did remember Dr. Bisgrove and that he was a good doctor. She remembers getting paid $2 per day to clean houses.

I asked Ruth, "Did Loretta go out to clean house just like you did?"

Ruth told us, "Loretta went out to the Elmwood Colony and others and stayed there longer than I did. They didn't let me stay with Loretta long because I would upset her for some reason. The matrons at the colonies thought I was a bad influence on her. It was probably true."

A Social Service entry on March 22, 1954, in Loretta's history states, "Miss Salensky is quite worried about Loretta as she is getting very nervous and upset about her sister, Ruth, who has been getting into some difficulties in the colony. Some nights she has trouble eating her dinner. She is very anxious and jittery. Miss Salensky feels that Ruth should be moved as soon as possible."

Another entry from Social Services titled a "Colony Interview" reads, "May 14, 1954—worker had a very nice talk with Loretta while worker was visiting the colony on this evening. She is getting along nicely at the colony. She told me that her eyes had been bothering her quite a bit and that she thinks she needs an eye examination. She has never been to Dr. Joy. Worker told her she would make an appointment sometime soon. The last letter she had from her mother, she had moved to 10 Washington Street, Mohawk, NY, and now lives next door to the aunt. The aunt and the mother usually come together to visit the girls at the school. Loretta asked about her sister, Ruth, and if she would be seeing her soon. She also asked if we had heard from her home and if they had requested her visiting them this summer."

Loretta never saw or had wet packs applied to her or anyone else that she witnessed. She had no recollection of any sick needles or was ever placed in isolation. Loretta was usually separated from Ruth. Ruth felt Loretta was a Goody Two-shoes and that she was always placed with the "bad kids."

I told Loretta that Betty said "Ruth was terrorizing the place."

Loretta replied, "That is the truth."

I asked Loretta the same question that I asked Betty and Ruth many times, "Who was the worst-behaved kid in the place?"

Without hesitation, she pointed to Ruth.

Loretta continued to discuss how she learned to knit and sew at the state school. She also went to school while there, unlike Ruth.

"I never went to school. I was always in detention probably. What school? In detention having bread and milk for breakfast, lunch, and dinner. My favorite food. Two pieces of bread and a bowl of milk, not even a glass, like I was a cat," Ruth replied.

Loretta told us she was released at twenty-three years of age and Ruth at twenty-five. Ruth was released as a test to live with her mother, and it didn't work out well.

To get started again after our second visit with Loretta, we discussed Ruth's early release history, which was to live with her mother

"All I did was work in Prine's Laundry and Supreme Dairy in Mohawk. All my mother wanted was the money I earned. I wasn't going to give her anything. She wanted me to pay her each month, and all I did was sleep there. I didn't eat there. I wouldn't eat there. We lived on Washington Street in Mohawk, the apartment was clean, but I didn't want to live there. I was there about a month, and I told her, 'Put my clothes on the porch, and I would pick them up after work,' because I was not going to pay her to stay there. I was leaving to go live with my uncle Wally on Orchard Street in Frankfort."

Being that Ruth was still on probation from the state school, Ruth took a train from Herkimer to Syracuse to meet with Dr. Sarno and inform her that it was not working out living with her mother and that she was going to live with her uncle Wally. Of course, the move had to be approved by Dr. Sarno. So, a social worker was dispatched to make a home visit/evaluation of the living conditions at Wally's house. Ruth's move to Wally's house was approved. Ruth worked babysitting for her six cousins—some biological, some by marriage—for her room and board. Everything was working out well while living at Wally's. While living at Wally's, Ruth met and married George, who also lived for a short time at her uncle's on Orchard Street. Ruth and George could save enough money to buy their house on Highland Avenue in Ilion in 1963, where she lived until today. Her first daughter, Mary Christine, was born in September of 1964 and was named after Mary LaGraff, one of the matrons at the state school who treated her with respect and helped her over the years while in Syracuse.

Further information concerning Loretta's release was cloudy. From the notes and Ruth's recollection, since it didn't work out with Ruth and her mother, Loretta was released soon after Ruth, but to her their mutual aunt Thelma's house across the street from Ruth's mother in Mohawk. Ruth was not aware that her sister was living at

Thelma's house; otherwise, she would have gone to live with her aunt instead of with her uncle Wally. If it had played out that way, Ruth and I would have never met, and we wouldn't be sitting here working on this project. Approximately fifty-six years later, fate showed her hand to me in that I never knew any of this.

As this was unfolding without my knowledge, Ruth and I had our paths crossed. It was all happening quickly in 1959. Being that I was born in 1955, we lived across the street from each other on Orchard Street when I was four years old.

I said to Ruth, "Those were the days."

Ruth repeated the same thing, "Those were the days."

I told her, "We were in our own little world, and everything just seemed to work out fine. We will probably never get another chance like that again."

"I'll never forget when Rose couldn't start her car. So, I told her to release the hood and unscrewed the air filter. I put my two fingers on the carburetor and tried it to open and close the air-intake valves a couple of times, and then the car started. Rose laughed so hard she couldn't believe that I got the car to start." Ruth giggled as she told the story. Funny thing is that my father laughed when he told the story also.

For my part of this part of the story, "Today again, the whirr of a vacuum cleaner sounds of cups and saucers "clinking" in the kitchen sink while being washed and a feminine figure outside my bedroom door, a broom or mop of dust pan in hand. Yet, the narrative begins much before my time. It begins much more deeply. It began with Ruthie and Loretta. It begins in 1934, in the throes of the Great Depression. It begins with "Ruthie...Deeply..."

In approximately 1959, at some point that year, Ruth and I moved into each's orbits. Although she was moving into what would prove to be unknown to her the best long-term arrangement she would experience in her life. All was not known to me since I was about four years old. My first real recollection of Ruth must have been in late 1963 when I was eight years old. Funny, now that we're here in 2017, I can't remember much, and Ruth should be able to remember everything. How is that for "simply a twist of fate"? Thus, in her still young life, Ruth began to feel some sense of control, some sense of freedom, and even some sense of fate. Most of her life, in other than specific situations like her contact with Mary LaGraff while at the Syracuse State School, Ruth was exposed to a lot more hate than help. She was rejected and exposed to complete abandonment at four months old, as delineated in page after page of reports about her life; even prior to being a ward of New York State, there were huge gaps of time—when she was residing with "a friend in Mohawk," when she was shuffled in and out of the House of the Good Shepherd to be with her mother, and times when her mother was supposed to pick her up at the House of the Good Shepherd and never showed up. It's a daily experience of rejection of abandonment and loneliness.

What I first do remember of my experience with Ruth was of her being very exuberant and always ready to work. She would do what is commonly called bullwork. I remember her always moving things, always busy, and being small in stature with light-red hair. I do remember her coming in and out of my parents' house mostly to work and occasionally come to my mother's beauty shop, still located in the basement of my parents' home, even though my mother hadn't run her business for the last three or four years due to aging. I remember Ruth bringing her daughters, Mary and Colleen, to Rose's Beauty Salon to get their hair done. I was older when Ruth brought her daughters. I remember Ruth's daughters even more then I remember Ruth when I was five or six years old. She always had the attitude of a fighter. Not a fighter in the negative sense like to hurt people, and yes, she could do that also if she had to. But a fighter to advance herself and not allow anyone take advantage of her or take things from her. That must be a lesson she learned immediately when just considering the type of environment she was exposed to from birth through the age of twenty-four, when she was released from the Syracuse State School. One of the oldest military strategies: form ranks and fight. The American pioneers circled their wagons and fought. Ruth didn't have any wagons or military, but Ruth quickly learned how to fight. She had to. It was the only way she was going to survive. I wonder when she came to the adult realization that she was going to have to fight? I guess around the age of thirteen or fourteen. I asked how she survived before she came to that adult realization. The notes clearly indicate, if nothing else, that there was little if any documentation, minimal adult supervision, no solid protocols, and it seems few if any legal considerations. That is certainly a recipe that you had to learn: fight to survive.

By the time I got to my teenage years, I saw Ruth at many places. I would see her in many places—my parents' house, the bakery on Orchard Street either working or visiting her relatives. But things had really changed. Most of the families that lived on Orchard Street had moved to other neighborhoods. I remember Ruth getting married when I was about thirteen or fourteen years old. I knew her husband, and I had been to her house numerous times. I remember her first daughter, Mary, being born. I remember her son Shawn. I vaguely remember when Colleen was born because she is much younger than me. I don't remember any information about her divorcing George other than she had gotten a divorce. Back in 2014 when we started this project, Ruth filled me in about fifty to sixty years later about the circumstances as to why she and George divorced. Even twenty years after the state school, Ruth still found herself embroiled in all sorts of controversy in her nuclear family and still and extended family out of control. Being that Ruth's mother was still alive, family controversy was most likely active also. Loretta was leading her life as wife and mother while working at Remington Arms. I vaguely remember Loretta's husband, whose name was Roger, but not any of Loretta's children. I don't remember Loretta resembling Ruth much then, and I still don't think she does even today.

Through my twenties and early thirties, I don't remember much contact with Ruth or Loretta. I'm sure I must have seen them or heard information about them but don't remember any direct interaction with either of them. Amazingly, from my early thirties through my late fifties, Ruth never crossed my mind. It wasn't until 2014 when I saw the local newspaper article about her winning a Volunteer of the Year Award for her work with the handicapped preschool children and her volunteer work with the local foster grandparents organization. Obviously, she had again survived on her own and was doing well. Contrary to what most people, all those years ago, in the New York State foster care system thought would happen to her. As she often said, "Not bad for a retard." Even to this day, although I think she sees it a much different light; after a lifetime of bad experiences, now she can find humor in it. She is still fighting as if she is still thirteen or fourteen years old for her voice to be heard and someone to notice that there is a real person inside her.

Ruth and Little Foot came today on a snowy Saturday in February. We started out with the donuts she brought from a local bakery deli named Holland Farms, which is the best in the area. Big flavorful donuts that are delicious. Vanilla and chocolate fingers that are huge, jelly buns equally as big and filled with jelly to the point the jelly oozes out of the hole it was put in with, custard-filled delicacies that are soft and burst with flavor in your mouth. Mix them all up with some tea or a glass of milk with ice—what a way to start a day. Probably not good for either of us with our heart situation, but as I told the cardiologist that treated me, "Of course not, but moderation is the key. You can't deny yourself everything."

So, I think we should enjoy these donuts, and we certainly did.

Ruth had a lot of energy this morning, and after our donut pause, we started with what she remembered about clothes at the Syracuse State School, considering the fact of the cold weather we have been experiencing lately.

"We wore tick dresses every day. We never went anywhere, so we never changed from those same old dresses. We never wore slacks—I never even heard of them. Never had a sweater, blouse, or skirts. When waxing the floors in the dorms, hallways, wherever, we would use safety pins to pin the dress up so they wouldn't get all wet. Pushing around twenty-five-pound weights, which was how heavy the polisher was, when we waxed the floor all day long. There was no motor, just brushes, and we were the motor. We had socks and shoes, like saddle shoes, and we wore the same things all year long. Winter, summer, spring, and fall. There was no shampoo. They put all the leftover little pieces of soap from showers in a jar with water. Then we shook the jar to make shampoo. It was gooey and slimy. It was so old, there was no smell to it. When Betty went over the wall, she had her tick dress on, and I was amazed she didn't get caught with that dress on. Someone must have gotten her clothes to change into because she didn't get caught. Her coat would cover most of it, but the dress went all the way to your ankles. It was spring time, so that's why she had a coat on. Norris's brother met her at the fence, and he took her to downtown Syracuse where Betty said she spent a few days. Betty may have even gone to see an employee of the state school. She didn't t turn her in and told her to run. At least that was what Betty told me the way she remembered it. Her daughter Gloria would know more. Can you imagine having the same dress on day after day after day until shower time once a week? Then we would get a clean one—same thing, same pattern, same everything." Ruth saw it all vividly, even today.

Carol asked her, "Were you cold?"

She thought back and raised her arms in disbelief. "I think we had enough heat, but it was hard to tell. All we did was work. You don't get cold if you keep moving. Work, work, work. No school, never heard of it. When I looked for a job, I would lie that I had had a high school diploma, but I didn't. If I got a chance, I could have gone to college, maybe been a lawyer. Betty would have done good too. There was a lot of us that could have done well. Even with a speech problem that at one time I tried to correct, but it didn't work. The Masons always asked me how I learned to read. I told them I didn't know, I just did."

We got into a long discussion about the Masons, who are also friends of mine. Ruth told me Irving was retired; they have closed the business and now spent a lot of time in Florida. Excellent people that Ruth worked for, for a long time. She thought the world of them, and so do I. They in turn thought the world of her also, and I hope even of me also.

We segue back to our visit with Loretta. Loretta's healthy had improved now that she was living a better lifestyle. After Loretta's release from the state school, she lived with her aunt Thelma on Washington Street in Mohawk. She worked for George Murtaugh in Frankfort and did very well there. George was a friend of mine, and I went to school with his daughter Melinda. Loretta really liked the family, and the feelings were mutual. While at the House of the Good Shepherd and the Syracuse State School, she found much more success than Ruth. Loretta mentioned a Jewish woman that she learned a lot from, but she couldn't remember if it was while she was at the House of the Good Shepherd or the Syracuse State School. Ruth said she was always in trouble, so they didn't send her to school, but Loretta did remember going to school on the grounds of the Syracuse State School. She remembered that she learned to be respectful to others.

The day we visited, Loretta was sitting in the chair with her dog, Cheyenne, on her lap. She worked for twenty-four and a half years at Remington Arms on a punch press that she felt was very dangerous and she could get hurt at any time. She had two sons, Roger and Kevin. With some sadness, Loretta mentioned that her granddaughter had died at the age of thirty-five, but she was not clear about the circumstances of her death. She told us that she agreed with Ruth that her mother never got any help, and that was probably why she struggled her whole life. Loretta didn't want to remember anything about her early family life, and possibly with her adult life issues, she couldn't remember much about her early family life. She did agree that their mother never thought much of either one of them, or she would not have so early abandoned them and quickly turned them over to the foster care system. While in the Syracuse State School, she lived in colonies on James Street, Westcott Street, and somewhere in Geddes. She tended to block a lot of those memories out but remembered some good friends and overall did well. While residing at the state school, she lived in the Main Building with the girls that behaved while Ruth was mostly housed in the Girls Building who refused to cooperate to a large degree. Ruth got a big kick out of those memories and said, "No one was going to bully me."

Loretta never remembered any kids getting wet packs, sick needles, or any kind of discipline. It's amazing that they lived about a half mile apart, but the worlds that they resided in could have been a thousand miles apart. Betty remembered it being set up the same for the boys—a building for the boys that behaved and one for those who wouldn't behave.

When I asked her how many buildings there were, she told me, "Too many."

It was difficult for Loretta to verify any of Ruth's experiences in that she lived in the other building where there were few if any problems with behavior. She talked about a good friend she made with Jean Robinson that she was friends with her whole life. She never saw any of the misbehaviors by Ruth or getting disciplined with wet packs or any other form. Loretta did hear the stories from other girls about the time Ruth got locked in the cold dark cellar and was frightened. When Ruth was released from the cellar, she was immediately wet-packed, and Loretta didn't even know what Ruth had done.

Ruth added in, "So they could have the sheets already for me and then placed in detention, so I could put the nightgown on. I think it was Jackson that set the whole thing up. She didn't like me, and I had no reason to like her."

Loretta told me that she asked about Ruth a lot, but she was always in trouble and at the Girls Building, and no one would tell Loretta about her sister. She knew why Ruth was always in trouble because Ruth's temper would cause problems for her.

Ruth wondered aloud, "Was it my temper or the people that worked there and took it out on us?"

That question was probably the crux of Ruth's entire experience in the Syracuse State School.

We had been at Loretta's for about an hour, and she really liked the Murtaughs. Her husband, Roger, and she were happy throughout their marriage. Roger passed away several years ago. The highlight of her life at the Syracuse State School was going to swimming lessons at the local YMCA. She didn't remember any residents or employees that were members of any other minority group. There was good medical care, good food, and the place was very clean. They had to clean the place, but it wasn't a punishment, it was part of the daily routine. She also felt like Ruth—that all that she learned was all on her own. She never harbored any thoughts of hurting herself or others.

An experience that defined why Ruth didn't feel the same towards her mother as Loretta did that Ruth bluntly related to us was when at some point when both children were very young, with neither her mother nor father anywhere to be found, she and Loretta were hungry. They may have been left alone overnight; at some point, she took her sister by the hand, and both children walked over to a Utica Police Department station in the area of Mary Street in East Utica. Someone at the police department made them both a breakfast of eggs and bacon. Ruth's recollection was that a police officer brought the children back to their apartment and perhaps waited a short time for the parents to return. Ruth couldn't remember what happened after that, but Carol remembered something in the notes to this effect, and we would research it further.

We ended the visit with a question: "So tell me, Loretta, if your mother was standing here right now, what would you say to her?"

"I would tell her that although she turned us away, it was the best thing for us. At least we had food, warm clothes, and a decent place to live. I would tell her that I love her," she replied with little thought.

For Loretta, that seemed true, having resided in what Ruth would call the Goody-Two Shoes Main Building. But, certainly not where Betty and Ruth lived at, the Girls Building—with the detention, wet packs, etc. Their life within those walls was markedly different and fully devastating.

Before we typed this exchange of our interview with Loretta, I whispered to Michael, "Watch Ruth's reaction when I repeat what Loretta would say to her mother if her mother were in the room."

He did. Ruth scoffed and rolled her eyes today just as she did on April 9, 2016, at 10:37 a.m. in Loretta's house in Ilion, New York. Obviously, Ruth's feeling had not changed.

Having finished our last session with a discussion of the meeting with Loretta on April 9, we turned next to the official record that was released to Loretta in much the same way as Ruth's. In that we contacted the Health Information Management Department of New York State Mental Health, and they released to Loretta the pertinent information that was on record. Much of the existing information mirrored the record that was provided to Ruth, often simply reprocessed from older records written by Oneida County Department of Public Welfare, the House of the Good Shepherd, etc.

Yet, there was, as always was the case, a great deal of conflicting information, gaps in the record, and a great deal of subjective comments that had little to do with either of the sisters' situations.

On November 21, 1936, at the age of seven months, Loretta was placed in the House of the Good Shepherd. At Loretta's placement, Ruth was approximately two years old—best guess is that she spent the first two years of her life being placed at home, in boarding houses, and in the House of the Good Shepherd. What was amazing was that even though there were no clear records where Ruth was the first two years of her life, even when Loretta came into the picture, there still was no clear record of where Ruth was that could be used to fill in the blanks of Ruth's placement at that early age. Loretta resided at the House of the Good Shepherd from November 21, 1936, through April 2, 1940, and then was released to a boarding home. Apparently, she was in the boarding home from April 2, 1940, through December 22, 1942, when she was discharged to her parents. From 1942 through 1946, there was no clear indication as to where Loretta and Ruth were, only that on September 30, 1946, they were returned to the House of the Good Shepherd. On March 12, 1947, Loretta was not doing very well in school. She had a D in reading and spelling and a C in writing and music. "However, she evades work and needs close supervision."

Ruth, on the other hand, was in special class. "Her number work is good, writing unusually good, reading and spelling fair. She is special class material." The same information on Ruth came up again. She was left by parents with a lodger in a rooming house. Ruth was termed "anemic, dirty and ill kept." At some point, Ruth was returned to the House of the Good Shepherd, and her parents returned five days later.

> Loretta's history is very similar to Ruth's. Loretta Jean Raymond was committed to the House of Good Shephard November 21, 1936, less than two months old. Mother was not giving the child proper care, and father was a transient worker. Family living in inadequate quar-

ters. It is noted in the record that the couple, on December 3, 1936, considered placing her out for adoption. When in boarding home, she was "brighter than Ruth, more vivacious." At times, she was moody and disagreeable, had temper tantrums, and talked baby talk. She was more of a behavior problem in school than her sister and reacted poorly to discipline. Health is good.

The children had not been questioned about conditions in the home at this time. They had seen and heard many things that they should not. Their mother said they were increasingly hard to discipline.

Chapter 5

Ruth's Mother and Father, Elizabeth and Ted Raymond

What we could determine as time had progressed. In Loretta's history, more information came to light about the children's mother.
A report from the Rome State School dated May 28, 1935:

> Elizabeth Richardson was admitted to this institution on February 9, 1928, from Ilion, New York, at the age of twelve years. The mother had died during that year, and the father, who was anxious to do all he could for the child, was unable to give her the supervision she needed. There were four brothers and sisters in the home, from two to fourteen years of age. On admission, Elizabeth was a restless, active child with a with a mental age of 7 years, 2 months, and an I.Q. of 55.
> Elizabeth was given school training here at the institution in Elementary Domestic work, Music, Story Work, and Physical Training. Teachers' reports state that she was interested, cheerful, and very neat about her work. She was

at times troubled by dreams which she talked about to the children, often frightening them.

She was a good student in academic work and did light domestic work well.

Paroled to her father, Mr. Wallace Richardson, 19 Elm Street, Ilion, N.Y.

The history next turned to Ruth's alleged father who Ruth denied as her biological father. Theodore Raymond was born in Rochester, New York, on February 1915. He had an alias and moved to Utica in 1921. Theodore's parents were divorced, and the stepfather deserted them. He attended school part-time till he was sixteen and had been self-supporting since then. He claimed many jobs such as watchmaking, painting, automobile body work, and roofing. He first became known to the Oneida County DPW after deserting an infant in a rooming house. After the second child was born, Loretta, he considered placing her out for adoption and had always been ready to allow someone else to assume responsibility for the children. Ted and his wife did not visit the children at Christmastime and did not bring them any presents. Under court order, he was ordered to pay $1 towards the children's maintenance. He never paid mostly due to the fact that he constantly changed jobs. He was taken on April 14, 1939, to adult mental health clinic to determine if he had the ability to ever provide for his children and his attitudes about ordinary situations. Dr. Bigelow recommended "no change to the children placement until he is steadily employed in private industry and shows evidence of increased stability." It was recommended that this family have continuous and intense Social Services supervision. In 1945, he was in the roofing business, employing several men, and was providing for his children. According to the records, William Ribyat was assisting Raymond in paying his bills and keeping his books. Mr. Ribyat had been attempting to have the children released to their parents. When Betty was taken to the hospital for an unknown illness, Mr. Raymond did not want to make a complaint because of

Harry Culver's family and was relentless in a request that the break in family life not be attributed to him. He was anxious about his wife and believed that sex between her and Culver had contributed to her illness. Mr. Raymond did not know his wife had been taken to the hospital until he came home and was told by neighbors. On late September, he called the police because Betty was hemorrhaging. He allowed Mr. Culver to take the children to his sister's house in Mohawk. A social worker asked him why he didn't get in touch with someone in the Children's Division about moving Ruth and Loretta. Mr. Raymond thought it was a temporary thing and did not want to antagonize the Culver family because they had been friends for years. He did not want to give the impression that he wanted to place the children out of his home at the first opportunity, and he would have allowed them to stay in Mohawk if the social worker would have allowed it. Ruth and Loretta would only be out of the house for the weekend till he could obtain more information about his wife on September 30, 1947. He again insisted he was not trying to get rid of his children at the first opportunity. At this point, a recommendation for the Syracuse State School was explained to him and that he did not object to this place and felt both girls needed training and especially supervision. However, since that office visit, he had not been seen and stopped calling.

The couple was married on June 4, 1934, by the Reverend Albert C. Judd in Ilion, New York. Betty was pregnant at the time of the marriage, but Mr. Raymond denied paternity. Several times he referred to the fact that he was married in June of 1934, and Ruth was born in December of 1934, and felt it was a bad reflection on him. He had known Betty for years and had been friends with the family. He felt he would give the child his name and that Betty will be able to keep a clean home. The marriage had never shown to be secure, and he had a weak personality and no support from his wife. The couple drifted into an unsatisfactory marriage and had been on relief many times. They mostly resided in furnished rooms, moving from place to place. In June of 1946, Mr. Raymond came into the social worker's office saying he wanted the children released and that he was earning enough money to support his family. Betty was doing well and was an exceptional housekeeper. Betty came in a few days later, and from her appearance, they were getting along well. At this point, Betty had the children with her dressed in identical clothes.

Ruth said, "One dress was green, and one was blue. I think I wore the green one. I remember because we have a picture."

Chapter 6

Loretta Progresses, Ruth Flounders, Elizabeth and Ted's Disarray Worsens, Deepening the Children's Problems

M. B. Cline reports on May 16, 1947, "The House of the Good Shepherd strongly recommends Syracuse State School for Ruth and Loretta. Prospects of rehabilitating home are poor. They do not adjust to normal school routine. It is difficult for them to keep up with the normal children at the House of the Good Shepherd. It is reported they are affectionate, nice girls, and training at Syracuse State School will be beneficial."

One end of the statement proved valid: "Prospects of rehabilitating home are poor." But the other end concerning not adjusting to the "normal school routine" and "difficult to keep up with the normal children" could not be more off the mark, as Ruth had proven day after day for over eighty-two years.

There was no writing session scheduled for today, March 11, 2017. It was very cold, five or six degrees, with windchills of zero or less. We had planned to attend the local St. Patrick's Day Parade today, but it got cancelled due to the weather, and it was rescheduled for two weeks from now, March 25. Hopefully it would be warm enough by then so that we can go and not be threatened by the weather. Ruth called this week to ask Carol what she charged per hour for housecleaning. Ruth was charging $6 per hour, which was less than one-third of what Carol charged. I bet the people that she cleaned for, ones that I have known for years, knew exactly what the going rate per hour was. Yet, no one offered to raise her rate. Ruth was unaware and would not ask for more. Again, as in much of her life, she was happy with what she got paid, and it worked for her, so she just kept going forward.

Perhaps, we should all apply that attitude as often as possible. It would probably make for a more content, fair world. If only we could all keep that ugly greed at bay.

The situation was equally an ugly example of how it cut the other way in that no one offered to raise her rate to the going rate or at least minimum wage. People were still taking advantage of her, but I bet after speaking to Carol this week, the paradigm would change, and it should.

It had always struck me that in this whole expedition, for every question or situation we can definitively find an answer to or describe wholly, it only opens more questions or a door to a less-describable situation. Elie Wiesel, in his 1986 Nobel Prize-winning book, *Night*, describes a conversation he had as a young boy with a man named Moshe the Beadle in his town. Moshe insisted that "every question possessed a power that did not lie in the answer" and "that you will find the true answers, Eliezer, only within yourself!" Moshe then went on to discuss that he prayed so that the god within him would give him the strength to ask him the right questions. Complicated concepts and deep thoughts that lend themselves to Ruthie's entire life. Again, that in for every question that gets posed and answered, there is another question that opens. "Every question possessed a power that did not lie in the answer." That power is long and wide and deep and undeniable and unknown to most people, but it is there. Ruth's story is complex and uncomfortable. The questions it raises are disconcerting and generate a lot of dissonance. Her story illuminates that we humans are not as far evolved as we think. That our laws, mores, and values are much less enlightened than, in all our conceit, we think they are. I fear that is even more true in 2017 than it was is in 1931 or 1731. Has there been vast improvement? Certainly, there has. On the other hand, all of that ugliness has not been defeated. Terrorism abounds on almost a daily basis. Serial killers, child abuse, bombings done in the name of God and religion have become an everyday occurrence. Stoning people, burning them alive, throwing them off buildings, and abortions happen all over the world at an alarming rate. I must wonder if it has or really has not changed. Possibly it all simply came more to light with the advent of the Internet and mass communication. Is there anything really "new under the sun"? It would not seem so reading Ruthie's history from 1934 through the mid-1960s and reading the newspaper today. I used to feel when I worked that the names changed and the faces changed, but the experience did not. Time went by, students, teachers, parents, etc. moved in and out of the school, but the behaviors and attitudes haunted the building year after year with little or no noticeable difference. Questions and observations just as uncomfortable as Ruthie's in 1931 and presently. I truly do not feel we are as far advanced as we're led to believe in 2017 or in 1817. Evolution, in all its forms, is a long process, and my instincts tell me we have only taken the preliminary steps. As much as humans, with all our arrogance, think we have come a long way through billions of years of time.

The adage states, "There is no fool like an old fool," and we, all humanity collectively, are truly old fools.

On April Fools' Day 2017, Ruth, Carol, and I, along with Little Foot, picked up again. Ruth came early with her first cell phone in her hand. Carol helped her set up the many different functions as we visited and caught up for the last two weeks. We decided it was time to pursue whatever we could concerning the man that allowed Ruth and Loretta to use his last name, Theodore Raymond. Ruth had professed since day one of this project that he was not her biological father, and the history clearly demonstrated that it was the case when at one point, Theodore only agreed to give the girls his name for reasons that to this day are not evident. For Ruth, through her early years, from what she remembered, he was rarely in the picture; and when he was, he was nasty about the entire situation. The most Ruth remembered about him was that after Betty died, she went to Albany to see Ted, in that he was in the throes of death and, soon after that, passed away. From there, Ruth never heard anything about him again.

More of Loretta's information appears again in the form of a report card. Loretta's 1948 report card from the Syracuse State School indicated poor to fair to very good school progress. "She is very fidgety and will not sit at a desk correctly. She makes six beds daily, dusts chairs, sweeps music hall, polishes floors, scrubs bathroom, helps little girls wash their feet after showers, straightens classroom before retiring, and washes underwear. She seeks attention by talking, is spasmodic in groups and if overconfident in her work. She has had friends consistently."

In June 1949: "Reading and Language work satisfactory. Overconfident; resents criticism. Very disagreeable under correction."

Reported in June 1950: "Is socially confident for her mental level. Makes her best effort. Cooperative, friendly, cheerful."

The report of June 1951: "Good work in all subjects and shows improvement in English oral and written expression." In June of 1952, the report stated, "Loretta is friendly, eager, and cooperative and works at a moderate and steady pace. Work is all good. Completely done the study on budgeting income and has done well. Cleans nursery and sets table in the children's dining room."

Continuing through her reports of 1951/52 school year, Loretta overall was doing well. Ruth, on the other hand, while residing in the Girls Building, was daily experiencing many forms of behavioral difficulties and was being subjected to many protocols of institutional discipline. The Syracuse State School record of hospitalization beginning in September of 1947 through June of 1957 indicated many common childhood illnesses such as cold, sore throat, injury to her right ankle, upset stomach, tooth extraction, etc. The record showed under the circumstances that Loretta was doing fairly well.

Even before the above reports from the Syracuse State School, there was a previous report from 1947 as an admission note that stated, "Loretta is a nice-looking girl and in good health, doing acceptable academic work, and her hymen is intact." Her classification was "Moron."

RUTHIE DEEPLY

Conference for Diagnosis and Certification report:

> November 14, 1947—Girl interviewed and records reviewed. Certification of Director approved. Moron IQ 68. Probable cause of Mental deficiency: Heredity. Clinical Classification: Familial.
> Loretta is making good progress at the Syracuse State School, is well behaved, and gets along with the employees and the other girls. She reads and writes letters to her mother, and she came to see Loretta at Christmastime. She is clean, cooperates, and likes to listen to the radio and especially likes to listen to the murder mysteries. Loretta says she likes the Syracuse State School better than the House of the Good Shepherd, where she was a resident for a year prior to coming to Syracuse. Loretta was allowed visits with her mother and allowed to go out with her mother while in Syracuse. She was placed in the Westcott Colony on August 12, 1953. She conforms to the Colony route and is very friendly. If she were placed in a home where the employer was truly interested in her, she would make a good adjustment in the community. In March of 1956, she is placed in convalescent care with Mrs. Ralph Prowda in Syracuse NY. Mrs. Prowda is pleased with Loretta's work, but Loretta was not pleased with the placement. In February 1957, Loretta is placed in the home of Reverend and Mrs. Halsey M. Cook of Syracuse NY. In May 1957, she is then placed in the home of her Aunt Mrs. Lawrence Scanlon in Mohawk NY. Loretta and Mr. and Mrs. Scanlon begin the discussing of a full release from the Syracuse State School. Loretta has been continually employed

working for a school teacher who will no longer need her employment in the fall as she is pregnant and will not be returning to teaching. Loretta also is working for Father Greenway, a rector of the Episcopal Church. She enjoys recreation with the Scanlon children, such as swimming, movies, and bowling. She has in her account $332.61, and she owns no property.

In view of this patient's apparently fine adjustment and her stable home situation, worker feels the patient should be considered for discharge at this time.

There seems to be little or no problem with Loretta's direction as we reviewed and composed all that was happening with her at this point. As we looked deeper into her history at the Syracuse State School, there were some simple problems evident, but nothing compared to Ruth's. The details, I was betting, would not prove as devastating as Ruth's. Yet, as with Ruth's case, we would follow them wherever they led, starting the next time. We broke for lunch.

Just as quickly as Loretta appeared on the radar again, she fell right off.

Excellent record-keeping by the New York State foster care system? Again.

We haven't seen or heard from Ruth lately. She had been going to numerous doctor's appointments in order to figure out her heart condition, and to add to the situation, she fell and hurt back. Now, she was having back problems that may require surgery. In any case, she and Little Foot came for a writing session. Ruth being Ruth, she came in still happy and vibrant; her optimism was something we should all emulate.

"I went to see Loretta this week.," she told me. "But I won't go in. I only stayed outside and talked. I'm high class, you know. Look at the purse Colleen gave me. It's Kate Spade with a matching wallet. I have class," she continued.

She certainly did.

We all got a big laugh out of that, including Little Foot. It was funny in light of the life she had led, but there was a message there we should all learn and apply all the time.

We started to discuss the experience at the Syracuse State School when Jackson would slap her repeatedly, and Ruth would tell her, "Why don't you just kill me if that would make you happy."

Ruth wanted to know if we read what happened to Eric Hernandez, a young NFL star that was convicted of murder and subsequently killed himself in jail.

She told us, "You shouldn't kill anybody. Yet I could have killed a few back then. They were never afraid of me because they were so big compared to me. They really had no idea what I was thinking."

Even though Ruth and Loretta were only yards apart on the grounds of the Syracuse State School, in the Girls Building or the Main Building, they were completely isolated from each other, at least from their perspective. Still, the foster care system saw them as a pair with the possibility, however remote, of returning them both to their mother.

As the history now returned to Loretta again, we decided to pick up again with a report on Loretta received on May 23, 1947, at the Syracuse State School that was the "Last Clinic Evaluation of Patient," written by Dr. Marion Collins on October 4, 1942. The report showed the turmoil that their mother, Betty, was consistently generating along with their father, Ted, Harry Culver, and oftentimes some unknown men that resided in Utica, one of them possibly being Bob.

The report began, "Discharged together with sister Ruth from B.H. to parents by O.C C Div. on 12/22/42. Supervision in own home continued. For time, seemed to be working out so well that O.C. Ch. Div. felt they might be able to withdraw from case entirely. In fall of '46, Co. Welfare discovered adjustment was not as good as they had thought. Mother, who is very low mentally, became involved with another man."

A county worker then suggested that Betty return to a mental clinic for treatment. One of Betty's sisters promised that she would take her for a mental evaluation but never did.

When the mother calls the HGS to see the children, it is usually very difficult because of the promises she insists upon making to the children regarding going home, etc. Despite everyone's effort to make her see what such promises are apt to do to the children's adjustments, because of the mother's "unbalance," she is not allowed to take the children off the grounds. However, she does call. Mr. Raymond has made a much better adjustment. He makes a very good impression although he is visionary and has little depth.

Loretta and Ruth are returned to the H.G.S. on 3-46 and was in the same physical condition as when she left. Loretta and Ruth look very much alike with blond hair and a fair complexation; "she is plainer looking than Ruth. She is bold and a behavior in school and behaves poorly to discipline. However, she is more vivacious and brighter than Ruth. Like her sister, it is felt that she has heard and seen happenings at home which would give her worldly knowledge far in advance of her years. While the other children in her group have noticed her "peculiarities," they "are bearing with her." She is not as carefree as Ruth and inclined to be more secretive. She is also a bed wetter. Her housemother has stated that "Ruth tattles to get attention."

The mother's visit disturbed Loretta more than Ruth. When Loretta returns to her group, she is angry. While when Ruth goes back to her group, "she just seems to forget about it." Loretta enjoys her father's visits and is not upset about them. Loretta made a remark to her housemother that "Harry is my father now."

While these two girls seem to be fond of each other, they are not especially demonstrative and do not seem to mind being in separate groups as they see each other on the playground and the way back and forth to school.

Loretta's progress notes as seen in the clinic:

> Physical: Well developed and nourished. Tonsils moderately enlarged. Teeth good. No secondary sex characteristics. Gait normal, heart normal.
> Psychiatric: Friendly and cooperative. Clean and neatly dressed. Not spontaneous. Cries when mother visits her because she can't see her all the time.
> Social: Is happy at HGS. Everyone is good to her. Likes the other children and they like her. Is in 4th grade in Kemble School. Thinks she is doing well except for arithmetic.

Progress notes from October 14, 1948:

> Loretta is 12 years old. She would like to be home. Does not like it here too much. Likes her attendants. Is in Junior Kindergarten, likes it ok in school. Gets along nicely with other children and has made friends. Parents visit her if she is good. No complaints. Does not seem well adjusted. She is in 3rd grade; learns well and likes to learn. Attendant states she is very good girl, very good, worked, cooperative; no complaints.
> On December 6, 1949, social service conducts a home visit at 101 Morgan Street, Ilion,

NY. The worker interviews Mrs. Harrison Culver, Ruth's mother, and finds her to be childish, emotionally immature, and with no insight into her children's condition and will not recognize the fact that both children need training and supervision in an instruction. In September of 1949, Mrs. Culver divorces the children's father and married Mr. Culver. He works at the Union Fork and Hoe, also known as the University of Frankfort, for 14 years as a skilled laborer, and his take-home pay averages $69.00 per week.

The home is located on the second floor of a shabby, old house about four blocks from the main street in Ilion. It is a small apartment consisting of two bedrooms, living room, and kitchen and bath. It is poorly furnished, and it is evident that Mrs. Culver is not too good of a housekeeper. Although it was a very cold day, there was no heat in either of the two stoves in the apartment, and Mrs. Culver was doing her work in a heavy coat.

Mrs. Culver stated that the children would attend the Baptist Church on Sundays and that she would supervise their recreation. Apparently, she does not realize what this means, but was just saying it for effect on the worker. She stated that the children would probably attend the West Hill School, which is not too far from the home.

Mrs. Culver is quite insistent that the children return home for Christmas and refused to recognize the fact that they might not be home for Christmas and sees no reason why they cannot be home. She stated her husband has started proceedings to adopt the children as he is very fond of them.

Worker feels that the home is rather inadequate and that the children would not receive proper care and supervision if they were allowed to go home.

At such an odd time, I noticed in the notes Loretta's care number: D-48555. We wondered if Loretta would know that. Ruth wanted us to check a picture, which we did. Sure enough, there was a picture of Ruth numbered D-48554 and sequentially Loretta's was D-48555. We wondered if the Nazis of the concentration camps numbered family members sequentially? Could there be a historic similarity here that those assigning the numbers may have been consciously or unconsciously aware of?

On the same date, the social worker left the home and went to West Hill School to discuss the possibility of the children attending school there. The principal was not in that day, and the worker meets with Mrs. Hoffman, the school nurse, who did not think the children would not receive enough personal attention in a regular class to allow them to progress at the same rate as the other children. She suggested a report be sent to the superintendent of schools for his opinion. According to Mrs. Hoffman, "Mr. Culver and his family do not have to good a reputation in the community. She knows nothing of Mrs. Culver."

The worker then called at the Herkimer County Department of Public Welfare and talked with Mrs. Delaney about the possibility of the children returning to their mother. Mr. Culver has been known to the public welfare system for many years. The current information showed that Culver's first wife was in the state hospital, one child in the Marcy State Hospital, one child in a foster home, and another in a tuberculosis sanatorium. It seemed that Mr. Culver was attempting to adopt Ruth and Loretta, but the Department of Public Welfare needed to investigate the arrangement. Mrs. Delaney questioned the advisability of the adoption but would be willing to cooperate with any plan they wished to make. The only condition that Joyce Murphy, social worker composing the report, made was that if the children could return home, then she would like a summary sent to the Oneida County Department of Social Services. No one was making any effort to get real control of the problem. It was one agency handing off a terrible situation to another agency. Neither county was making a solid effort to resolve anything. Any attempt by the family to resolve Ruth's and Loretta's situation was ludicrous.

December 14, 1949, Summary for Consideration of Convalescent Care to the Mother:

> Loretta has temper tantrums and is a behavior problem. The mother and father did not get along very well so that the children were at home and in institutions at different periods. The mother has divorced the father, and the home conditions are not favorable. The mother is considered not bright enough to support the children. At some point, a vote is taken, and the staff unanimously disapproves of the girls being returned to the mother's house for a short visit.

December 14, 1949, Social Service:

> On this date, letters were sent to Mr. Howard J. Blaugrund, attorney-at-law, 618-19, 1st National Bank Bldg., Utica, NY, and to the Raymond girls' mother, Mrs. Harrison Culver, 101 Morgan St. Ilion, N.Y. It was stated that the request for the girls to go to the home of their mother had been reviewed by our Staff, and it was felt due to the lack of school facilities in special class in Ilion and the fact whether the mother could adequately supervise the girls, it was felt the girls should remain under the care and supervision of the school.

We all knew what the level of turmoil was taking place throughout this narrative so far, but suddenly we were all more appalled than ever, Ruth included. The children tended to stay in one spot for anywhere from a few days to a year and then were moved as out as quickly as they moved in. No one person, agency, county, or family member ever made a serious attempt to help these two children. It was similar to the child abuse scandal in the Catholic Church whereby bishops shifted priests from one church to another when rumors of the priest concerned abusing children surfaced. It was apparent that the same situation occurred way back when with Ruth and Loretta. They all were very quick to hand off this terrible situation to another person or agency as quickly as they could or when they had run out of options. It was evident no real attempt was ever made on the children's behalf. I suspected the same occurrence happens today, even in larger numbers with even greater frequency. Bigger and more appalling than ever. Bigger and sadder than ever. Goodness help us.

All clogging the system, this narrative and many narratives for generations passed. Like the most common cry of the dying and wounded on a battlefield, "Mother." Never changing, never stopping. Like the honey badger, while he hunts getting stung and bit, slogging through the brush and weeds and the water. Never being deterred from his goal of finding food. Honey badgers don't give up. Honey badgers don't give a shit. Neither does the system. Just turn on your television—not yesterday, not today, but hopefully tomorrow.

Carol and Ruth spoke on the telephone a few times over the past week. Ruth was doing all sorts of testing during the past month due to her heart situation. She had a nuclear stress test this week and got sick in the midst of the process. The attending nurse saw her condition and asked if she was all right, and Ruth told her no. She was then given three shots at the end of the test to relieve her symptoms. She was also getting shots in her back at a pain management clinic due to falling at work and injuring her back. Couple all of that with having to have her heart shocked at some time soon in order to restore the normal rhythm. Obviously, a lot of problems, especially in light of her age, yet she still had that same cheery attitude as she and Little Foot came bouncing through the door.

She sat at the kitchen table and told us, "I feel good because I have to be. These tests and doctors are stressing me out. Whose sneakers are those?"

I told her, "Mine."

She replied, "If they are gone when I leave, you will know where they went."

The attitude never changed. That's what kept her going all those years.

Ruth's mother paid a visit to the school on June 22, 1951, to attend a graduation. She requested that Ruth be allowed to return home and was advised that it would not be the best idea for Ruth. Mrs. Culver asked that both girls be allowed home for a vacation, and a letter was forwarded to consider that vacation. Herkimer County Department of Welfare approved a vacation at her mother's home from July 28 to August 12, 1951. The record indicated that another vacation was not approved until July 2, 1952, through July 9, 1952. A Christmas vacation was considered on December 9, 1952, for Loretta to visit her mother but was denied because of unpredictable weather and crowded traveling facilities.

In July of 1951, Loretta was admitted to detention on July 9 for being disobedient and stubborn when she was reprimanded. "She uses vile language and calls the attendants vile names." She spent eight days in detention from July 9–16. A psychological exam by Dr. Fink classified her as a "moron." Ruth's mother paid a visit to the school on June 22, 1951, to attend a graduation.

Progress notes:

> May 30, 1953—Loretta was formerly saucy, defiant, and resented orders, but during the past year, she has shown much improvement and appeared more mature. She is interested in her schoolwork, is polite, and respectful. Loretta asked about convalescent care, and she was informed that we planned for her to have a vacation with her mother this summer for a short period. She was informed, however, that

>we planned for her to be placed in a colony on her return from vacation. Loretta's mother, a former patient of Rome State School, is childish, immature, and a poor housekeeper. Mr. Culver, Loretta's stepfather, has a good work record and a good reputation. Loretta stated that an aunt is interested in her, but she was informed that we have not received any requests from the aunt.

Loretta was baptized and received her communion at the Onondaga Presbyterian Church, thus completing her religious education. Loretta was granted vacation with her mother from June 22, 1953, to July 5, 1953, and was returned on July 5 as agreed.

A colony employee, Jane Wheeler, filed a report, an interview, on October 20, 1953. It seemed during the first few weeks Loretta was in the Colony, she did well. Then things took a turn towards being a "little ill-tempered towards the other girls." When Loretta got angry, she said little or nothing.

>One night she would not come down to dinner on time after the bell had been rung, and she had been asked 2 or 3 times before the bell was rung. When she came down, she would not say the evening grace with the rest of the girls, and when Miss Dwyer spoke to her and asked her to say it with them, she said in a hostile manner that she had. Eventually Miss Dwyer had her say it with the rest of the girls. Later she punished Loretta for this and had her dry dishes for the rest of the week to remind her that when the bell rings in the colony, she should be down on time and that she needs to show more respect to her matrons.

Approximately eight weeks later, Jane Wheeler filed another report on December 11, 1953.

> On the whole, Loretta's adjustment has been good. Is an excellent worker and is well-liked by employers? Fond of children. Occasionally Loretta has been sassy to Miss Salensky. Has gotten upset about little things. For instance: she came to the dining room with a comb in her pocket. Miss Salensky asked her to please keep it upstairs. Said she didn't know where to put it. Miss Salensky told her where, and she answered sarcastically, "Oh, I knew that." Miss Salensky has asked that a social worker talk with Loretta about improving her disposition.

Physical exam was conducted on Loretta at age sixteen. Dr. M. Lohaza described her as a "16-year-old blond, slightly pale-looking girl, and does not complain about any physical conditions. She is 5 foot 2 inches tall weighing 126 pounds. Her teeth are in good condition along with her inner organs. Does not show any gross pathology. Her urine specimen is normal, her blood pressure 100 over 60, and her heart rate is 72 beats per minute." Dr. Lohaza deemed her "fit for the Colony." Her adjustment to the Colony was good, and she was cheerful and willing to help. From 1952–1953, Loretta worked as a "Senior Parole Cooking and Laundry. She is a competent worker, nice mannered, truthful, obedient worker, and alert. She always does more than her share and requires minimal supervision."

Mrs. Salensky in spring of 1954 was worried about Loretta about being upset about her sister, Ruth, that was having problems in the Colony. "Loretta is anxious and jittery and is having trouble eating her dinner. Mrs. Salensky feels Ruth is causing the problem and should be moved as soon as possible." Loretta received a letter from her mother asking if Loretta's aunt Thelma could come to visit both girls at school. Loretta was interested in seeing her sister soon.

Social Services conducted a home visit on October 14, 1954. The purposed of the visit was to determine if both girls could live with their mother and her second husband, Harrison Culver. Mrs. Culver was dressed in a nice house coat and explained that she had an operation in her stomach and rested in the afternoon.

> Mrs. Culver is a nice-looking person and a neat housekeeper. After talking with her for a few minutes, it is quite apparent that she is not any brighter than her daughters. She rambles on from one subject to the next with no coherent point. The social worker informs her that Loretta has settled in to the Colony nicely. A consideration is being made to release the girls home, but Ruth would be given the chance first. The final decision could take a considerable amount of time and was asked to not say anything to the girls because if the decision was not approved, it would upset the girls.

In a colony interview on May 20, 1955, Loretta asked to see a social worker. Loretta wanted to know if Ruth was still at the Syracuse State School. Loretta had heard from other girls that Ruth was sent back to the school. Loretta began to tell the social worker that her mother was in a car accident in February and was severely injured and spent some time in a Utica Hospital. Loretta felt that Ruth's upset condition was a result of Ruth's being worried about her mother's condition. Loretta was also concerned that she had not heard anything from her aunt Thelma. A consideration was now being made to place Loretta out of the Colony. Loretta has had several arguments with another patient named Louise Christano. The writer of the report, Mrs. Wright, felt that Mrs. Salensky protected Loretta and always blamed the other girls.

> Loretta is very concerned about her sister, Ruth, who at one time was at Westcott Colony.

She visits her occasionally, and the supervisor feels that Loretta worries about her sister quite a lot especially when she hears she has been in difficulty.

The girl's mother has again requested a summer vacation with both girls in that her husband, Harry, now has a car and will be on vacation at the same time. Mrs. Culver feels that the access to a car will allow the family to get out more to see friends and relatives and that the visits may help the girls.

October 13, 1955, Social Service Progress Note:

> Loretta is a good type of girl who gives an impression of being more self-sufficient than most of our girls. She has now been in the Colony over two years and is obviously getting rather discouraged at her seeming lack of progress. She spoke most sensible and with surprising understanding of her home and said that she realized the impossibility of her ever going home. She would very much like to get out on convalescent care in the near future. Worker thinks that Loretta is becoming very discouraged, and there is a danger of her slipping back if she is not placed out soon. She is quite a competent girl and should do very well.

February 28, 1956, Social Service Summary of Contacts:

> Loretta has been at Westcott Colony since August 12, 1953. She is well adjusted in the Colony and seems to get along with all the girls and supervisors. Loretta asked on many occasions about going to a private home. Worker feels that if Loretta is not placed on convalescent care in the near future, she will become very discouraged, which will hinder her further progress.

Loretta appears to be self-sufficient, and it is felt that if she got a home where the employer was sincerely interested in her, she probably would make a good adjustment in the community. She likes little children, and it is felt that she would enjoy a home with them.

On March 20, 1956, Loretta is placed on convalescent care at Mrs. Ralph Prowda of Syracuse New York at wage of $8.05 a week with $2.50 weekly spending money.

A home visit is conducted on April 2, 1956, with Mrs. Prowda and Loretta. Loretta states that she felt left out because she did not eat dinner with the family. Loretta feels that it is the right amount of work and it keeps her busy all day. Mrs. Prowda reports that Loretta is a sweet girl and needs little supervision. Mrs. Prowda reports that she heard from Mrs. Farchione, who Ruth is residing with, that Loretta was not too happy in her home. Mrs. Prowda states that it makes "her feel a little hurt." Mrs. Prowda feels that new placements are always hard to get accustomed to as the girls have to get used to the work routine and the family. Another social worker is assigned to supervise the case.

On April 25, 1956, Loretta is given permission to visit Mrs. Louis Eddy on Lenox Ave in Utica New York. Loretta informs the social worker that Betty Lehman, at some point, was a resident of the Syracuse State School and discharged. At Christmas time, Loretta saw Mrs. Eddy and renewed their friendship and caused Mrs. Eddy to request the visit. She was given permission by Dr. Sharno and Mrs. Prowda for the visit at 2:00 p.m. in the front hall of the school. Soon after that visit, Loretta comes to the school to pick up money for uniforms that Mrs. Prowda has requested. Loretta appears to like the home but is not very enthusiastic about it. There are two sons in the home, ages 8 and 10. Loretta is interested in moving closer to home to be near her mother, who is now residing on Main Street in Mohawk. Ruth Raymond came to the school on May 31, 1956, and reported to a social worker that she is not happy in her home. The social worker intends to investigate next week.

A discussion with Mrs. Prowda reveals that things have not been going very well and would like to talk in detail with the social worker about these issues. The social worker then contacts Loretta, who agrees she is not happy in the home. Loretta complains that on Sunday, she does not know what hours she will be given time off. Some Sundays, it's at 1:00 p.m. or 2:00 p.m., sometimes at 4:00 p.m. Loretta complains that it is too late and leaves her no time to go anywhere. Loretta has also written several letters to her mother, and she has not heard anything back. Loretta definitely wants to return home, but a placement is made at a job in Syracuse first to see how it would work out. Her doctor agrees that she should concentrate on doing a good job in Syracuse first before returning home. Mrs. Prowda feels that at times Loretta is unreasonable. At one point Loretta is ironing in the basement, and Mrs. Prowda requests that she stop. Loretta continues to iron as if it was her choice to continue or not. Mrs. Prowda feels her attitude is very hard to understand. Loretta gets angry over little instances, gets angry, talks back, and throws things around. In the most recent incident, Loretta made a big scene about something Mrs. Prowda asked her to do. Mrs. Prowda suggested that she stop being so touchy and resentful. She further stated that if Loretta continued to behave this way, she did not want to keep her. Her social worker Mary Marks explained to Mrs. Prowda that it is very important to the girls that they get off at 2:00 p.m. promptly. Mrs. Prowda promised to correct the situation and pointed it out that Loretta was making plans to return home to her mother but that she had not heard from her mother in a while. The social worker discussed the problems with Loretta, and Loretta decided to go back to the Prowda home.

It was now the middle of June, and it looked like summer had finally arrived. As Carol and I began to type and discuss today's topic, Ruth and Little Foot arrived. Both were glad to be here. Little Foot was very happy, and Ruth was out of breath.

She told us, "The doctor shocked my heart this week to try to get it back to a normal rhythm, but they can't promise that it will work. How smart are they that they want me to take the risk, but it may not work. I don't think they honestly know what they are doing, but I have to take the risk. They will walk out of the room, and I might die. They are fools, and I am a bigger fool to do it."

I told her, "Maybe it will work. It is worth a try."

She was not convinced.

She brought with her, her mother's and Harrison Culver's death certificates that the local funeral director, who buried them both, gave her. She also had her mother's obituary with a picture. My dad had told me right along that I knew Betty, but I could never picture her. Now I did recognize her and clearly did remember who she was. My recollection of her was pretty poor. Always around but never accomplishing much. Just kind of killing time.

I asked Ruth, "From reading the obit, it seems like the other brothers and sisters did okay. What do you think pushed her over the edge to the lifestyle she led? Was it the birth order being the youngest? Was it drugs or alcohol or sex?"

Ruth thought for a second then replied, "I think it was the fact that she got pregnant young. She may have not been able to learn very well."

I asked, "Was she handicapped?"

"Probably," she replied.

I was betting she was more than we will ever know. The lifestyle and the dysfunction coupled with the spin-off effect on her family certainly would indicate that she was.

After the issues were somewhat resolved at the Prowda home, a social worker visited the home on June 11, 1956.

> Worker called at the Prowda home to find out if the situation had improved. Loretta appeared cheerful and displayed a much different attitude than on her recent trip to the school. She told me their differences had been worked out and that she wished to remain on the job. Mrs. Prowda also gave a similar picture of the situation and said that things were much improved and that she and Loretta seemed to have a better understanding. Loretta is looking forward to going home on her vacation. We discussed this together with Mrs. Prowda. Loretta would like to go the first week in July. This would be from July 1st through July 7th. Worker suggested that she write her mother about it and have her mother get in touch with Dr. Watts so that it could be cleared as soon as possible. Loretta has always gone home for a vacation during the summertime, and she is more interested in this than going to Sandy Pond. Mrs. Prowda feels that it is very important that Loretta gets home as she knows she is looking forward to it, and Mrs. Prowda will do everything possible to see that Loretta gets off at the time we feel is desirable.

Loretta was interviewed in the Social Services office at the Syracuse State School in July 9, 1956. She had gone home for a vacation from July 1–8, 1956. Upon her return, she voluntarily came to the Social Service office. She had indicated she had a good vacation with her mother, stepfather, and her aunt. She also indicated that she would like to return home but understood that for the first year she would have to remain on the job for the first year in Syracuse. Betty is not working, but her aunt is working at a Duofold factory, only a block or two from her home. "From appearances, Loretta accepted the matter of coming back to her job and appeared to not be upset."

Loretta is enrolled at a swimming class at the YMCA. Mrs. Prowda feels that Loretta should "take the dips" every Thursday, and Mrs. Prowda feels that swimming lessons would benefit her. Mrs. Prowda is given permission to schedule swimming lessons for morning or early evening. There still are still ups and downs, but everything seems to be going smoothly.

October 8, 1956
Visit with mother, October 3, 1956
On this date, Loretta's mother telephoned to state that she was planning to be in Syracuse that afternoon and would like to see her daughters. Worker called Mrs. Prowda and gave her this information, and since Loretta was scheduled for a polio shot the day, it worked out very nicely. Worker saw Loretta's mother for a few minutes. She is working at the present time and had asked for the day off to come to Syracuse. Loretta appeared to have a nice visit with her mother. Loretta was planning to come into the city the following day as it was her birthday, and Mrs. Prowda was giving her a birthday party at Edwards Tea Room.

The plan was then developed based on the fact that Social Service that received a letter from Mrs. Culver that Ruth and Loretta be returned home for Christmas and be placed on convalescent care with her. The request was discussed at a departmental staff meeting, and the census was that the Christmas visit be taken up with the employers and, if it was convenient, that both girls could go; but prior to release, the Department of Public Welfare should do a home visit. If the home visit is satisfactory, Loretta would be released from the Prowda home, and Mrs. Prowda has already requested a replacement. Mrs. Prowda was also against the Christmas visit because Loretta may soon be permanently released. Mrs. Prowda also quickly requested a permanent replacement if Loretta was to be released. In a matter of three weeks, the possibilities suddenly reversed. On December 30, 1956, Loretta was returned to the Girls Building by patrolmen Myers, and attendant Jankowski. Mrs. Prowda had called Dr. Semshyn that she was having trouble with Loretta and wanted her to be returned immediately. Ruth's opinion was that Loretta must have done something pretty bad for them to call the police and be returned to the Girls Building instead of the Main Building, or, as Ruth called it, the Goody-Two Shoes Building. Soon after she was returned, Loretta was hospitalized in mid-January after complaints of weight loss, anorexia, and fainting. The physical showed, "No pathology on her lungs and coughs a lot, experiencing night sweats."

On January 13, 1957, Loretta was placed in the home of Mr. and Mrs. Halsey Cook, earning $8.05 a week. Loretta made a quick adjustment, and she liked the family, and the family liked her. There were visits by the state school offices and telephone calls checking on the placement. Loretta was active in the church group and continuing with swimming lessons. The worker making the visits felt that Loretta was making a great deal of improvement in the last year.

Loretta in late June was sent on one week's vacation to her mother's house, 16 North Washington Street, Ilion, New York. Loretta returned to Rev. Cook's house after vacation with her mother, and the Cooks took Loretta with them to their camp in the Thousand Islands, New York. When she left, she was complaining of a sore throat and was admitted to the hospital with laryngitis. She was quickly released back to the Cooks' home. There were continuing problems with her knee, and surgery was a possibility. As indicated time and time again by Ruth and Loretta's mother and employers, Mrs. Cook had requested a temporary placement if Loretta had to have surgery. Loretta was very happy at the Cook home and requested some money so she can begin her Christmas shopping. The social worker approved releasing some money due to Loretta's pending surgery. Loretta had developed a cyst at the lateral joint space on her knee, and a letter had been sent to Mrs. Culver to gain approval for this surgery. The operation was scheduled for December 3, 1957. Mrs. Cook would like Loretta returned as soon as she was able to go up- and downstairs, so she could take her meals in the kitchen. Loretta was released from University Hospital on December 10, 1957, and was placed in the Girls Building. She was trained on how to remove and apply her cast and was discharged on December 13, 1957. At a dance in early January in 1958, Loretta commented that she felt well, and she was impressed on how the girls were dressed, and she was pleased that they could groom themselves so well. Loretta was conscientious of her appearance and was tidy.

On another occasion, when discussing her hospital bills, Loretta spotted an error. She was being charged for being at the hospital for nine days, but she was discharged on the ninth day before 1:00 p.m. and should have only been charged for eight days. Worker contacted the hospital, and they said they would adjust the bill. These incidences among others seemed to indicate that Loretta was making an excellent adjustment. Mrs. Cook continued to be very satisfied with Loretta and indicated that the Cooks would like Loretta to stay with them after she was discharged.

In the middle of January, Loretta's knee was healed, her leg could bear full weight, sutures had been removed, the wound was well healed, and it was safe for her to go without crutches. There were no further reports written until March 10, 1958. When a social worker did visit in March, Loretta appeared to be somewhat run-down. She did not do much physical work but did have a great deal of responsibility. Loretta fed the children breakfast, clothed them, and played with them. The children were all school-age and very lively. It was evident to the social worker that Loretta did not get enough rest during the course of the day. Mrs. Cook was pleased with Loretta, but she and Reverend Cook did not wish to take Loretta with them should they leave town. Loretta was informed of this decision; the social worker felt that her case should be studied to create a suitable plan for her future. Soon after that, Loretta was hospitalized for again fainting; no coughing was found or night sweats but rough breathing. Chest X-ray was performed and showed no pulmonary disease.

A Stanford-Binet psychological test was performed on March 14, 1958. Loretta showed a chronological age of 21.5 and a mental age of 9.0 and an IQ of 60.

> April 21, 1958—Social Service
> Progress Note
> Loretta has known for about five weeks that the Cooks are moving out of the state and that she will have to have a change of placement. She is very confused as she would like to have the freedom that comes with being on convalescent care at home but does not want to live with her mother. Dr. Sarno has suggested that she write to an aunt who lives near her mother to see if she can live with this aunt. The alternative is to remain in Syracuse and be placed in a new home. Several people who are aware of the Cooks leaving town have expressed an interest in having Loretta come live with them.
> All this time, Loretta is still uncertain as to what she really wants, and she is very much on edge. She is planning to go to her aunt the weekend of May 3 to see what the job opportunities are in that area.
> In late May, Loretta visits her aunt, Mr. and Mrs. Lawrence Scanlon, who have agreed to have Loretta live with them when she is released. Loretta is apprehensive about finding employment but is assured that she can return to a working home in Syracuse if the current plan does not

work out for her. Herkimer County Department of Welfare will assist with Loretta's adjustment. Rev. and Mrs. Cook and Dr. Sarno are satisfied with the plan for Loretta.

May 25, 1958—Social Service
Placed on Convalescent Care with Aunt

On this day, Loretta was placed on convalescent care with her aunt, Mrs. Lawrence Scanlon, 59 E. Main Street, Mohawk, New York. Room and board payments will be arranged when patient secures employment. Until that time, she will receive free room and board.

Staff Note: May 27, 1958
PRESENTED AT STAFF MEETING FOR CONVALESCENT CARE CONSIDERATION RECOMMENDED

Loretta is a 21 1/2 year old girl admitted to this school in 1947 from Oneida County. She was doing 5–6th grade work at the time she was removed from the academic department. She completed her vocational 21-5; she had an MA of 9-0 and an IQ of 60 on the Stanford-Binet (L). She had made a good adjustment to the school although she is a rather immature girl. Loretta's mother has shown an interest in her and has visited her frequently, and Loretta has been permitted to visit at home. However, Loretta does not feel secure in her mother's home and does not wish to go there on convalescent care. Her aunt, Mrs. Lawrence Scanlon, has expressed an interest in having Loretta stay with her. The aunt is employed in a factory; however, she does not wish to have Loretta work in a factory. She stated that she would help Loretta obtain work possibly in the same factory. She stated that she would help Loretta obtain employment doing housework or something similar to that. Loretta's present employer is leaving the city of Syracuse, and that is the reason why other plans were being made for her. In as much as she had to leave her employment home this past weekend, Loretta was permitted to go home with her aunt at least until a definite decision was made by the staff.

May 27, 1958—the staff's recommendation that this patient be placed on convalescent care with her aunt is approved.

Upon Loretta's release to her aunt, she quickly obtained work at the home of a now-deceased but longtime friend of mine and my family, George and Martha Murtaugh. Loretta "lived in" the family and had Wednesday and Sunday afternoons off. She usually spent her free time with her aunt Mrs. Scanlon and her family. If Loretta returned to the house late, she would stay at her aunt's house so she didn't disturb the Murtaugh family. Loretta attended the Episcopal Church either in Ilion, Frankfort, or Herkimer. Mrs. Scanlon reported that Loretta attended services regularly and read her Bible every night before bed. She has adjusted very well to the community and was closely associated with the Scanlons. She was very dependable and "even more so than Ruth." During a social worker's visit, July 3, 1958, Loretta was not present in the home but called to ask permission if she could have dinner at her mother's house.

On October 1, 1958, the Herkimer County DPW requested a report on Loretta.

The report of October 16, 1958, read as follows:

Report from Herkimer County Dept. of Public Welfare and Home Visit

October 10, 1958—Herkimer County DPW reported that patient is continuing to make an excellent progress. She is still working for the Murtaugh family in Frankfort: likes her very much, and she enjoys working for them and living in their home. Patient attends church (Episcopal) regularly, visits her aunt Mrs. Scanlon quite often.

On October 9, 1958, this worker made a home visit to patient at the Murtaugh home in Frankfort. Patient appeared in good health and was pleased to tell worker about her recreation activities. She belongs to a bowling team and to a Moose Youth Group. Since Mrs. Murtaugh does not know that patient is from the Syracuse State School, worker could not interview her concerning patient's adjustment. However, Mrs. Murtaugh appeared to be a very pleasant woman who was satisfied with patient's progress in her home.

In May of 1959, Loretta takes it upon herself to get another job. She works for Mrs. George Barney of Mohawk, New York, taking care of her two preschool children until 5:00 p.m. then returns to either the Murtaugh or Scanlon home. She also works on the weekend in the home of Father Greenway, the rector of the Episcopal church in Mohawk. Mrs. Scanlon feels that Loretta is ready for a full discharge and wants to come to Syracuse to talk to a worker about discharge. The topic of Loretta's discharge will be discussed at the next meeting. A discharge interview with Loretta and a physician's exam will be required before any discharge can be finalized. Mrs. Scanlon will bring the patient to the school, Saturday morning, July 18, 1959, to discuss a full discharge.

On July 20, 1959, Loretta receives a physical from Dr. A. Zyznewski. She is 5'2" and weighs 112 pounds. She has no physical complaints. Loretta describes a fainting spell on March 1959 in this way: "As she went to communion without breakfast, she became weak in church and fell to the floor, but she did not bite her tongue, urinate, and no one observed shaking of her extremities." Loretta's skin is clear and teeth are in good shape. Her heart is alright. Her BP is 110 over 70 and pulse is 82 beats per minute. Dr. A. Zyznewski reports her as good-natured and with a clean appearance. She is able to carry on a good conversation, read simple material, and do simple sums. Loretta is mentally and physically fit for discharge from this school.

A final discharge interview is conducted with Loretta's aunt and uncle in July of 1959. According to reports from Herkimer County DPW, Mr. and Mrs. Scanlon is very pleased with Loretta and fits in well with their family. They consider her like their daughter. Loretta never does anything without asking and gets along with their children. Loretta no longer works for the Barneys because she is expecting again and will not need her services, and she will not return to teaching in the fall. Mrs. Barney has written an excellent letter of recommendation for Loretta. Mrs. Barney helped Loretta secure a job working in the home of Dr. Carney four days a week. Mrs. Barney points out that Loretta was able to toilet train her children, which she was unable to do. Loretta's recreation revolves around bowling and swimming. Loretta continues to read her Bible every night. She likes movies and visits her mother regularly. The report writer was very impressed with Mr. and Mrs. Scanlon. She felt them warm and friendly and have a great affection for Loretta. The Scanlons accept her limitations but treat her like a normal individual. They could not be prouder of Loretta even if she was their own daughter. The worker recommends discharge.

August 19, 1959—Social Services
Summary for discharge consideration on greet sheet.

September 17, 1959—Social Services
Discussed for Discharge—Approved
This case was discussed for consideration of discharge at the Departmental Staff Meeting. The case was reviewed, and the patient was recommended for discharge.
Date of Discharge: September 22, 1959
To Whom Discharged: Aunt Mrs. Lawrence Scanlon, 59 E. Main Street Mohawk, N.Y.
Condition on discharge improved—capable of self-support.

To this day, July 8, 2017, Loretta resided in Ilion, New York. She was once married to Roger Hall and had two sons, Roger Jr. and Kevin. She worked at Remington Arms Company for twenty-five years, retiring in her early sixties. The last time we visited, she was healthy and happy in the house she owned, living with her significant other. Ruth, Carol, and I agreed to go visit Loretta again soon on or about July 22, 2017, in order to visit and bring even more life to her personal history.

As we had planned, we went to visit Loretta again on a warm, sunny July, Saturday morning after Carol and I attended Kiwanis for the meeting and breakfast. We picked Ruth up at her home at about ten o'clock. When we arrived at Loretta's house, she was sitting on the front porch with her dog, Cheyenne. It was such a nice morning that we decided to sit outside while we talked. It was early in that the neighborhood had not started to wake up yet. Loretta offered us coffee, which we all turned down.

We began by discussing Loretta's notes from the Syracuse State School as opposed to Ruth's. Loretta was fully aware that Ruth's notes were about an inch thick, and hers were not even a quarter of an inch.

Loretta knew that it was a direct result of her behavior as opposed to Ruth's.

Loretta quickly added, "She didn't take any shit, and she still doesn't. Right, Ruth?"

Ruth nodded her head in agreement.

I asked Loretta, "Is bad attention better than no attention?"

She agreed wholeheartedly.

I asked Loretta, "How did you get along with your mother?"

She quickly replied, "Pretty good, but she never took care of us. No one ever helped her. But, she was also never there for us, nor was my father. She rarely, if ever, came to see us. Harry was pretty good. Ted Raymond was my biological father. He was supposedly a roofer or contractor, but he never had any work."

In terms of her mother, that was almost the same as Ruth's reply every time I asked her about her mother.

As we typed, I could see the look in Ruth's eyes that she was thinking—deeply.

I asked her, "What are you thinking about?"

With a large degree of sadness evident, Ruth said, "If you had known my aunt Thelma that lived across the street from my mother, I would have definitely gone to live with her. My aunt Thelma was special. She tried to adopt us, but my mother refused to sign the papers. We would have had a much better life and better education."

I said to Ruth, "Have you ever seen the movie *The Hundred-Foot Journey?*"

Ruth replied, "No."

I told her the story is about an Indian national that moved to France and opened a restaurant across the street from a famous restaurant that had been there for 150 years. When he finally crossed the street and met the owner of the other restaurant, they become good friends and eventually got married. The families blended together, and everyone was happy. I suggested to Ruth that if she had gone twenty-five feet across the street to live with her aunt Thelma, I agreed that she probably would have had a different life. On the other hand, my neighbor next door told the story that he was living in Syracuse and bought a ticket for a stag party in New Hartford. Often when he bought stag party tickets, he didn't attend the party, and the price of the ticket was a donation. For this party in particular, he bought the ticket and went to the party. As it would be, he met his future wife that night, and as they say, the rest is history. So, I guess it can play out in a thousand different ways. No one knows for sure what happens in five minutes or fifty years. The only thing that doesn't change is the fact that things change.

Loretta knew about Ruth with the sheets, sick needles, and sleeping needles. The girls in the Main Building knew something was going on in the Girls Building by watching the employees going from one building to the other. When Mary Le Graff went to the Girls Building, it was usually after lunch; and someone, usually Ruth, was in trouble and was probably going to get the "sheets," formally known as *wet packs*. Loretta remembered Beverly Davis and Betty Cable getting the sheets and the sick needles also. As we have discussed numerous times, "Betty and Beverly were bad, but Ruth was the worst." Loretta spent most of the time with the other kids, mostly playing Hula-Hoops and jump rope. She said she heard of the sick needles and sleep needles but never saw it. Loretta did a lot of cooking and crocheting, which kept her busy. Loretta also felt the employees aggravated Ruth and made matters worse. They never really tried to help Ruth; in fact, they made it worse for her.

Loretta was convinced, "If they gave Ruth something to do, she would have been better. Instead, all they did was aggravate her."

Ruth described the Girls Building, "The first classroom was where epileptic children were, and the detention room was right near there. As you continue down the hall then go past the dining room and the hall, there were two more classrooms. In those rooms, they held kids who behaved a little better but were still in the Girls Building."

Loretta never had any contact with the epileptic kids, but her recollection was that sick children were placed in an infirmary.

Loretta then made a statement that probably summarizes both her and Ruth's experience during twenty-five years of residing in the New York State foster care system, "We were just a little bit above slave labor."

When Loretta left the Murtaughs, she married Roger Hall, who worked at the Union Fork and Hoe Company. They lived in a trailer for a short period of time and then bought the house that she resides in to this day. She worked at a local company named Duofold for two years that manufactured cold-weather clothing, gloves, and outerwear. After two years, she applied for a job at Remington Arms and worked at Remington for twenty-five years. I mentioned some friends' names, and she knew some of my friends that worked at Remington for many years also: Bob Spoor, Billy Evans, and Bob Bracken. They worked as a punch press operator. Loretta felt it was a very good job, and she enjoyed the people she worked with, especially the people in the office. She always enjoyed the after-work hours at the bowling alley right next door to Remington, more commonly known as the BA. She always made money working at Remington, and the company was always willing to help her. Loretta did a dangerous job with the punch press because it could pull your fingers or arm into it and crush them. She now supported herself with a Remington Arms pension and Social Security to pay her bills. While working at Remington, she went to work every day, never using a sick time. Loretta, Roger, and her family went on vacations and even went on a very expensive cruise.

About two hours had gone by, and we all had other places to go in the afternoon, so our visit was about to end. We turned to Loretta's wedding and marriage. Loretta remembered Ruth wearing her wedding dress when she got married and leaving for the church from my dad's house.

I asked her, "How long were you married?"

A fast/definitive reply: "Too long. We did have some good times though. Ruth and I were good sisters even though we didn't see much each other for over twenty years, just little bits and pieces here and there. Our real contact didn't start until we were both released from the Syracuse State School."

As with all people, there is in every one's life something that makes them proud. Loretta had hers. At some point, she received a plaque from the local Moose Club for fifty years of strong membership. It made her strong. It made her proud.

Speaking of which, Ruth came in today with a letter that also made her strong and proud. It was written by her daughter Colleen on Colleen's wedding day, June 17, 1995.

RUTHIE DEEPLY

Mom

    I just thought that it was about time to write you a letter and express some of my thoughts and feelings.

    First, I would just like to say, "thank you," for everything you have done for me throughout my life. I love you so much more and I can't thank you enough. I know that growing up I wasn't always the best kid, I did say things that weren't always right. At times, I even made you feel like I was embarrassed of you. I was just young, and I didn't know any better. I am not embarrassed of you, more in fact I am so proud of you. I don't think that God could have given me a better Mom. You have always tried so hard to give us children the best you possibly could. Working two and three jobs for us. I love you and admire you so very much. I hope that when I have children, I can do as good as you have. You are my breath, Mom. Without you, I wouldn't be here. You're always there when I need you. Even now when I'm 25 years old. I still go running to Mom for comfort. You're always there when I need you. Please let me do for you the next 25 years what you have done for me. I know I can never do that, it would be impossible. You have done too much. I do intend to start taking care of you for once. We (me and Rob) love you and have you here with us, so whenever you're nearby, come home.

                                    I love you Mom,
                                        Colleen

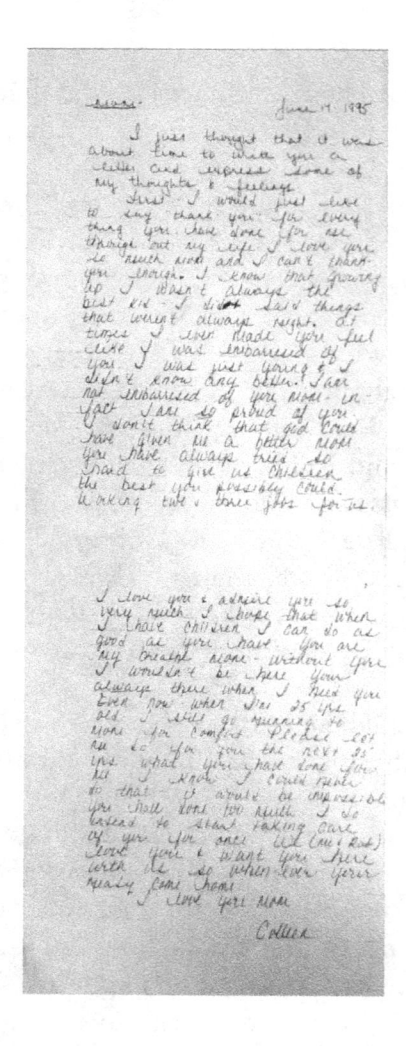

A wonderful testament to a woman that really struggled, and still did to this day, by a women that witnessed it all.

"Ruth, tell me the story about the food stamps," I asked.

"When we went to the grocery store, and it came time to check out, I would stand in between the kids to count out the food stamps so the other people in line couldn't see me counting them. I am sure they did see me, but what else could I do?" she replied.

Embarrassing to her kids and her, I bet, but necessary to survive. To Colleen, embarrassing then but not now.

Part 2

Chapter 7

A Teenager in Syracuse State School: Ruth's World Implodes

At some point around the year 2001, Betty and Ruth decided that they both "wanted to see how nice they treated us, not like we didn't know." To the best of Ruth's recollection, she and Betty drove to Syracuse to request that their histories be released to them. Ruth remembers speaking to an employee, she believes was named Bob, concerning their request for information. Again, to the best of Ruth's recollection, Bob provided Ruth with the records that are the basis of her story. It is now painfully obvious to the writers and readers that Ruth's life through age thirteen and her placement in Syracuse was certainly not very consistent, to put it mildly. Yet, the true horror of her story is yet to be told. In light of her experience in Syracuse, her life up to her placement there was made up mostly of bouncing from institution to institution, home to home, boarding house to boarding house—until it all became a tangled web that was still hard to follow, even with Ruth sitting here, to the best of her ability plugging holes.

When we first started this process approximately three years ago, we started with a letter Ruth received from a then active Syracuse State School social worker that came to her home to deliver a computer. The first thing I noticed about that original letter was that it was not dated. The letter was nice and very apologetic for the treatment/mistreatment she had received as "children at the hands of adults."

Thus, a good place to start the Syracuse State School portion of Ruth's life may be at the time in the year 2000 with an undated letter, which when I first saw it struck me as undated. It reads as follows:

> Central New York Developmental Services Office
> 800 South Wilbur Avenue
> Syracuse, New York 13204
> Ruth Morgan
> 39 Highland Avenue
> Ilion, New York 13357
>
> Dear Mrs. Morgan:
>
> I have finally copied your old record. I apologize for my slowness.
>
> You were certainly a young woman with a lot of spunk. I think it is wonderful that you knew your own mind and were working very hard at becoming independent. There were many instances when I think we treated the persons who lived at the old school unfairly, and we sometimes showed very little understanding of what it must have been like to be young and far away from home. I apologize for the past.
>
> I was also relieved to discover that there were even back then some attendants and other staff persons who seemed to really like young people and did their best to act in ways that showed friendship and compassion. I hope you remember some of these people as you read through this material.
>
> Our whole service system has changed, and if a person with your abilities had come to us today, they would never be institutionalized.

They would be given the support to stay in their own home and attend the school in their community. Hopefully they would be allowed to experience a normal childhood.

If you have any questions about anything that I have sent you, please call me (315-473-6371). Bob and I enjoyed our morning with you. You have a beautiful home. Thank you also for the doughnuts.

Sincerely yours,
Keith P.
Social Worker

Carol and I woke up this late August morning about eighty thirty to a gloomy sky after a huge rain last night.

First thing out her mouth was, "Any flooding after all that rain last night? Those poor people in the village. This rain is killing them. They must have spent the whole night watching that creek. Poor Will's grandparents at their age they have to go through this again."

It is true; the time they were having was horrible.

About fifteen minutes later, Ruth and Little Foot come in; and sure enough, the first thing out of Ruth's mouth was the same thing out of Carol's.

"Do you believe it is raining again? Those poor souls with all this rain destroying their property again." She truly felt sorry for them.

It startled me that she could have empathy for people she didn't even know when very few people—with the exception of my mother and father, the Masons in Herkimer, and a few others—ever showed empathy for her.

As Carol showed Ruth the furnishings that we bought for Alaina's dorm room, one of those sad comments Ruth often made popped out. When Carol explained to Ruth all the "little things" we had bought for Lana's room and how they worked, she quickly stated, "That's great. I never had 'little things.'"

Carol, being the greatest that she is, replied, "But you do now."

The story unwound further.

We discussed briefly that the real story of *Ruthie Deeply* started now with her experience at the Syracuse State School and the fact that she was a teenager through age twenty-five while a resident. She had a full recollection of her experience there and was willing to tell the story. Whereas others, such as Betty, tended to block out the whole thing as they moved along in their lives.

Although the first entry in the record from the Syracuse State School was out of chronological order, as I would expect, it started with a detention record, starting on admission to detention January 3, 1949, through January 7, 1949.

Problem stated briefly, for a long period of insubordination.

> Dates and times in wet pack: January 6, 2:30–4:30 PM and then January 7, 2:30–4:30 PM.
> Dates in single room: January 3–January 7.
> Dates in seclusion: none.
> Dates and time in restraint: none.
> Dates on bread and milk diet: January 3–10 Inc.
> Dates deprived of dessert: January 3–10 Inc.
> Occupation during stay and effort attended school: 3 days.
> Dates taken outdoors: January 4 to school.
> Unusual occurrences: none.
> Result of above therapy upon discharge and recommendations: placid and calm now.

I asked Ruth, "How did this all come about?" Here was where the story came to life. This was the writer's voice starting now.

Ruth said, "I believe it started with me not feeling good. The matron said that 'you better eat your breakfast. If you don't eat it, you'll get the same food for lunch and supper, and if you don't eat it, then you will get the sheets for three days.' I wouldn't eat it, so I got the sheets for three days."

I asked Ruth, "Did you give them hell for three days?"

Her reply was, "Not really, because you're wrapped up in those sheets. You're too weak to do anything, especially after you get out. Then they put you in a cell in detention."

I asked Ruth, "How long did you stay in the cell?"

She replied, "Unusually about three days while they were giving you the sheets. It was a small room, big enough to hold a cot. It was probably dingy gray from what I can remember. It wasn't too hot or too cold, it was okay. Solitary was a different thing. Solitary had a long radiator with a pipe running down the wall, and the window had bars. No bed, no pillow or blanket, just a bare floor where I slept. They would come in three times a day to let you go to the bathroom and delivered the bread and milk. They would bring the bread and milk when they fed the rest of the ward. The bread was fresh and the milk usually cold."

Oddly, the second entry in the Syracuse State School was another detention record: June 9, 1949, through June 22, 1949.

> Problem (State Briefly)
> Attempted to escape, didn't get off grounds.
> Dates in single room: June 9–June 16.
> Dates on bread and milk diet: June 9, 10, 11.
> Dates deprived of dessert: June 9–16.
> Occupation during stay and effort: rag teasing.
> Dates taken outdoors: none.
> Dates and time of wet pack: none.
> Dates and time of restraint: none.
> Dates medicated and drugs used: none.

As we sat and talked about the January 3, 1949, incident, I perused through the records; and sure enough, the date showed. January 3, 1949, showed up as the first indication of wet packs being applied.

> Detention and Wet Packs
> January 3, 1949—Ruth has been very insubordinate over a long period of time. She

has periods when she is excitable. It was necessary to give her wet packs on January 5 and 6. Discharged from detention January 7, 1949.

The primary source seemed to be an admission ticket to a detention and a record of what happened while there and her condition upon release. The full history that we later located wasn't really specific, but again, to the best of Ruth's knowledge, it involved refusing to eat her breakfast, which they then threatened to feed her for lunch and dinner. Until she ate it, or as it played out, she ended up in detention with wet packs.

To the best of Ruth's recollection, she went from the House of the Good Shepherd to the Syracuse State School at the age of thirteen years old in 1947. The first recorded wet pack was in 1949. Is it possible that Ruth behaved for over two years? Ruth felt she was "casing the place," although she cannot be certain, and she doubts that she behaved for two years. In any case, it was simply a matter of time before the "real Ruth" emerged, and the Syracuse State School would get the full dose.

I asked her about those two years.

Ruth told me, "I don't really remember much, but I must have behaved pretty well since there is no record of wet packs and detention until 1949. I think I was so scared that I behaved until I got to know the place. Then all hell broke loose. Once I started, I was in detention and seclusion so much that I lost track. I think I might have been in the colonies working. I am not sure, but I am sure of what happened after that, and boy, it wasn't fun. I might have even been on vacation. I really don't know."

As we looked a little forward in the notes, the whole idea of behaving went out the window. The in-depth record was full of wet packs, detention, fighting, hospitalization with scabies, and so on.

There was pretty much a rehash of Ruth's early history when she was admitted to the Syracuse State School in May 23, 1947. For a while, it seemed to be working so well at home that the case was considered to be withdrawn entirely. In the fall of 1946, the county social worker visited the home, and the adjustment didn't appear as good as first thought. Ruth's very low functioning mother became involved with another man. At this time, Ruth's mother was admitted to the hospital with severe hemorrhaging. Betty was supposed to be living in Mohawk with her sister Thelma and her boyfriend. The worker urged Betty to return to the mental health clinic for treatment, and her sister promised to take her, but as of yet, that had not been done. When Betty went to the House of the Good Shepherd, it turned out to be a very difficult situation because of the promises Betty made to take the children home. Despite everyone's efforts to inform Betty of the damage that those promises were doing to the children, due to her imbalance, she was not allowed to take the children off the grounds. Although she came to visit on numerous occasions. Mr. Raymond also visited and was allowed to take the children for rides on occasions. Mr. Raymond was happy with the placement, and the children were safe. He was also glad he could come and see them when possible.

The report by E. H. Ferguson, case director, House of the Good Shepherd, concluded with the following:

> On the outside, Ruth looked very nice when returned to HGS. However, her body was very dirty, and her head was badly infected with lice. Her worldly knowledge as well as her language was far in advance of her years. However, she was an affectionate youngster who seemed to want to do what was right if she only knew how. She had a rather blank expression on her face and seemed to be bewildered. Housemother reports she feels Ruth will always need supervision. She talks constantly, is energetic, and does things well after having been shown how.

As we got ready to end our discussion for the day, I turned on television to watch the pregame show for the Yankees. I told both Ruth and Carol about an interview I was reading with Joe Torre, former manager of the Yankees, concerning retired Yankee star Derek Jeter's recent purchase of the Florida Marlins.

The question posed to Torre was how he thought Jeter would do as an owner of the Marlins. Torre felt that he would do very well in that he was a "tough smart kid that had a great upbringing."

When I tell Carol and Ruth that, in a flash, Ruth said, "I had no upbringing. Alone, that was the only one I ever had."

All truth, half of her life, in thirteen words.

One week ago today, Saturday, October 14, 2017, my father, Ben Palmieri, after a brief illness, passed away. He was a strong man with a big heart, which Ruth will verify in that he and my mother were some of the few in this world that treated her well. Obviously, his death had gotten us off track. Yet, as we started today, we were all more determined than ever to complete this project. My daughter Alaina came across an online tribute to a long-ago writer pen-named Nellie Bly, who about seventy-five years ago, with the help of an attorney, got herself admitted to Bellevue Hospital in New York City to report on the conditions there. In the background of the video, there is a grainy split-second video of what looks like a wet pack being applied to a patient.

Ruth was obviously interested. For obvious reasons. We would locate it again.

The next detention record didn't show up until June 9, 1949, and ran through June 22, 1949.

I asked Ruth with a chuckle if she behaved from January through June since there was no other detention entries.

She replied, "I could have. I was younger then. When I was older and bolder, probably not."

The full documentation was received in the Syracuse State School on May 23, 1947, from a clinic at the House of the Good Shepherd, dated January 8, 1947.

> Original admission information:
> Raymond, Ruth Laura
> D-48554

Admitted September 24, 1947—Oneida County—Protestant
Born December 18, 1934

September 24, 1947—the above-named girl was today brought to the school by Mrs. Marjorie B. Cline, Special Deputy of Oneida County Department of Public Welfare, Court House, Utica 2, New York, from the House of the Good Shepherd, Utica, New York. Ruth is well developed, well-nourished girl of about 12 years of age. She appears in good physical condition. She answers questions readily and presents a pleasing appearance.

S. W. Bisgrove, M.D.
Senior Director
SWB/E

October 2, 1947—from Hospital to M.B.
Admission Note

October 1947—Ruth is a nice-looking girl in good health. There are no skeletal deformities nor signs of endocrinopathy. Hymen intact. Ruth is nervous but cooperative.

Blood taken for Wassermann.

Dr. Hauser

September 1947—School Test

Grade 2-2 trial—Ruth's academic abilities are quite evenly distributed at high second grade level. Knows the mechanics of addition and subtraction. Can solve simple thought problems. Spelling poor.

H. Cashore/rw

Psychological Exam
October 6, 1947

VINCENT PALMIERI

Stanford Binet: M. C.A. 12-10, M.A. 8-2, I.Q. 64
Goodenough   Man 6-3
             Woman 8-0
Purpose: New admission.
Classification: High moron level of general intelligence.
H. Green/rw

The intake of information continued with a visit to a Syracuse hospital for further evaluation of Ruth's physical condition by the City Health Department. She was administered an x-ray on October 7, 1947, which indicated "no evidence of tuberculosis."

City Lab Report
   October 1947—Examination of September 24, 1947—Examination of vaginal smear for G.C. Results: No puss cells. No gonococci seen.
   October 1947—Exam of September 24, 1947—Examination of throat and nose cultures for diphtheria and hemolytic streptococci. Result: Negative for diphtheria.
   October 1947—Examination of the specimen of blood for the complement fixation test for syphilis. A titer of No Reaction was obtained.

On November 14, 1947, Ruth was interviewed by Dr. M. Naples Sarno, and all of her records were reviewed. Ruth presented a moron IQ of 64. The probable cause of her mental deficiency was heredity, and her clinical classification: familial. On November 17, Dr. Sarno completed a certificate of director. When we googled the meaning of *certificate of director*, the Childcare Education Institute states, "The director provides skills and knowledge of child care in order to identify appropriate classroom settings, define appropriate performance-based assessments, identify communication strategies, and manage a child developmental center." On November 12, Ruth was seen by Dr. Benjamin Pollick and awarded the privileges of the statute. We googled what *privileges of the statute* means, and we couldn't find any clear-cut definition, but it seems that the Syracuse State School employees were able to communicate with each other confidentially without any fear of lawsuits or repercussions. The whole idea pretty much gave the employees to do whatever they felt was necessary to deal with the resident.

Ruth quickly said, "It gave them the right to abuse you or send you away to another place." From January 13, 1948, through January 18, 1948, Ruth was moved three times from the Main Building, Girls Building, to a ward for detention. The next day, she went back from the Girls Building to the Main Building. Two days after that, she went from the Main Building to the hospital.

I asked Ruth if the hospital meant a hospital in Syracuse, or the infirmary on the grounds of the Syracuse State School.

Ruth's reply was, "That's where they make the sick needle or the sleep needles. They go from the infirmary to the Girls Building, where the detention area was. Then if you don't behave, they give you either the sick needle or the sleep needle, but mostly the sick needle. The sick needle makes you very sick. They lock you in a cell by yourself. You throw up as soon as they give you the needle. Within a few seconds, you start vomiting. You continually vomit right through the night. No one checks on you. They didn't care if you died. In the cell, the floor can be covered with vomit. You sleep on the floor—with no bed, covers, etc. The next morning, they come in and make you clean it up. You are tired, exhausted, and then you have to scrub the floor. You continue to stay in the detention however long you were assigned by the doctor in charge. You were given bread and milk and are allowed to use the bathroom three times a day. When they wouldn't let me go to the bathroom, I would pee in the bowl that they gave me milk in and then pour it down the hole. The pipe for the radiator came through the floor, up the wall, to the radiator about eight feet up the wall. The hole in the floor had a slight gap, and that is where I poured my pee. I had no idea what was below me, and I didn't care."

About five months after she was admitted in January 1948, progress notes were drafted. Ruth was not getting along with the other girls and the employees. She was always fighting and using bad language. She has good morals. Ruth wondered, how can you use bad language and fight with the other girls and have good morals? Her teacher's reports: "She scores at a second-grade level. Well displaced from her chronological age of 14." Her mother wrote her letters, and her teacher and the other girls in her class helped Ruth reply. She was not neat in appearance and liked to play cards with the other girls. Ruth did not like the radio in general but liked *Blonde* and *Baby Snooks*. Ruth said she liked it at the state school and had no complaints. Generally, she was in good health.

Ruth felt, "That's not me saying I was content there. Always in trouble—how content could I behave? The only time I was happy was when LaGraff was there."

I told Ruth, "I would hear bits and pieces of what happened to you when you were in the state school, and I would ask my mother or father, when you were younger, what happened to you? They both had the same answer, 'She was there and wouldn't behave.'"

Ruth chimed in, "I wouldn't behave, they wouldn't behave. So, who was at fault? I didn't like their attitude, and they didn't like mine. That goes to show you how retarded I was."

We googled the *Baby Snooks Shows*, which, ironically, was about a mischievous young girl. It began on CBS Radio on Sunday evenings at six thirty in 1994 and known as *Post Toasties Time* and also called *Baby Snooks and Daddy*. At some point, it moved to television and then ended the series.

Ruth was sent back to the hospital in late January 1948 with rash on her arms and legs, which was diagnosed as scabies. She was put in isolation and was provided with a polysulfide ointment without bathing for three days. Ruth laughed at the idea of no bath for three days, as "they only let you take a bath once a week." In late February, she was rehospitalized with impetigo contagious. From February 12 to March 22, she was again back and forth to the hospital. March 11, the scabies came back on her fingers and arms. Again, no bathing and isolation.

Ruth remembered, "Betty and I were in the hospital together. Betty was in the hospital, and I was in the isolation because I behaved so well. They made you look worse than you really were."

She was discharged from the hospital in late March and continued back and forth from the Main Building to the Girls Building right through the end of July. Including detention from July 7 through July 28; "further stay not beneficial," according to Dr. Naples Sarno. As Ruth remembered it, she was a resident of the Girls Building for behavior issues, but they would move her to the Main Building if she was better in terms of behavior.

Ruth recalled, "Betty must have done something wrong to get her permanently placed in the Girls Building. That is where the epileptic kids are, and they expected us to take care of them. I wouldn't do it, and Betty wouldn't either. So, they kept us in the Girls Building permanently. It was nice and close, so when we did something wrong, they could place you right in detention, which is located in the Girls Building."

> Progress Note
> August 9, 1948—Attendant states:
> No trouble, behavior good—gets along nicely with other children. She states she is coming along here not too good—some of the girls fight with her. She says she gets along well with some of the attendants—likes school and will be in the third grade. Has no complaints.

Ruth felt, "They constantly contradict themselves. How can I have no complaints if I am always in trouble or detention or solitary? I was never happy. Only when I saw Mary LaGraff, and I still miss her."

Sad for her to this day. Poor women had nothing, did pretty well, but still suffered from the long-term effects of her early life. Sort of crushes my spirit along with hers. Yet we soldier on, we fight on.

On September 24, 1948, Ruth was admitted to detention for misbehaving for over a period of time. She was discharged on

December 28 because Dr. Sarno felt it was not advisable to leave her out of school for a long period of time.

Ruth said, "School? I haven't seen school since I got here, which was fall of 1947. It is September of 1948, and I haven't even been in school. What school? Betty said the same thing. If I was spending all that time in detention, how could I be going to school? If they had kept me in school instead of all that time in school, I would have learned something. That's coming from a moron."

> Progress Notes
>
> October 14, 1948—Ruth is 14 years old. She is very miserable [statement of attendant]. Bad character; is slow, obstinate, emotional, not a very good worker, very lazy. Likes it here ok; no complaints. Likes her attendants, is in gym and likes it there. Likes the teachers; has made friends and gets along nicely with other children. She has been here about one year. Seems to be well adjusted.

Carol needed to add her opinion now, "Vinny, how can she be 'slow, obstinate, lazy,' and so on? But 'she likes it here, no complaints, likes the other kids, and, after a year, seems well-adjusted'?"

"It seems total inconsistency. What could they expect from the residents with this constant turmoil? There is no rhyme or reason to any of it. Like Scott Smith said, it tells you more about the writer of the report than the person the report is about. It says nothing about the person—how they feel, how they act. It's more employee-centered information. No one is going to get anywhere like that. The employee just gets another paycheck, nothing is resolved, nothing is improved, and every day is dragged on from the day before. Or in Ruth's case, another sick needle, wet pack, detention, or sleeping needle," I stated.

Ruth said, "You never see anything mentioned of the sick needle or sleep needle because I bet it was illegal, and no one is going to put that in writing."

I was betting she was 100 percent right.

We picked up again in early November on a snowless but very cold Saturday.

We begin with Ruth's release from the Girls Building to the South Wing, which was a classroom building where Mary LaGraff worked as a supervisor. From January 7 through February 12, approximately five weeks, there was no mention of any behavioral/disciplinary incidents.

I wondered aloud, "Why such good behavior?"

"Because of LaGraff. Since she was in charge, and I liked her so much I behaved. I would do anything for her. She treated me and all of us with respect. I think she really tried to help us, not like everybody else. She was a good person but never showed any partiality. If there was a problem, she let you know about it but was fair and tried to help. Some workers, I just wouldn't behave for. When they came in the building, I would try to trip them. I was terrible. Some of them I hated so much, even when they tried to help me, I was still mean to them. I also liked Mrs. Bowman. She would put candy under my pillow, when the other kids were asleep, I would eat it. Then flush the wrapper down the toilet so no one would know that she was being nice to me. I wouldn't want her to get in trouble. I didn't even tell the other girls she gave me candy. Usually, when someone wanted to get rid of something, we flushed it down the toilet. There was no one else to get rid of anything. We had a little poem that went along with what we did. It was:

> Walls got ears,
> Pipes got holes,
> Back to the boss
> Everything goes.

"We put in the last line because if anyone heard anything, they would turn you in, and then there would be some type of punishment. Betty really liked Mrs. Ryan and Mrs. Gephardt. Betty behaved pretty good compared to me, and so did my sister. They all knew that I was the instigator. There was a whole underground of communication even from building to building. My sister told you that she always knew when I was in trouble—in detention, getting wet packs, etc., and she was in the other building. I have no idea how she found out, but she did. We all seemed to know about what was going on with everybody else. News travels."

On February 12, sure enough, Ruth went back to the Girls Building for detention for some sort of unspecified incident. The light went off in Ruth's head. I could see it.

"I bet Mary LaGraff went on vacation or was sick or whatever because she left, especially if she was out for a long time, so I started making trouble," was her take on it. I bet again she was 100 percent correct.

From the Syracuse State School notes:

> DETENTION
> February 12, 1949—admitted to detention because of defiance and insubordination and disrespect. Discharged February 21, 1949.

Not much information in terms of the reason for the placement or what took place while in the Girls Building for that time, but chances were it was very much the same thing: wet packs, isolation, bread and milk, etc.

Ruth was then released from the Girls Building on February 21, 1949, and apparently behaved through June 9. Again, we were guessing about the good behavior only because the record had no information about disciplinary infractions or disciplinary actions. Ruth felt Mary LaGraff was working during that time, in that the employees had maybe two weeks off per year, and Mary's were in February of 1949. That February through June, Mary was working, so Ruth behaved, she guessed.

On June 9, certain issues led to big problems.

> Mother Given Custody
> June 9, 1949, a letter was received from Mr. Howard J. Blaugrund, attorney-at-law, dated

June 6, stating that the mother was granted a divorce from the father, and the mother was given custody of the two children. Letter filed in Ruth's record.

Detention Note
June 9, 1949—admitted to detention because she attempted to escape. She was apprehended before she got off the grounds. Discharged from detention June 22, 1949.

Could Ruth have heard from that underground communication network, which certainly existed, that her mother had been granted custody, and that stress caused her to act out, even attempting to escape? Might all be a coincidence but might all be a fact too. Although Ruth does not remember any connection, it also was approximately sixty-eight years ago. Time does weird things to a person's memory. Or maybe Mary LaGraff was gone on vacation again? We will never know now. Only fuzzy memories—and ugly fuzzy memories at that.

Carol and I did some Christmas shopping on Wednesday night and some birthday shopping for Ruth's birthday on December 18. As we got two jobs done at once, Ruth's birthday and Christmas presents, the discussion inevitably turned to Ruth's past birthdays and Christmases.

So, when Ruth came on Saturday, December 9, to continue our project, we began a discussion of those past birthdays and holidays—of which there really wasn't any. The details certainly were not pretty.

She told us, "I don't remember there being any birthdays or Christmas gifts or celebrations throughout the years as far back as I can remember. I never remember opening up a present. There was never a Christmas tree or lights in my house or at the state school. My mother would never decorate anything, but it wasn't as commercialized then either. She never baked cookies or even cooked dinner. Maybe she did, but nothing I can remember. I was too young to know if she was an alcoholic, because most of time as a child and teenager,

I spent at the House of the Good Shepherd or at the Syracuse State School. Even though my aunt Thelma, who lived right across the street, would celebrate birthdays and holidays with her own children, my mother never really got the idea or chose not to. My first birthday memory was when I worked for Dr. Farchione in Syracuse when I was twenty-three years old. The party was with Dr. Farchione and his family. They also invited Mary LaGraff because they knew I really liked her. We had cake and ice cream. I'm pretty sure they gave me a present. I have a picture of the birthday party. I still can't understand how they could be so mean to children. How would they feel if someone did that to their own children, or maybe they did? I see these days how they do 'Stuff the Bus' for children. I never had any of that, and why don't they do anything like that for older people? How would I go about starting something to benefit them? We were by the Burnet Park, I would be in solitary and could hear the hyenas laughing. Do you believe I thought they were laughing at me?"

What a shame for a twenty-three-year-old adult woman to have her first birthday cake all done by total strangers. Years of rejection finally resolved by strangers, certainly not family. I can only speak for myself, but I know I sure take a lot for granted. I have to wonder how many people at this moment in the world are still in Ruth's formerly horrible situation. It's beyond my understanding of how people working at the Syracuse State School could deny the residents any type of acknowledgment of birthdays or holidays and then go home and celebrate birthdays and holidays with their own families. Perhaps it was institutional in that in New York State guidelines, there could not be any celebrations for wards of the State. What makes it greater irony for me is, if it was the case, then it was a formalized policy preventing those types of celebrations for children and young adults in the long run; subtleties as denying celebrations probably hurt more than helped the effectiveness of their programs and cost more money. No one got any feeling of attachment or normalcy, but maybe that was by design too. Right to this second, Ruth could show benevolence for other people.

"How would I go about starting something to benefit them?"

In December 1949, a social worker contacted the Herkimer County Department of public welfare and spoke with Mrs. Delaney regarding the possibility of the Raymond children returning home. Mrs. Delaney also knew Mr. Culver, stating that his wife was in a state hospital, one child in the Marcy State Hospital, one in foster care, and one in a TB sanatorium. Mrs. Delaney questioned the possibility of the children returning to their parents but felt the parents would be willing to cooperate with a plan to place the children in their home.

A final summary for these visits was produced on December 14, 1949, and a return to the parental home was denied. Again, research on Theodore Raymond indicated he had very brief employments. It noted that he was unstable but was willing for others to take responsibility for his children.

In 1945, things seemed to be going pretty well until Mrs. Raymond began to have an affair with Mr. Culver. At that time, Mrs. Raymond was very ill, and the children were returned to the House of the Good Shepherd. After Ruth's initial abandonment and placement at the House of the Good Shephard, Mrs. Raymond discovered Ruth's whereabouts. When Mr. and Mrs. Raymond arrived at the House of the Good Shephard, Ruth was immediately returned to them. After just abandoning a four-to-five-month-old in a rooming house, she was returned to the parents as soon as they showed up. What were the people at the House of the Good Shepherd thinking about?

A staff meeting was then held and chaired by Mrs. Murphy. The report outlined the children's placement at various institutions, the other's remarriage, unfavorable conditions in the home, and the mother was considered not to be bright enough to supervise the children. At twelve years and ten months sold, Ruth made poor adjustments at the school. She was disgraceful, disobedient, and uncooperative. Loretta on the other hand made a better adjustment. The staff objected to the children being returned home. Howard J. Blaugrued submitted a request to have the girls' places in their home. But it was denied due to the facts that there was not a special class at the school in Ilion and that the mother could not adequately supervise them. The community opted to keep Ruth and Loretta at the school.

Ruth was bounced back and forth from the Girl's Building to the South Wing, both locations being in the Main Building. Then circumstances were as follows, directly from the notes:

> Detention—Insubordination
>
> Mary 31, 1960—admitted to Detention April 20, 1950, because of a long period of insubordination, impudence, and insolence. She was not permitted to idle the day away but was put to scrubbing and was very submissive when discharged on May 24.
>
> Progress Notes
>
> June 13, 1950, interviewed June 10—states she is 16—does not know if she will graduate because of her behavior; is admonished to behave from now on in a better way. She wants to know if she can go home during the summer vacation, would like to start parole classes in the fall. She promises to try to behave from now on in the proper way, wants in particular to talk to her sister, Loretta, who is in the gym. Ruth is in S. W. 1 and would like to be with her sister; sometimes in trouble with her attendants. She likes the girls. She thinks she had only two fights in one year.
>
> Parole sewing terminated, 5/26/50—was not in class very much due to behavior outside of school, which detained her in the detention Department. Ruth is capable but has episodes of emotional tension, which upset her comprehension and retention. When she is calmed down, she can learn, but not in her disturbed attitudes. Given credit for Junior term. Class Attendance for the whole school year was 81 days.

VINCENT PALMIERI

September 11, 1950—report from September 1949 to June 1950. Junior term Parole Sewing completed. Ruth has ability but doesn't always do good work. She could not understand much of what one tried to explain to her. Also, it is difficult for her to express herself. Poor concentration, talks instead of giving attention to project, resents criticism, likes praise but does little to prompt it. Bold and impudent, aggressive and quarrelsome. Seems difficult for her to conform or behave for any length of time.

Today, being two days prior to Christmas, we decided to meet again for some Christmas fun and some writing. In light of the fact that it has been snowing with sleet and freezing rain almost the entire time since our last session, we decided to cancel until next weekend. After spending another forty-five minutes snowblowing my driveway, which has become a daily ritual, I decided to do some writing without the aid of my trusty cowriters Ruth and Carol. Before I began writing, I checked my email, Facebook, etc., and found a post/short video by a relative of mine of a young boy, probably thirteen or fourteen, suffering from cancer. He was without hair lying in a hospital bed with various ports, tubes, etc. all over the bed. I was not certain what he was saying to whoever was filming, but the boy was obviously in tears and had been suffering a great deal for a long period of time. The post asked people seeing the video to pray for him. I couldn't watch. I was immediately brought to tears. I immediately made a silent vow to him, all cancer patients, people suffering in this world, God, and myself to pray every day of my life, even if only for ten seconds, for these people and everyone in the world. The same thing happened to me the other night while watching *The Color Purple*. Then five minutes later on the History Channel, a documentary about the Holocaust was airing, which had the same effect. A concentration camp survivor was discussing how while in the camp, the Nazi ordered the Jews to not use their names any longer but only their numbers since they no longer existed and did not deserve to own a name. The audio of the interview of the survivor was being played over a grainy actual video of perhaps ten children, ages seven to twelve, standing in a group. Someone off the camera must have given them an order to show their numbers. In unison, those poor helpless children all pulled up the sleeves of their ragged clothes and jackets to sheepishly display their numbers. I was paralyzed. My eyes filled with tears, and I began to weep. My wife and children were safely asleep in their beds, and I was paralyzed. Both the boy in the hospital and the children in the concentration camp were victims of something beyond their control. The full point being, so was poor Ruth. At four months old, abandoned in a boarding house? She could have easily died from freezing, starvation, or numerous other incidents. Again, something completely beyond her control. Then thrust for over twenty-four years in literally a penal system that destroyed her, as best it could, almost every day. The efficiency was nowhere near that of the Nazis, and it wasn't meant to kill her, but it certainly inflicted harm most every day. As she had stated numerous times, "We were children at the hands of adults." In the case of her mother, "I can't understand how anyone could do that to their own children." Or the general statement, "I would kill a person before I would let them harm my children." Those were raw emotions coming from a person that had been there. There was no denying those emotions were real and, to some degree on numerous levels, legitimate.

Where is the love?

I think most people would agree that change is inevitable. I think we all at some point in our lives come to that conclusion and must learn to deal with it. Given that fact, the only option we really have is to do our best to shape the change as it is occurring in order to reap the maximum benefit of that change. It is where the best happens. It is where the future is, where the action lies. Much like a butterfly on a pin. It has transpired. The butterfly is there. Now how do we fashion it in order to bring something positive from it? The change, as in 90 percent of situations, has to come from the bottom up. From the butterfly up, in order to gain some sort of positive benefit. It is obviously a huge change for the butterfly, and for all observers, a chance to shape something positive from it.

Where is the love?

Another reference to the Holocaust comes to mind. In the book *Night*, at one point, some young children were caught stealing food. They were starving and, against great odds, trying to survive. The Nazis decided to execute all of them by hanging. The entire camp was brought to witness the execution of perhaps four children. The victims were paraded up the gallows for execution and were hanged. The Nazis then ordered all prisoners in the camp to walk up on the gallows to get a good look at the victims.

As the line was progressing to view the victims up close, someone in the line questioned all of those moving up the gallows, "Where is your god now?"

To which someone in the line pointed to the executed victims, being children, mind you, and stated, "Right there."

As in the case of an innocent Jesus, two thousand years prior, having been executed too for committing no crime whatsoever.

Where is the love?

Same issue as the young cancer patient, the children in the concentration camp, and Ruth. Obviously, not certain what will happen to the young cancer patient. Can make a good guess what happened to the children in the concentration camp. Yet, I do know for certain what happened to Ruth. She fashioned all the terrible things that happened to her, as they happened, whether she knew it or not into something positive from the ground up.

Where is the love?

There is the love.

After a week off, due to the weather, we started again the next Saturday with really not much improvement in the weather. Ruth was here bright and early with Little Foot ready to go. Carol and Ruth had coffee and muffins. We started again with a review/discussion of the notes from the Syracuse State School.

Naturally, the first entry we started with again was a wet pack. Ruth was placed in a wet pack on October 6, 1950, due to the fact that Ruth was in a very excitable state. There was a gap from

October 6 to November 22 when Ruth was moved from the Main Building to the Girls Building. Apparently, she behaved in the Girls Building for five days, because on November 27, she went back to the Main Building. For those five days, Ruth could not be sure what happened, but she felt the chances were she wanted to go back to the Main Building because Mary LaGraff worked in the Main Building. The notes further stated that Ruth was placed on November 22 in the Girls Building because "Ruth had been insubordinate for a period of time and caused a disturbance in class for quite some time."

From the end of November to the end of March 1951, there was no indication of any problems. Yet, that only lasted so long.

The next entry from the notes:

> Detention—Excited—Wet Pack Given
> March 29, 1951—admitted to Detention on March 1, 1951—Discharged March 28, 1951. Ruth has had episodes in which she has become excited. She is not too bright a girl, and it is felt that this excitement is due more or less to lack of understanding. During one of these periods, she was placed in Detention. Wet pack was given on March 1, 1951, and on March 9, 1951.

That is approximately one month in a detention environment.

I asked Ruth, "What could have gone on in that detention for one month?"

Ruth said, "I was probably in solitary confinement for a week. In solitary confinement, you are locked up all the time, and you can only go to the bathroom three times a day, with two matrons in the hall waiting for you to escort you back to your cell. Then a regular cell where you could use the bathroom when you wanted, regular food, take a bath, then probably two weeks on the ward but still in detention. But you're moving back to a classroom. The classroom was teasing rags. It was not classroom like a school classroom. With me, they were just wasting their time. That's worse than jail.

When they told me I had to go to the Sewing Room, I went for one day and wouldn't go back. I wouldn't give them a chance in the Sewing Room. There would be three teachers and probably just a few people. I didn't want to give it a chance. I wanted to work in the Canning Factory. It was hard work, but I liked it. Betty and I used to raise hell there. We used to do the canning, we would talk and have fun. It was hard work, but we had fun. No one was really watching us that much, they were too busy. There was a conveyor above our heads with big racks of canned food, which we pushed in to the cold bath as part of the canning process. It may have food that was grown by the boys in the school. The boys did all the farmwork, and the girls did all the canning. When you went back to the Main Building, if you behaved, you would stay there. If you didn't behave, you went back to the Girls Building, and the same routine started all over again. I just didn't behave. I doubt anyone misbehaved more than me. I never went to the movies or dances. Betty said I was the worst behaved, and Loretta agreed with her. Vinny's mother always told him that I wouldn't behave."

That had to be the truth some sixty-six years later. Her memories were strong. Strong enough to almost bring her to tears or fire up her temper to the point that if the people involved were standing in my kitchen, she would probably have decked one of them.

It is amazing that people bounced in and out of her life: Ann Meyersberg, a psychology intern, Ms. Cashoe, E. Allen, and always Dr. M. A. Sarno. They continued to give her psychological exams, like Stanford-Binet, Wechsler-Bellevue, all indicating an IQ of 69 and a mental age of approximately a ten-year-old. She was constantly classified as a high-grade moron. The inconsistencies were stunning. Ruth's history indicated she was baptized when she was about five years and baptized again on March 15, 1951, by the Reverend Charles Baker in Syracuse, New York. There was a full-scale effort to "save" Ruth. She couldn't get a bath in solitary confinement to save her life, but now they wanted to baptize her every time she turned around.

On June 22, 1951, Ruth's mother, Betty, suddenly came back into the picture.

> Mother Interviewed
> June 22 1951—Mrs. Elizabeth Culver, mother of Ruth and Loretta, visited the school yesterday to attend the graduation exercises. She was interviewed by the writer, and she requested that Ruth be permitted to return home on convalescent care. She was advised that this was not the best thing for Ruth. Mrs. Culver then asked that both girls be permitted a vacation at home. I informed her that we would consider the matter. Letter written today to the Herkimer County Welfare Department.
>
> Dr. M. Naples-Sarno/b

Document now jumped backwards from June 22, 1951, to May 22, 1951, where Ruth was subjected to a wet pack because of a highly excited state.

No incidents reported, and on June 11, 1951, Ruth was granted a two-week vacation by way of a letter from the Herkimer County Dept. of Welfare, dated July 6, 1951, approving a short vacation for Ruth and Loretta. The vacation would be with the girls' mother from July 28, 1951, through August 12, 1951.

There seemed to be some sort of vocational education taking place, indicated by the notes dated July 13, 1951.

> Vocational School Report
> July 13, 1951, September 1950 to June 1951, Junior Parole completed, Junior diploma issued. Ruth is an extremely unstable girl. However, this year she has put forth an effort to improve. When asked to be quiet, she will be deliberately noisy. Keep herself neatly groomed

and is usually cheerful. Socially inadequate and requires guidance.

Again, Ruth remembered no form of academic education. There was no instruction in math, reading, writing, history, or science of any sort. The vocational education was a name attached to "teasing rags," canning, scrubbing floors with 25-lb. weights to polish the long hallways, sewing, and laundry. No academics to the best of Ruth's knowledge ever took place, and Betty verified it. No preparation for a successful life in the outside world ever took place for Betty or Ruth. That lack of academics may have been a result of lack of appropriate behavior on Betty's part, Ruth's, and others, yet still it seemed they should have been given at least a chance to succeed academically. Especially in light of the fact that even without any academic preparation, Ruth and Betty did pretty well over the course of their lives. With even the smallest chance to academically succeed, only time would tell if both of them could have gone 50 percent to 75 percent or even 100 percent further. In order to be fair, perhaps they both were given a chance for an academic education, and they both wasted it. Neither one of them remembered anything of the sort, but it was a long time ago, and they were both young.

The inconsistency on behalf of the Syracuse State School's part and Ruth's part again was evidenced when on July 19, 1951, through July 24, 1951, she was sent to detention.

> July 19, 1951—over a period of time, Ruth has presented a problem. It has been felt that many of her actions are for attention getting. She has been impudent although her behavior improved until a few days ago. Attendant Sansone was to relieve one of the South Wing classes for a few days, and Ruth was one of the girls involved in saying they would not cooperate with the attendant and would "get after her." Ruth was interviewed concerning this. One day she brought a knife up from the dining room,

and when asked for the knife by the interviewed, Ruth relinquished it without difficulty. At the time she relinquished the knife, Ruth was reminded that she had been given permission to visit at home, but unless her behavior changed, we might retract her permission. In spite of this, the following day, Ruth scratched her arms and legs. It was felt she might profit by a stay in Detention, and if her behavior improved, we would still consider a vacation.

July 24, 1951—discharged from Detention to Main Building.

Carol and I were discussing our next session for *Ruthie Deeply* this past week after we had both returned from a vacation in Savannah, Georgia. I was watching television in the living room with a liberal or conservative congressman babbling on about some inane topic on CNN or whatever. As he spoke, I said to Carol, "This guy needs a 'come to Jesus' moment."

With a true Carol Palmieri comment, she replied, "You need a 'come to dinner' moment. It is getting cold."

I had to think how many people that Ruth came in contact during her twenty-four years in the New York State foster care system ever had "a come to Jesus" moment, and how things might have changed for them, and more importantly for Ruth.

So, we picked up the history again on January 27, 2018, with an interview on October 29, 1951. The interview began with a worker visiting Ruth at a home where she was working that day. The worker spoke with her behavioral difficulties at the Colony. There had been various infractions at the Colony. The worker characterized the infractions as attention-getting devices, but they were bad enough to undermine the disciplinary structures at the Colony. The worker informed Ruth that although she many not understand the reason for the rules, she still had to obey them. Ruth had been stopping at another girl's, named Joan, day employment home. Although she had been told not to do it, she continued to stop and was noisy while she was there, thus attracting attention. Ruth tried to keep some of the tip money and not turn it into the state. She also used the phone in some of her work homes to call Dr. Sarno at her home. Ruth claimed she did not know some of those rules, and the worker pointed out that she had broken many of the rules after she had known about them. Ruth asked the worker if she could go home for Christmas, and she was informed by the worker that she could not go because of her responsibility to her job and her employers. Ruth was granted to visit her mother on Christmas Day only. The worker explained to Ruth that for more approvals to leave, she would have to make a good adjustment to the Colony. Ruth was characterized as very immature and attention seeking. It was noted that you had to be very firm when dealing with Ruth. On November 6, 1952, Ruth was given permission to visit her sister, Loretta, on November 11, 1951. The telephone booth, matrons storeroom, institution patrolman, and Colony were notified of the visit.

Ruth picked right up on the conversation, immediately knowing that all these situations occurred at the James Street Colony.

She stated, "Most of the girls in the Colony knew they were on the way out and they wouldn't be there much longer. The colonies were the last stop before going out to their own homes or a private home, like the Farchiones'. Most of the girls that went to the colonies behaved well enough to go to their home or a private home. With the exception of me. I went to Elmwood, Geddes, Westcott, and James Street about three times before I earned a chance to go to a private home. I was usually sent back for my mouth, using the phone to call LaGraff, talking back, being stubborn, and not doing what I was supposed to do—with a little chuckle I might add. Most of the girls that got out behaved better than me because they knew they were going to go out. They had people who cared about them. They probably were with some family members. I tried to call anyone I could, especially Mary LaGraff. I wasn't supposed to, but that is how I got her to come to my first birthday party I had at age twenty-four at the Farchiones'. That is the photo we have. I had nowhere to go, so what difference did it make if I behaved or followed the rules? The only one I had to talk to was Mary. That is why I named my oldest daughter after her. I was happy for the other girls who had a chance to leave the Colony, but I knew it was going to be a lot different for me. Westcott was the only colony that Loretta was in. Then she went to two different private homes, then she was released to our aunt Thelma in Mohawk."

On December 11, 1951, Ruth's mother was given permission to visit Ruth and Loretta at the state school.

> January 15, 1952, Social Service
> Interview with Girl
>
> Worker called at Ruth's day employment home to talk with her about her recent adjustment in the Colony.
>
> Ruth is very immature, and she causes a great difficulty in the colony by being loud and boisterous and by deliberately breaking a great many of the minor rules. If she knows something is forbidden, she immediately goes ahead and does it, and the Colony girls are complaining; they do not want to be with her on the street since she tries to attract attention by her loud boisterous laughter and talk. Ruth laughed gleefully and spoke to worker about these infractions of rules. She does not like Mrs. Keller, the Assistant Matron at the Colony, and sees no reason why she should obey her. She said if the matron ignores her when she speaks to her, she will ignore the matron "to pay her back." Worker pointed out to her the necessity for rules in order to keep the Colony running smoothly and explained to her that the matrons are there to help the girls and that each matron is different and has a different way of handling the girls.
>
> Ruth wants very much to go home with her mother and still talks about the fact that she was not allowed to go home to visit her mother at

Christmas time. Worker tried to point out to her, her responsibility toward her job and explained the necessity for colony training before she is allowed to go home. Ruth finally agreed that she would try a little bit harder to act a little more grownup and ladylike. She is very immature, but she is a very likeable girl and is showing some slight progress in the Colony, and it may be possible that she will get along better in the Colony when Mrs. Lee, the regular matron, returns on duty.

Joyce Murphy/HGH

January 18, 1952
Progress Notes

While worker was in the Colony talking with some of the girls, Ruth became almost unmanageable. Worker again talked with her about this behavior, and Ruth became very silly, laughing boisterously at her misbehavior and reacting in a very immature fashion. Following worker's talk with Ruth, it was time for the girls to go to bed, and Ruth went upstairs but immediately came down again, and when the matron told her she was to go back upstairs, she kept trying to evade the matron, and it was necessary to become very firm with her.

This is just one sample of Ruth's behavior in the Colony. Mrs. Lee reports it goes on like this all the time, and it is becoming a big problem.

Following worker's return to the school, she discussed this with Dr. Naples Sarno, and it was felt that Ruth might need a little more discipline than she was getting in the Colony since she apparently thinks rules are made only to be broken. She has done nothing really bad, but it is a series of small things that proves a continual source of aggravation in the Colony. Ruth has been warned this behavior cannot continue. Dr. Sarno has given permission for Ruth to be returned to the school and placed in detention for a few days.

Ruth wondered aloud, "What for?"

I wondered the same thing. I also wondered what a "few days" was. A few days for me may be three for Carol, it might be eight. Was it purposely written that way to leave a lot of wiggle room for the employees? The inconsistency of treatment was, I would guess, what led to the behavior issues that manifested themselves daily. Instead of lending to appropriate behavior, it lent itself to inappropriate behavior. A job-saving tactic? Whether consciously or unconsciously, the system itself was generating the issue it was meant to resolve.

Mrs. Culver was again granted permission to visit both girls at the school on February 21 and March 7, 1952. Ruth and Loretta were taken to Edwards Department Store for shopping. Ruth wondered if she behaved while shopping at Edwards, and the notes indicated, ironically, she did. Ruth commented that when she was in the various colonies, at times, she would purposely misbehave so she would be placed back at the state school—to see Mary LaGraff.

A classic situation of the tail wagging the dog. The system was trying to change Ruth's behavior, and in the end, she was changing their behavior.

In the entrance to the Baseball Hall of Fame Plaque Gallery, where those enshrined are indicated by plaques, there is a quote above the door by a former Yankee pitcher named Jim Bouton. The quote reads, "I spent my whole life gripping a baseball and, in the end, I found it was the other way around."

Fully similar was that it was becoming more apparent with each session that the same thing happened to Ruth. The foster care system thought they were changing her, but in the end, she was changing them.

I mentioned to Ruth there was no mention of *wet pack* for a period of six to eight months.

She explained, "When you're in the Colony, you don't get the wet pack or sick needles because you are working your way out of the system. Unless you do something like try to escape, talk back, use a phone at one of the homes without permission, or break one of the many rules. If you break enough rules, you will be sent back to the state school—that's when you would be subjected to the detention, wet packs, sick needles, and like in Betty's case, dunking. I'm surprised I never got that. I would have pushed them in the tub and held them down underwater so they couldn't breathe. I wish I could have been there to see them do that to Betty. I would have dunked the bitch. I would have held her head so far down, she would have never come up until she was dead. I bet it was Jackson."

> March 25, 1952
> Social Service
> Colony Interview
>
> While worker was in the Colony for the evening, she talked with Ruth about her attitude toward Mrs. Keller. Ruth had become very unmanageable, had been very impudent to Mrs. Keller, and had been very loud and boisterous. Just before going upstairs to bed, Ruth came to the matron's desk, threw a letter on the desk, and in a loud tone remarked that this had better go out right away. Mrs. Keller told Ruth that the letter would go out at the same time the other letters went out in a few days, and Ruth became very disagreeable saying that her mother had to have the letter right away, and she did not see why it could not go out the following morning.
>
> Mrs. Keller has reported many incidents similar to this, when Ruth has deliberately tried to provoke an argument with Mrs. Keller. Ruth is so immature that it is almost impossible to explain

things to her. She can see nothing wrong with her behavior, and although she finally promises to do better, it has no meaning to her. She needs very firm but understanding guidance.

We were starting to come to the end of today's session, so we closed with some of Ruth's famous state school ditties:

> Lemonade, lemonade,
> Five cents a glass,
> If you don't like it,
> Shove it up your—
>
> Ask me no questions,
> I'll tell you no lies
> If you get hit with a bucket of shit,
> Don't forget to close your eyes.
>
> April fool, go to school,
> Tell your teacher she's a fool.
> If she hits you with a broom,
> Take your hat and leave the room.

Through all this, so far, what became most apparent was this: in a system when most everyone else was slowing down, Ruth stepped on the gas. Still was as we met today, and tomorrow and next week and the week after that—for the remainder of her natural life, just as she always has, and it has served her well.

It had been a long week. Carol had surgery on her foot, which she was recovering from along with a plugged gland in her eyelid, which was also being treated. The weather cooperated, so Ruth and Little Foot could get here. Ruth had called about eight o'clock and that someone had shoveled her driveway for her. She wasn't sure who, but she would be on her way soon. At about nine, she arrived, had some orange juice and muffins. When we stopped on January 27,

2018, we talked about her mother and how she was given permission to visit Ruth and Loretta at the school on April 20, 1952.

In the spring of 1952, Ruth was residing at the James Street Colony. Mrs. Lee from the Colony called Dr. Fink at the Syracuse State School and reported Ruth has made "considerable disturbance at the Colony." Mrs. Lee reported that she was very well-liked by her employers, but her behavior in the Colony was such that she could no longer reside there. Mrs. Lee felt that Ruth was very immature and did the exact opposite of what she was told to do. Ruth was loud and boisterous on the street; she insisted on talking to the other girls while at church services. She was always trying to attract attention to herself. Ruth was described as insolent to another worker at the school; she continued to talk back as she was being reprimanded. The social workers had discussed these issues with Ruth on many occasions, and she promised to do better; but within two or three days, she returned to the old behavior.

As for the future: "Ruth is so immature that it may be sometime before she is placed in the Colony again."

I told Ruth that was the official position.

Then I asked her to describe her unofficial position.

She said, "I think I have to agree with some of the things they said, but I think I was being miserable because I wanted to go back to the school to be around Mary LaGraff, a matron there. First, I went to James Street, then they sent me back to the school. Mrs. Lee and I got along, but Mrs. Keller and I never got along. For example, if I came home from work and didn't take a shower right away, when she asked me why, I told her, 'I will when I'm ready,' and she didn't like that. I can see her now—that stupid fool. She never liked me from the beginning. When the others would go upstairs to take a shower before watching television downstairs, I would crochet and watch television first, and Mrs. Keller did not like the idea. She wanted everyone to do it all at the same time, and I didn't want to. Just little things that were stupid is what she didn't like. Keller knew that I had been sent back to the school. She thought I was trouble before and I would be trouble again. So, my opinion is that she wouldn't let it go. When people knew Ruth was going to the Colony, everyone ran for cover. I surely gave them a run for their money. Good riddance to bad rubbish. They would pick on little things and make a big deal out of them. It was all so stupid. I am amazed that I made it through all the nonsense. I think they made me out to be a lot worse than I was. Like I said before, they tried to make you think you were crazy. But I fooled them."

From June 1 through June 5, 1952, when Ruth was back at the state school, the situation must have quieted down because Ruth was granted a home visit.

> Visit at Home Permitted
> June 5, 1952
> Mrs. Elizabeth Culver, 101 Morgan Street, Ilion, New York, mother of Ruth, inquired about the possibility of Ruth being permitted to visit her this summer. It is rumored that Ruth has bragged about being sent back to the school so that she would be permitted more than a week for a visit at home. Mrs. Culver has been informed that Ruth will be permitted to visit her this summer. Ruth will be permitted to visit her the week that James Street Colony is on vacation and for that week only, even though at that time she may be a patient at the School.

Starting on about June 20, Ruth was placed in a wet pack for being in a highly excited state. The only mention was the one disciplinary action, and on July 2, she was released to her mother for her planned vacation.

I told Ruth that Dr. Sarno signed off on the wet packs, bringing her back to the state school from the Colony and approving her vacation.

Ruth explained that Dr. Sarno used to let her go to her office and talk to her and explain that the wet pack, sick needles, and other punishments were not working. Dr. Sarno owned a Catholic store on Salina Street in Syracuse, and when Ruth was at the Colony, she would stop at Dr. Sarno's store to see her. When she was at the school, Ruth went to her office because she was probably in trouble, and she gave her a cross-stitch tablecloth to work on and stay out of trouble—at least that was her hope.

    July 9, 1952—returns to the School from a week's vacation with her mother.

    July 15, 1952—patient was placed in detention on July 14, because of her behavior. She has been highly excited and abusive to the other patients and to the attendants. She also created disturbances throughout the building.

Detention Report
    July 18, 1952—admitted to detention on June 4, 1952. Patient was belligerent, roaming all over, bragging about her bad behavior etc. Worked during detention time. Discharged on trial June 30, 1952.
    July 14, 1952—from Girls Building to Detention

Wet Pack
    July 16, 1952—Ruth was given a wet pack on this date as she was highly excited and disturbed.

From Detention to Girls Building
    July 21, 1952—patient was admitted to detention from the Girls Building on July 14 because of her impossible behavior in keeping the dining room and dormitory in a turmoil.
    July 21, 1952—from Detention to Girls Building

September 2, 1952—from Girls Building to Detention

Detention note
September 3, 1952—admitted to detention on September 2, 1952, because she has been going through period of insubordination. Threatened to assault an employee. She used vile and obscene language to everyone whenever corrected.

Wet Pack
September 3, 1952—wet pack was given to Ruth this date as she was highly excited.
September 20, 1952—from Detention to Girls Building

Detention Report
October 3, 1952—Discharged from detention on September 20, 1952. Behavior in detention: fair.

Wet Pack
October 3, 1952—wet pack was given on September 19. Excited and causing a general disturbance.
October 9, 1952—from Girls Building to Detention.
October 10, 1952—from Detention to Girls Building.
October 14, 1952—Ruth was put in seclusion on October 9, 1952, because she was very excited.

Detention Report
October 14, 1952—admitted to detention on October 9, 1952, from Girls Building for

fighting with another girl. No amount of persuasion could stop the fight. Kept the entire east side on an uproar. Ruth is rather an excitable girl. Discharged from detention to Girls Building on trial.

October 15, 1952—from Girls Building to Detention

Wet Pack

October 21, 1952—Ruth was put in seclusion on October 16 because she was highly excited and rang the fire alarm, also on October 17 because she was very excited.

Seclusion

October 22, 1952—Ruth was put in seclusion on October 18, 19, and 20 because she was highly excited.

Seclusion

October 23, 1952—Ruth was put in seclusion on October 20 and 21 because she was highly excited.

Wet pack

October 23, 1952—Ruth was given a wet pack on October 21 because she was highly excited.

Seclusion

October 27, 1952—Ruth was put in Seclusion on October 22, 23, 24, 25, and 26 because she was highly excited.

Wet Pack

October 31, 1952—Ruth was given wet pack on October 29 because she was excited and threatened to assault an employee and threw food in employee's face.

Seclusion

October 31, 1952—Ruth was put in Seclusion on October 28, 29 because she was excited.

Seclusion

November 6, 1952—Ruth was given a wet pack on November 3, 4, and 5, 1952, because she was excited.

Wet Pack

November 6, 1952—Ruth was given a wet pack on November 4, 1952, because she was highly excited.

Seclusion

November 13, 1952—placed in Seclusion on November 6, 7, and 8 because she was highly excited.

Wet Pack

November 13, 1952—given a wet pack on November 6 and 7 because she was highly excited.

Detention Report

November 17, 1952—admitted to Detention on October 15; rang the fire alarm in an excited state. Prolongation of Detention time inadvisable. Discharged on November 12, 1952.

"An awful long period of punishment with no discernible appreciation in behavior.," I said to Ruth.

Ruth replied, "That's when Dr. Sarno told them all that nothing was working, and I am not sure what happened next. Dr. Held, who Ruth never heard of, just signs off that 'prolongation of detention time is inadvisable.'"

Same old, same old. No one was listening to Ruth, no one was reading the doctor's recommendations. Ironically, Ruth again paid the price. Just as she had, for at that time, the entire eighteen years of her life. That price in a variety of ways would continue to be paid right through about 1974, when after ten years of an inconsistent married and family life, Ruth finally decided enough was enough and struck out on her own in order to do everything for her children and herself as her only priority.

We had intended to meet today, March 1, 2018, but a number of unforeseen circumstances prevented that from happening. The biggest issue being the unexpected death of my father-in-law while spending the winter in Myrtle Beach, South Carolina, last Tuesday. Nick was ninety and in very good health. For the past seventeen years, two of his friends, Bob and Eddie, both widowers, also spent January through March on Myrtle Beach really enjoying themselves. Playing golf often, shopping, out to dinner almost every night, volunteering, and doing a lot of socializing. Really an excellent time. We got a call last Tuesday about 4:30 p.m., which Carol answered. Not that I listen to her telephone conversations, but this one I did hear. She was discussing that she wasn't Carol Palmieri, then she was—I was not certain what was going on, but it was a strange conversation. She abruptly told the other person she couldn't talk anymore and handed the phone to me. It was an emergency room doctor from Grand Strand Regional Medical Center who was looking for the next of kin of Nick Ciufo. I told her, "That would be my wife, who you just spoke to, but she can't talk anymore, and I am then the next of kin." Sure enough, poor Nick had passed away. I asked her what we should do next. She gave the phone to a nurse that informed me that we needed to contact a funeral director licensed in South Carolina that they could release the remains to, but until then, they would keep the body in the morgue. We exchanged phone numbers, and I told them I would call back soon.

Carol and I discussed what to do next in that I had mentioned to Nick it may be time to set up a funeral director, funeral, wake, etc. He told me when the time came, Carol and I could do what we feel was best. Probably not a good idea in that under the circumstances we now had no idea what to do. I suggested we call a cousin, Vincent Iocovozzi, who was in a funeral business that was started by my uncle of the same name in 1946, VJ Iocovozzi, whose home was in Frankfort, New York. She agreed. When I called, Vinny's son, also named Vinny, answered. After the usual pleasantries, I informed him that my father-in-law had died in Myrtle Beach, South Carolina, and I wanted to know where his father was. Vinny informed me his father was on vacation in, of all places, Myrtle Beach. What were the odds? Huge. I then called Vinny Sr. Again, the usual pleasantries. We then discussed that my father-in-law had died. He wanted to know where the body was. When I told him at the Grand Strand Medical Center, he practically dropped the phone. He could see the building from where he was standing. Again, what are the chances? Double huge. Vinny then proceeded to contact a local funeral director that proceeded to the hospital to get the remains released, embalmed, and so on. Nick's body was then flown home for a wake and funeral; both very well attended, by people from his great-grandchildren to men in their seventies that played on his football or golf teams or were in his class, had played golf with him for years, knew him from the local gym he belonged to, or wherever. Nick led a long life and accomplished a lot. Much like my father or literally millions of Greatest Generation men and women. Sadly, there are only about five hundred thousand of such men still alive, but dying at a rate of about four hundred per day. Doing the math shows that there is a very short time before all are gone. Sadly, people my age and my children's age are the last generations that will hear the stories directly as a primary source from the people that were there. Rest in peace, Nick and Dad.

Next issue that kept us apart today was those invincible Upstate New York winters. When I put my garbage out this past Thursday about 11:30 p.m., the temperature was about forty-five degrees with literally no snow on the ground. The rain started about midnight and, within twenty minutes, turned into a blizzard with snow falling at about two inches per hour. By the time it ended, twenty-four hours later, we had received about seventeen inches of snow. When I had my taxes filed on Tuesday, there were no snowbanks. When I drove by my accountant's office seventy-two hours later, the snowbanks were three feet high, and the snow piles were ten feet high. Extreme weather was now the norm. Next four days were predicted in the forties, and the snow may well be gone again. Global warming? I was not certain, but something had definitely changed.

Last issue: in true Ruth Morgan style, even with all the snow, there was a local Great American Heart Run/Walk that was taking placing this weekend. The legend goes that when these walks/runs first started up in America after the fact, national meetings were held in various cities to thank all involved, total the proceeds, and celebrate success. Local chapters sent representatives from the biggest cities in America, such as Boston, Los Angles, etc. When the individuals from these cities saw the amount raised in Utica, New York, they all had never heard of Utica, wanted to know how many people lived here and why they had never heard of it. When the information was provided, they all expressed shock that such a vast amount of money could be raised in such a small area; upwards of one million dollars was not unheard-of. This local area was extremely generous when given a cause they feel strongly about. This all played into Ruth in that she went there at eighty-three years old to volunteer for the first time. Since she, along with me, at the same time suffered a heart attack in 2016. I should follow her example. Great idea for next year.

All that kept us apart today. Yet still pulled us together tomorrow. As we continued to pursue *Ruthie Deeply* to the end.

Though we missed a week, we started again today. Carol and Ruth were discussing how it was nice to have both of our children home in that it was spring break from Lemoyne College.

Carol said, "It's nice to have both kids at home in their own beds."

Ruth's reply was typical. "I never had the chance to sleep in my own bed. I never had my own home. When my kids were small, I couldn't afford a refrigerator, so I kept a cooler with ice on my back porch to keep milk and eggs cold. My friend Beverly bought me a crib for my Mary. I told little white lies to get what we needed. A lot of people helped me, and I couldn't have gotten anywhere without them. Your mom and dad always helped me too."

Absolute truth, and she was fully aware of it. Thank goodness. Since most people are not.

Social Services interviewed Ruth on December 1, 1952.

> Progress Notes
> Worker talked with Mrs. Lee about Ruth. Mrs. Lee feels that Ruth has shown a great deal of improvement since her last date in the Colony. She appears much more mature and much more amenable to advice and suggestion.
> Worker also talked with Ruth, who said she had had a chance to talk things over with Mrs. Keller.
> Ruth told Mrs. Keller she was sorry for her behavior before and that she would like to get along with Mrs. Keller. This pleased Mrs. Keller very much. Ruth said she is very happy to be back in James St. Colony, and she is getting along well in all her homes.

Ruth was scheduled to have a Christmas vacation at her mother's home in Ilion. Of all the bad luck, the weather took a turn for the worse, and with crowded travel facilities, the vacation was denied. The text again showed the inconsistencies because having approved vacation and then denied because of the weather, the next line was "Colony girls have no vacation." So, was she approved for the vacation, or was she not approved? Is it all just a cover to keep Ruth and the other residents under control? The veracity of all most any policy begs to be questioned. Was there ever any policy in writing, or was it all at the whims of the workers?

Oddly and for no documented reason, on December 31, 1952, Ruth was placed from the James Street Colony to the hospital. The hospital apparently being an infirmary. She remained in the infirmary until January 2 and then went back to the James Street Colony.

> Aiding Escaping Girls
>
> January 5, 1953—Elizabeth and Agnes escaped from James Street Colony on December 27. The girls stated that Ruth listed the clothes that they were packing. Ruth admitted this but stated that she did not know that they were packing to escape. This excuse was very flimsy, and she was reprimanded but permitted to return to the Colony.
>
> On January 6, 1953, was admitted back to the hospital from the Colony due to inflammation and a diagnosis of Otitis Externa.

Now the real story became evident.

Ruth explained, "We all had to get up at seven a.m., eat breakfast, do dishes, and get ready to go to work by eight. We would come home at five, take a shower, and get ready for dinner. After dinner, we all would do cleaning up. Once the work is done, we could watch TV, crochet, or anything you wanted to do until about eight at night. When I got up in the morning, I had the honor of making breakfast and waiting on the staff at the Colony. I think they were trying to keep me out of trouble. But I broke all the rules anyway. When we came home from work about five p.m., we were all supposed to take showers. I didn't want to take a shower then, and when Mrs. Keller insisted that I take my shower now, I resisted. I had no use for her, and she knew it. She would report me, which I didn't care. I think they were trying to get me out of there more than anything else, and I didn't care. The one I liked even less than Keller was Jackson. Betty and I argued with Jackson all the time. Jackson is the one that locked me in the cellar. Then I got the sheets for three days because I wouldn't tell them that I had given one of the other matrons money to buy me something. They wanted the name of the other matron I had given the money to. I refused to tell them. So, they would keep me or anyone in the sheets until you told them what they wanted to know. The money came from washing cars for the state school employees."

"Sounds like torture to me in order to get you to provide some information. Like something you would see the Greeks or the Romans or at some point the US Military was doing in Afghanistan. Sounds like a milder form of waterboarding," I suggested.

"I agree," Ruth emphatically agreed.

Hasn't this been the crux of the whole period of residency in the Syracuse State School? The goal being to sublimate these people, especially that they had no one to defend them or represent them when they were mistreated? Especially someone like Ruth that refused to comply?

Ruth got a big laugh out of that.

Ruth said, "The only one I would behave for was LaGraff, but she wasn't there all the time. As soon as she went on vacation or had the day off, I would start. Right in detention, Ruth goes."

She was telling us this as she punched her fist.

She continued, "Right into detention, right into the sheets, right in to the bread and milk, and sometimes the sick needle—right into everything. Even when Dr. Sarno told them it wasn't working, they continued to do it. They would call another doctor or whoever until they got the right to do it again."

What protocol was followed? It was more or less "doctor shopping," which is a modern phenomenon. These people were way ahead of the curve.

Ruth told us, "When Jackson hit me with her fist until my face was black-and-blue, I went right up to her and told her, 'Why you don't just kill me?' Coincidentally, she placed me in solitary confinement on the weekend my mother was scheduled to see me. In the solitary, I could have no visitors. What a great cover for something plainly abusive. It didn't happen often, but it did happen to me.

When the night matrons came to work, I didn't have a mirror to see what my face really looked like, but I could tell by the matrons' reaction that something was wrong with my face, and I could feel it. That's why they wouldn't let me see my mother. They made you out to be worse than what you really were."

I asked Ruth, "Why do you think they were trying to make you look worse than you really were?"

She replied, "Because I think I wouldn't follow the rules. I would sass back or wouldn't eat the dinner they tried to give me for three days. I would be rude and disrespectful, but they were just as rude and disrespectful in my opinion. Most of the mistreatment was unnecessary, no matter what rule or infractions were."

The notes went back to the escape attempt on December 29, 1952, and read as follows:

> Involved in Escape, December 29, 1952
>
> Ruth Raymond and Elsie were brought into the school to talk with Dr. Sarno regarding their being involved in the escape of Agnes and Elizabeth. Ruth had helped them pack their bags and helped them carry them downstairs. Elsie, who is house girl and knows where the keys are kept, had obtained the keys, unlocked the cellar door for the girls, and relocked it after they left. Elsie then attended the furnace, which is Agnes's job, in an effort to conceal this escape and give the girls further time to get away.
>
> Ruth readily admitted her part in the escape and after worker left. Dr. Sarno talked with her. She was returned to the Colony. She has been warned that such behavior in the future will result in her return to the school for punishment.
>
> Elsie was in a very disagreeable mood. She was feeling very sorry for herself because she had been caught for this misbehavior, and when Dr. Sarno questioned her, she was quite impudent,

so she was placed in detention and not returned to the Colony until Jan. 22. Elsie has no insight into her behavior. She blames the school and the other girls for holding her back, and she cannot see it is her own misbehavior which has prevented her from getting along. She is very bitter because she has not been placed in a private home, and although it has been explained to her that her failure to comply with the rules has resulted in her being kept in the Colony, she does not seem to grasp this explanation. She was returned to the Colony and has been warned that further misbehavior will result in her return to the school for punishment.

No further action was documented, but on February 24, 1953, another incident exploded.

> Returned to the Girls Building Overnight, Refused to Work
> When worker called at the Colony on February 24 to take some girls to the dentist, Ruth was seen in the kitchen with her jacket on in a very hostile mood. Mrs. Keller, Assistant Matron at James St. Colony, reported Ruth had refused to go to work that morning and had been impudent and defiant to the matron. When it came time for Ruth to go to work, she went up into the attic and would not come down even though the matron and the first called her several times. Ruth was to go to work that day for Mrs. Rizzo, 210 Wendell Terrace, and she has made many complaints to Mrs. Lee about this woman, saying she does not like to go there. Mrs. Lee had discussed this with worker a few days previously, and it had been agreed as soon as Mrs. Lee

returned from pass, she would try to rearrange the schedule so another girl could be sent to Mrs. Rizzo. Ruth knew such arrangement was going to be made in the near future. Ruth's complaints were that the woman constantly found fault with her work, making her repeat her work three or four times, did not allow her sufficient time to eat her lunch, to go to the bathroom, and continually nagged her about something. Ruth said this makes her so nervous she cannot do the work properly, and that is why she makes so many mistakes.

Worker returned Ruth to the Girls Building to talk with Dr. Naples Sarno. Ruth cried bitterly all the way back, saying she had been trying very hard to get along, that it did not pay, that even if you were good, you did not get anywhere. She has been trying very hard these last few weeks, and Ruth is a good worker. There have been no other complaints except from Mrs. Rizzo about Ruth's work.

Dr. Naples Sarno spoke to Ruth at length before she was returned to the James Street Colony. Worker will talk with Mrs. Rizzo in an effort to discover what is causing the difficulty.

Carol, Michael, and I attended a Utica Comets hockey game last night that the Comets eventually won in overtime and moved closer to a playoff spot. The game was sponsored by Frankfort Kiwanis but open to the public in a setting called the Stage and attended by about forty people. Most of the attendees were Kiwanians and their families, but probably fifteen people were non-Kiwanians. About halfway through the third period, someone told me that a very pretty—about forty years old—woman in attendance was a longtime friend of mine, Ray's daughter. The irony of *Ruthie Deeply* never stopped amazing me. Ray's daughter was also Thelma Richardson's daughter. Thelma Richardson, Wally Richardson's daughter from Orchard Street. Wally Richardson, Ruth's uncle that she came to live with on Orchard Street, where I first came in contact with her—I was about the age of five—after she was released from the Syracuse State School. When she couldn't live with her mother, who had thrown Ruth out of her house and put all of her minimal possessions on the porch. Needless to say, I went right over to this woman and immediately introduced myself, told her I have known her mother and father, her uncle Terry and Larry, her aunt Sharon, her grandfather Wally, the infamous Tommy Stone, whose firecracker incident was discussed early on, and of course Ruth. Who all those years ago was the Stone kids' and my babysitter? We went on and on about Orchard Street, of which she had no recollection of, being that she was not born yet, and so on. The irony was amazing. The world is smaller and smaller. All day. Every day.

The next day on Saturday, we started again with Ruth and Little Foot. Although Ruth didn't remember much medical care while residing at the Syracuse State School other than the infirmary, she did remember good medical care while in the colonies. For example, February 25, 1953, she was taken to Dr. Joy's eye clinic and found not to need glasses. On March 12, 1953, she was seen by the in-school dentist, and about the same time, she was complaining of pain in her breast; she was then referred her to Chappell's to purchase special support bras. While shopping at Chappell's with a worker, the discussion turned to Mrs. Keller at the James Street Colony. It seemed as soon as Mrs. Lee left, "Ruth immediately takes great delight in provoking Mrs. Keller by many small mischievous acts, and that has been very upsetting to the Colony. Ruth realizes that these acts are wrong and promises to do better in the future. The worker will talk to her again in a week or two."

Ruth got a big laugh out of that quote. Although she promised the worker to change, she had no intention of leaving Mrs. Keller alone. Ruth called it "a joke on them." At eighty-three years, she still laughed about the whole ordeal, yet at times, it seemed she wanted to cry.

Beginning on April 12, 1953, through a vacation granted on June 22, 1953, the situation deteriorated rapidly. From the notes:

>April 14, 1953—from Girls Building
>April 15, 1953—from detention.

Wet Packs
>April 21, 1953—Wet Pack was ordered on April 17, 1953, for patient being highly disturbed. Inciting other girls to misbehavior.

Wet Packs and Restraint Orders
>April 30, 1953—wet pack order was written 4/13/53 for reason "Excited disturbing detention" and on 4/21/1953 for excited—Inciting to deface room and create disturbance" (was written by nurse K. McCann).

RESTRAINT ORDERS:
>4/22/53 for "Excited—Inciting other to deface"
>4/23/53 "Excited. Defacing single room. Inciting others to misbehave"
>4/28/53 "Highly excited. Extremely belligerent to employees."
>A WET PACK written 4/28/53 had the reason "Excited—Abetting other girls to make a disturbance."

RESTRAINT ORDERS
>May 8, 1953—restraint orders were written on 4/29, 4/30, and 5/1/53 for patient being highly excited, abusive, and belligerent to employees.
>May 18, 1953—from Detention to G.B.

Detention Record
    May 19, 1953—patient was admitted to Detention on 4/16/53 from G.B. for being highly excited and concealing money in G.B. and refusing to hand it to the office. Prolongation of detention time would not help the patient, so she was discharged on trial on 5/18/53 back to G.B.
    May 24, 1953—from G.B. to Detention.

Restraining Sheets
    May 27, 1953—on May 24 and May 25, Restraining Sheet was ordered for patient being highly disturbed. One administered on May 26 also.
    June 11, 1953—from Detention to G.B.

Detention Record
    June 17, 1953—patient was admitted to Detention 5/24/53 from G.B. as she "Refused to go to religious services." Abusive to attendants and supervisor of Bldg. Ruth is determined to have her own way regardless of the rules. Has not been good since her recent release from Det. Prolongation of detention time would not help the situation. She was discharged after admonition on 6/11/53 back to G.B.
    June 18, 1953—from G.B. to Detention.

On June 20, 1953, Ruth left on vacation with her mother and was scheduled to return on June 28. Oddly, the notes showed that Ruth was admitted to detention on June 18 because she refused to work the next day, the nineteenth, reason being "rather disturbed because she was denied the privilege of going home. She will only work at jobs she selects herself." Again, the statement "prolongation detention will not change the attitude of this girl, so she is discharged on 6/20/ 1953 back to the Girls Building." Apparently, Ruth left that day to go on vacation with her mother. The detention report of June 23, 1953, was written by C. S. Held, MD. Dr. Held was the second doctor that stated that the detention was not going to help.

Confusion reigned when the history stated Ruth returned from vacation to the Girls Building on June 28, 1953, but also returned on July 9, 1953, as "Agreed." When what was agreed on was a June 28 return. No one had a handle on when she went in and when she went out. It appeared no better than the situation Ruth was in as an infant when she was constantly shifted around from boarding house, relatives, her mother's home, and the House of the Good Shepherd. Only difference being that twenty-one years had passed, and Ruth was now in New York State—approved living arrangements. Obviously, no better than the informal living arrangements she was born into.

Ruth's behavior was spiraling out of control. Beginning on July 22, 1953, through August 14, 1953, Ruth had three incidents that caused a lot of concern.

>Detention
>
>August 7, 1953—in detention from July 21–27 because of impudence. Over a long period of time, Ruth has been impudent. In June she was informed that she would not be able to visit her mother unless her behavior improved. It was the impression of the writer that Ruth does not comprehend all this. On some occasions, she does not realize her impudence. Ruth was permitted to visit her mother for one week but not for two weeks, as previously planned, because she was informed that her behavior did not warrant it. Upon her return, Ruth's behavior was fair. She had hopes of being permitted another week's vacation with her aunt. Although she was informed that this would only happen if she was well behaved, Ruth did not feel that she needed to better her behavior. Therefore, the vacation with the aunt was not permitted. On occasions,

Ruth has become excitable. On July 5 and on July 31, it was necessary to give her wet packs because of this excitement.

WET PACK
August 11, 1953—a wet pack was given on 8/9/53 for continued state of excitement. Struck another patient in the face.

WET PACK
August 14, 1953—a wet pack was given on 8/13/53 for continued excitement. Broke glass in fire door with heel of her shoe.

As for the Comets game last night, I recently read a quote from the writer Jim Harrison, "Sometimes God hands you a novel. You have to write it."

I had just repeated that quote to a fellow Kiwanian when he asked me if I was going to the meeting this morning. I replied I was not, in that Ruth was coming to work on *Ruthie Deeply*.

Next thing I knew, there was Thelma's daughter.

"Sometimes God hands you a novel. You have to write it."

Ruth had recounted to us numerous times when, out of frustration, she got so angry that she broke with her shoe what she originally thought was a light bulb. Sure enough on August 13, 1953, at the age of nineteen, the incident showed up in the notes. She still thought it was a light bulb, but the notes recorded it was the "glass in a fire door." Ruth felt she had to think about it more, but she definitely broke something made of glass. That incident was the crux of Ruthie's story.

The notes simply recorded, "Broke glass in fire door with heel of her shoe."

Another inappropriate incident, and that was the end of it.

Hardly. The obvious anger of a nineteen-year-old woman that had been minimized, manhandled, and rejected since birth was the real issue. A nineteen-year-old woman that was far past the age of reason and was tired of her lot in life. An eighty-three-year-old woman who sat in my kitchen still bubbly, full of life and fight. Pretty much the same as I recalled her in 1960 at five years old. While living with her uncle Wally across the street from my grandmother Mary and my own mother and father on Orchard Street in Frankfort. Those people are all dead now, but not for Ruth and me. They are just as alive now as they were in 1960. Just as real for Ruth now as the day she "broke the glass on the fire door" in 1953.

Again, a simple incident in a long excruciating history. That was what the formal history would indicate. Yet, not that simple because Ruth has the real history in her head just waiting to be told. There was no mention of the follow-up sick needle, the sleep needle, etc. Or how the glass incident then snowballed into the incident when Ruth provided one of the employees with some money to buy her something, which was against the rules, and how when she wouldn't divulge to individuals who the employee was, she was locked in the cellar for punishment and threatened with being sent to another facility in Hudson, New York, that housed criminally adjudicated individuals. All for breaking some glass in a window or trying to purchase some personal effect for herself at nineteen years old? Ruth didn't think the glass even broke due to the mesh woven through it.

All of it was pure intimidation aimed at getting her under control. Nothing diagnostic. Nothing therapeutic. All intimidation at its worst. It still didn't work, as at least two doctors pointed out it wouldn't. Sheets, solitary, sick needles, sleep needles, food deprivation, sleeping on closet floors without a blanket or pillow, using the bathroom three times a day, and so on. All with no appreciable effect other than the opposite of what was intended. Rather than making her comply, it all amped up her resistance. But still they plugged ahead, often mercilessly. Still Ruthie resisted just as mercilessly, if not more so.

A classic Mexican standoff.

The real winner, in the long run, called me once or twice a week, came to my house to work on *Ruthie Deeply*, fought it all off right to this day on many more levels than most people can understand. Just as she did, unbeknownst to her of course, upon her abandonment at four months old. Just as she did right through the House of the Good Shepherd and years of rejection by her mother. Just as she did right through the Syracuse State School. Just as she did on August 13, 1953, and through a bad marriage. Just as she did in the fall of 2016 following a heart attack. Just as she did in the spring of 2018 as we composed *Ruthie Deeply*.

All considered a larger-than-life "irresistible human tale that begs to be told and teaches timeless human values."

We last met on March 24; due to a perfect storm of circumstances, we were unable to meet again until June 2. Nevertheless, here we went again with the infamous "heel of the shoe" story.

> Wet Pack
> August 14, 1953—a wet pack was given on 8/13/53 for continued excitement. Broke glass in fire door with heel of her shoe.

A simple entry in the history, but Ruth had her own version of the incident.

I asked Ruth to tell us what she remembered.

She stated, "You can't break it. There is wire in the glass. It's impossible to break it with a shoe. There are two panes of glass pressed together that are very strong. They put me in a wet pack because they said the fire alarm went off. If I didn't break the glass, how could the fire alarm go off? It was all stupid. They were probably upset with me about something, so they had an excuse to do it. Same old thing with the wet packs. How long did I stay in the wet packs? Sometimes they would apply wet packs two to three hours at a time over a course of two or three days. They wouldn't do all that work for an hour. They left you in there until you surrendered. Just like Betty, they dunked her until she gave up and told them what they wanted to know. If you didn't surrender, they kept you in until you did. Every two or three hours, someone would come in and see if you were ready. If you said no, they would close the cell door and leave you there. Someone might come back an hour or two later and see if you were ready yet. If you said no, they left you again. First, they call you, and you have to go to detention into a cell. Then they give you a nightgown, then they come after you and slide your arms behind you in a pillowcase and pull it up to your shoulders. Then the girls that are on the ward in detention filled a bathtub with cold water and put about fourteen sheets in the tub. Then two girls stand on either ends of the tub. They wring the sheets out. They did it so they could get out of detention. When I was in detention, they tried that shit on me, but I wouldn't do it. I wouldn't do anything for them—let them get another sucker. After the girls wrung the sheets out, they would give them to the matrons and lay them on a wooded table. Then they came and got me, and I had to lie on the wet sheets. On either side of the table were four matrons, and they took each sheet individually, wrapped them on me tight like a mummy. Poor LaGraff, she liked me but had to do it—it was part of her job. At least I got to see her. It seemed like they never talked to each other. When you put someone in the sheets like that, what are you going to talk about? There was always a cop standing there watching. Nothing is going through my head now, I'm so used to it. I always told them, 'Whatever you do to me doesn't bother me.' I bet they thought, 'I'll fix your ass.' They push the table into the cell room, and they have a metal with springs on the bottom. They take two straps, one at your chest and one at your feet, and they strap you to the cot. Once you're tied down, they cover you with at least fifteen army blankets and lay them on top of you. Then they put an ice pack on the back of your head. Betty told me they would turn the heat up in the cell and leave you for two or three hours at least. Again, they wouldn't go to all that work for nothing. This could go on for two or three days or until you gave in, surrendered. When they took you out after each two or three hours, they would keep you in the cell and feed you bread and milk until the next day when you got the sheets again or you give up. As the sheets dried, they would wrinkle your skin and get stuck to you. When they finally unwrapped you, it was very painful. Most of the time after removing the sheets, I would pass out from weakness, exhaustion, screaming, and crying. This went on regularly for ten years. Even when they got done giving me the sheets, I was so stubborn that I would still fight them. Even though I knew they would give me the sheets or the sick needle or whatever again. I was a stinker. I wouldn't give in. I told them if it makes them happy, they could kill me. I was right up in their face. It never made me hallucinate. I was out of my mind before they even got to the sheets. I was desperate. When you were out of the sheets for the day, they took you to the bathroom, locked you in the bathroom by yourself. When you were finished, you knocked on the door, they let you out, and then they locked you back in the cell, and you slept on the floor. I was supposed to get the clothes for teasing, but I wouldn't do it. Let someone else do it that was afraid of them. I used to take threads from the others that did the teasing and make it look like I was doing what they wanted me to do. They were so stupid they didn't even know."

Powerful. Hurtful…for us all.

What long-term experiences that most of us would never dream of. Experiences that few or any people, I bet, even knew was happening. Ruth's best recollection of the thirty girls in her ward—everyone got the sheets at least once. Most of them learned their lesson and started to behave. Except a few that were really bad, like Beverly, Betty to some degree, Elizabeth, Adaline, Mary, and Ruth, who set the record for the most sheets ever applied.

Ruth felt absolutely it was abuse, felt clearly some sixty-five years later it was torture. There was no question in her mind.

We started to read through an autograph book from Saranac Lake, New York, that Ruth had no idea where it came from but still had in her possession. There were some very nice notes from the employees when they signed the book.

On January 6, 1956, Mrs. Thomas wrote:

> Ruth,
> Keep on trying, for you have improved. I know you got what it takes. You have surprised us, so surprise us some more. Orange Juice, Lemon Juice.

Again, on January 1956, Mrs. Wyne wrote:

> Ruth,

Remember this: The road to success is full of disappointments. Learn to accept the things the Lord has destined for you graciously, and you will be much happier. Don't forget your prayers.

These were positive full endorsement statements from the people that Ruth felt—and I agree with her 100 percent—literally tortured her on a regular basis? Day after day, hour after hour of sheets, bread and milk, sleeping on the floor, screaming, yelling, crying, and passing out—now they were wishing her the best of luck? Did any of them ever see any irony in the whole situation? If not, they had to be in denial. Or possibly sadistic torturers? Just doing their job? Or for the love of money?

Was this happening to possibly thousands of people of all ages all across the United States?

I bet it certainly was, and as terrible as this all is, in Ruth's case, I bet it only scratched the surface of what was really happening to possibly thousands of people all across the United States. Ruth's situation was in the New York State foster care system. She was not an adjudicated criminal. It frightens me to think of what was happening in the New York State penal system that long ago. It frightens me to think what is happening in the New York State penal system at this moment.

After all these incidences with sheets and punishments and bread and water, Ruth still hadn't given up on playing these people.

Hospitalization: Observation for Abdominal Pain
Sept 30, 1953—patient was admitted to the hospital on 9/24/53 from G.B. having been ambulatorily examined a day ago because of a history of pain in her lower abdomen. When examined, she did not act as a sick person. She talked incessantly, laughed, and stated that she feels fine. Her physical examination was essentially negative. Her abdomen was soft, not distended and not tender to palpation anywhere. Her last menstrual

period was 9/5/53. Her temperature by mouth was 98.4, by rectum 99.6; pulse 96 per minute. As patient continued to complain of her abdominal pain, later on in the G.B., she was brought to the hospital and was admitted for observation for a few days. Her examination in the hospital has been negative again. Her temperature remained normal. In the hospital, she did not offer any complaints. She was discharged 9/26/53.

About one week later, Ruth was at it again.

Progress Notes
October 6, 1953—Ruth has been back from the Colony for a while, and her general behavior has not been good. Rose stated that Ruth was planning on running away and had asked her to go along. Ruth admits having asked Rose to go along but stated that she was jesting about this and had no plans to escape. Ruth has talked about running away on more than one occasion; however, she has not followed through with these thoughts. Ruth enjoys antagonizing people. She also wishes to do as she pleases, and most of the time, this is contrary to the rules and regulations, and it is the opinion of the writer that this is willful on her part.

The next day on October 7, 1953, throughout January 12, 1954, Ruth bounced back and forth from the Girls Building to detention and the James Street Colony. There was no mention of sheets being applied during that period, but Ruth thought there probably was and it wasn't documented. If she was in and out of detention that much, there must have been sheets at some point.

Nonstop. All fight. All the way through.

For the first time, in this, so far, almost four-year venture, we met for two consecutive weekends. Something we should probably have done more often in order to more quickly get this project completed before something happened to any of us, which in reality it already had, back in November 2016 when Ruthie and I suffered heart attacks. Yet in characteristic fashion, more in Ruthie's case than mine, we both fought right through and were still sitting here today, with Carol's help, composing *Ruthie Deeply*.

> January 8, 1954
> Social Services Office Interview
> On January 8, Ruth Raymond came from the Girls Building to talk with the worker about her placement to James St. Colony. Ruth wanted to know why she had to go back there when she had been there so many times before. Worker explained to her that the girls at the Colony supervisor was also a different supervisor. Ruth promptly informed the worker that she was a "problem child" and that she misbehaved many times before. She added, however, that the worker probably knew this already and that this was nothing new to her. Worker tried to get her to define what a problem child was and why she felt she was one, and she said she was always getting into trouble and that she did not know why she did misbehave but that most people just did not understand her. She seemed to accept, rather reluctantly however, her placement at the James St. Colony. She was anxious to go to a colony but felt that perhaps it was going to be difficult for her to work at James St. as she and Mrs. Keller had not gotten along very well in previous placements there. She wanted to know if she was going to be able to work with a Mrs. Bizell, a former employer who had had her as day help.

> Worker had learned that Mrs. Bizell's relationship with Ruth was not what could be termed a wholesome one as she seemed to be overprotective and over-expressive in her affections to Ruth. Dr. Sarno felt that she should not be allowed to work for this employer, and Mrs. Wynes at the Colony was advised of this.

I asked Ruth, "What was the situation with Mrs. Bizell?"

As in most cases, Ruth's take on the situation was markedly different from the "official version."

Ruth replied, "I worked for Mrs. Bizell once a week while at the James Street Colony. She liked me, and I liked her. I would always do extra for her. Mrs. Keller called Dr. Sarno and complained about me working for her for no reason. I guess Dr. Sarno took Mrs. Keller's work and pulled me out of there. If I knew at the time that Mrs. Keller was the reason I would have punched her and probably got the sheets for two or three days. Detention, bread and milk for a long time. Keller had no reason that I was aware of doing that. Here I am getting along with someone, and they send me off to Mrs. Rizzo, that I couldn't get along with and wouldn't work for her. I can still see her face, and I would like to smash it. I don't know why she did it. I liked the woman, and what do they do—take you out of the job. Just when everything was going well, they take you out of the job to make you miserable. They would make it my fault, and then I would get in trouble, and then the same old pattern would take place. Detention, sheets, bread and milk—the usual process with no good results. When you are doing good, they take away a situation that is working. Then I would get mean and miserable. Same old, same old. It was so terrible, and I was the type of person that would not take no for an answer, especially when I was getting along with someone, and they never explained."

After that incident, it seemed that Ruth was sent back to the Girls Building and then back to the James St. Colony. Ruth didn't want to go to the James Street Colony because she probably wouldn't be welcome. During the ride to the James Street Colony, Ruth agreed that she would have to adjust and do her part. Apparently, there were several incidents during this placement between Mrs. Bizell and the James Street matrons that it was deemed "wise to move Ruth from James Street Colony to Westcott Colony." Six days after her placement at the Westcott Colony "to avoid further friction with one of Ruth's former employees, Ruth expressed fear that everyone would know her record, and then no one would accept her willingly. Coincidently, Ruth's sister, Loretta, was at the Westcott Colony.

A progress report in late February 1954 portrayed a happy, cooperative Ruth as trying to do the right thing. At this time, Ruth had a visit with her mother and her aunt. Both Ruth's mother and aunt wanted the girls placed at home. Indications that there would be more trouble because Ruth would be allowed to go to her aunt's and not her mother's. Ruth was advised that she didn't need to worry about these issues because she was not ready to leave the Colony yet. When she was ready, they would carefully consider the best option for her. Ruth frequently complained about leaving her bathrobe at the James Street Colony, and she wanted it back. Ruth said she paid about ten or fifteen dollars for it and loaned it to a girl at the James Street Colony who was sick. After supper, the residents took baths, put on their pajamas, and put on their bathrobes. She didn't like the fact that she had to wear her old housedress over her pajamas and wanted her bathrobe back. Now, in 2018, we all laughed about it, but it really was sad.

March 9, 1954—a progress report from Social Services that Ruth had been giving Ms. Salensky difficulty. Ruth was dissatisfied with the Colony and acted disagreeably in various ways. Ruth had packed her suitcase and announced she was going back to the school. On March 9, Ruth and another resident didn't go to work and went back to the school. When Ruth arrived back at the school, she was interviewed by Dr. Sarno and discussed why she was dissatisfied with the Colony and wanted to change. Ruth agreed to go back to Westcott and stay there until there was an opening at Elmwood. Since the bus incident, Ruth was still dissatisfied but not as disagreeable. Ms. Salensky suggested Ruth be removed from James Street because she was upsetting her sister. Ruth had earned some tip money for a total of $13.64, which she voluntarily surrendered to be put in her account.

Ruth remembered, "At the end of the month, you could use the money you saved to purchase shampoo, soap, and personal items because the Colony does not have these."

Ruth spent some time in late April 1954 in the infirmary complaining of stomach pains but was never diagnosed with any severe illness other than constipation.

> Detention—escape and return
> April 30, 1954—patient was admitted to detention on April 23. Claimed she lost her way back to the Colony and stopped at Mrs. Thater's house and asked her to call colony matron. As no further benefit was derived from detention, she was discharged on April 26, 1954.

First entry on their part. Totally different story on Ruth's part. Right down to the color.

Ruth's view of this incident: "I went to work. On my way home, at the end of the day, I got lost. I stopped at Mrs. Thater's house and asked her to call the matrons at the Colony to let them know. The Colony called the school, and the school sent the police to pick me up. I was put directly into detention. They proceed to put me in a seclusion cell, for no reason or any explanation. I was so mad because I was being punished for doing nothing wrong, when I did the right thing. I decided to throw my shoe at the light in the cell and broke the bulb. That obviously created a problem. The next thing I knew, Jackson came in with a small tray. On the tray was a syringe with an orange liquid in it. I was injected with what I call the sick needle. In less than five minutes, I was sick with diarrhea, vomiting. I was sick for about fifteen to eighteen hours, but eventually I fell asleep. You are not allowed to use a bathroom either. When I finally wake up about eight hours later, I had to clean and scrub the entire cell of my own vomit and excrement. No one else is going to clean it, so you are forced to clean it, and they won't let you out until you do. While you are in the cell, you wear your usual ticking dress, and when you are finished cleaning up the cell, you wash yourself with a washcloth in the bathroom down the hall because you can only take a bath once or twice a week. Then they would give you a clean ticking dress. I'm not sure…or after the April 30 situation…but at some point, I had the same thing happen to me in a classroom full of other patients. It also happened to Betty in a classroom. They wanted me to take care of an epileptic patient. I had no idea what to do, so I refused. A matron came into the classroom and gave me the sick needle. The tick dresses had short sleeves, and without even realizing what was happening, she injected me with a sick needle. I think it was also orange, but it happened so fast I couldn't even see it. Instantly I started throwing up with no control. I think I was in line for breakfast or lunch. There were at least thirty other people in line. So here I am sick and as embarrassed as can be, throwing up and with diarrhea, with thirty people watching me. I don't remember if they carried me out or dragged me out, but when I came around, I was in a classroom lying on the floor. I was left on the floor in the classroom until the next day, when I became aware again, and I had to clean it all up. People could have been hitting me or kicking me for all I know. How much can they embarrass me? I was nineteen years old, in front of all of these people, and nobody cared one bit. How did these people sleep at night? What if this happened to their kids? What would even my mother think? I take care of my dog better than they took care of me."

Then a second entry of the April 30 situation, with much more detail, became evident, but still nothing that matched Ruth's description.

    4/30/54
    Social Services return to school (Detention)
        Mrs. Wright reported that Ruth had been most uncooperative. She called the assisting supervisor insulting names, swore loudly in front of the other girls, calling the Colony names, and telling them she would not stay. She refused to eat

and disturbed the girls in the dormitory. She also refused to go out to work today and finally left the Colony saying she was going back to school. The supervisor's attitude was to ignore her as much as possible and to maintain the morale of the other girls.

Worker picked up Ruth on Glenwood Ave. She was nonchalant about getting into the care and apparently expected this. We told her every opportunity was given to her to get along, that people wanted to help her, and she was sure this was what she really wanted. She said she did not like the colonies. We told her it was her decision and that no one else was responsible. She was very quiet on the return. Detention was recommended, and it was felt that Ruth would have time to think over her behavior and not have the attention of the other girls and bragging about her ability to manipulate situations. It appears that Ruth reacts on impulse and does not have judgement to reason out her responsibility in her behavior. Retesting may be helpful at this point."

Retesting? Retesting? Sounds like doublespeak. Is that a code word for *sick needles*? For drug-induced vomiting? For drug-induced diarrhea? For injections that took away your coherence so you didn't know where you were? Code for embarrassing a twenty-year-old in front of thirty of her peers? Were the matrons rationalizing the punishment meted out to Ruth and possibly hundreds of other residents all across New York and the United States? How about in the prisons? How about in the psychiatric hospitals? Thank goodness Ruth is still alive and coherent enough to put her experiences on a piece of paper. Thank goodness Ruth is alive, coherent, and has the gumption to tell her own true-to-life details. Consider Ruth's strong opinion that the only reason that she got the sick needle on April 30, 1954, as opposed to the sheets was because the Syracuse State School, or was it the Syracuse Sick School, was short-staffed that day, and there weren't enough people to apply the sheets? Consider how many people took their story to the grave with them?

Ruth came in today limping. I was betting she hurt herself doing some work around her house. Sure enough, she fell off a ladder backwards on her butt. Not really any serious injuries, at least it seemed, but she told me there were lots and lots of bruises.

Ruth's story resumed on April 9, 1954, with a new placement attempt at the Elmwood Colony, where her sister, Loretta, was also residing.

Elmwood, Ruth told me, was the place for all the Goody-Two shoes.

"So, I obviously didn't last long." The liberating truth for all to know. No fear. No remorse.

Loretta, being one of those Goody-Two shoes, her only placement was in the Elmwood Colony then to a private placement and finally home to her mother. Seems like you could make it work if you tried, but Ruth wasn't going to try. Just fight.

On that date, Ruth was looking forward to going to the Elmwood Colony. She allowed another girl Mary Jane to go before her because Mary Jane had been waiting much longer than her. Ruth was taken shopping with two other girls, and she selected two attractive outfits but needed some help with making her decision. She gave an impression of indifference but really seemed to enjoy the day, especially lunch.

Things changed quickly for Ruth and changed just as quickly right back.

> April 16, 1954
> Social Services Colony Adjustment
> Mrs. Wright, acting supervisor, reported that Ruth was making a difficult adjustment, although, like the other girls, had tried to cooperate at the time of the Colony supervisor's death. In general, Ruth has resented all the rules—walking in bare feet, refusing to eat, wearing her gir-

dle, etc. She commented in front of the other girls that she could do as she pleased, at which time Mrs. Wright quietly told her she had to do the dishes. Mrs. Wright has tried to gain her confidence by not forcing her too much and with talking with her about her behavior in front of the other girls. Today she departed for work in good spirits. Ruth has seemed to conform after resisting the rules. However, two of the girls particularly resented what they felt was the supervisors overlooking Ruth's behavior. Mrs. Wright has tried to make them understand and that this is a new placement for Ruth and maybe hard at first. Ruth has some difficulty pleasing one of her employers on April 17 but returned to the Colony and talking about it to Mrs. Wright and accepting Mrs. Wright's suggestions for getting along.

From April 20 through the 22, 1954, Ruth was in the infirmary for an upset stomach.

All this was before the previously described incident when Ruth, Mary Jane, and Helen got lost on their way back to the Colony from Mrs. Thater's house because they were mixed up by the streets. They finally got back to the Colony, when an assistant matron and a patrolman picked them up. It seemed, according to Ruth's recollection, that Mary Jane and Helen went back to the Colony, but Ruth recalled being sent back to the school, immediately placed in detention, and given a sick needle because she broke the light. The history did indicate, not specifically, that after the lost incident on April 24, she returned to the Colony on April 29. Which fit with Ruth's recollection of the "sick needle, broken bulb" incident. Which would further indicate that the broken bulb situation resulted in five days in solitary, sick needle, vomit, etc.

This whole incident after the fact: "As no further benefit was derived from the detention."

Really?

Upon her return to the Colony on April 29, 1954, after the solitary, sick needle, and so on, Ruth was sent back to the Colony because it was felt she should not remain at the Girls Building too long. She was reluctant to go but viewed it as a step to return to convalescent care, as other girls had gone to convalescent care without colony placement.

From April 26 through May 11, it's a constant placement from detention to the Girls Building to Elmwood Colony, back to detention and back to the Girls Building.

> Detention Record
> May 19, 1954—patient was admitted to Detention on 4/30/54 from Elmwood Colony. She refused to cooperate in the Colony. Abusive to Colony Matron. Left without permission and was picked up on Glenwood Avenue by Mrs. Tucker. No further benefit could be had from Detention, so she was discharged on 5/11/54 to G.B.

From August 11, 1953, to June 21, 1954, there was no application of wet packs.

Suddenly on June 21, 1954, an entry appeared that Ruth was given a wet pack on June 16, 1954, because she was "highly disturbed, inciting others to misbehave." Another period of July 3 to July 27, 1954, was "Girls Building to vacation to hospital to detention to Girls Building etc."

On July 28, 1954, an entry appeared that a wet pack was given on July 17 "for being highly excited. Threatening to assault another patient."

> August 3, 1954—Ruth is admitted to detention for going to the playground without permission. She refuses to live by the rules of the

building, has done nothing but misbehave since returning from her vacation.

A violent altercation occurred on August 6, 1954.

> Accident, Injury—Incomplete Fracture Left Little Finger
> August 6, 1954—at about 7:30 p.m. on August 1, 1954, this patient had an altercation with another patient, Shirley D-55261 in the day room of the Girls Building, and during this altercation, she apparently injured her left little finger. Examination, including x-ray, revealed an incomplete fracture of the middle phalanx of the left little finger. The finger was immobilized by means of a proper splint, and the patient remains under care in our hospital building. Staff Attendant Mrs. Helen Jackson and Attendants Mrs. Patricia Clarke and Mrs. Gladys Guernsey witnessed the altercation. Mother, Mrs. Harrison Culver, 16 North Washington Street, Mohawk, New York, notification.

> Hospitalization—Incomplete Fracture of Left Little Finger—Pharyngitis
> August 10, 1954—patient was admitted to the hospital from G. B. with an incomplete fracture of the left small finger. On 8/4, she had a cough and pharyngitis. She was given gargles and aspirin. The throat was cleaned out, and on 8/7, with a splinted finger, she was sent back to G.B.

I said, "Jackson, Clarke, and Mrs. Guernsey."
Ruth said, "I hated them all. I can see their faces right now. Clarke is the one I gave the box of crap. I asked everyone to contribute. How gross is that? I got the sheets for quite a while. No way

would they let me get away with that. That is what happens when you feel hopeless and trapped with nowhere to turn. You're hopeless, so you do crazy things. I might have gotten the sick needle too. It really was pretty bad, and I must admit that whatever the punishment was, I deserved it. Of all the things I did, that one I deserved, but most of them, I did not."

August 7, 1954—from hospital to G.B.

Seclusion Order Wet Pack
August 10, 19554—patient was given a Wet Pack when she became highly excited; fist fighting. Order dated 8/2/54.
August 10, 1954—from G.B. to Detention.
August 25, 1954—from Detention to G.B.

Detention Impudence
August 1954—Ruth has periods during which she misbehaves. She has caused general disturbance in the classroom being boisterous, disobedient, and impudent. Placed in Detention on August 10, behavior improved and discharged on August 25.

Wet Pack Excited
September 2, 1954: On this day, Ruth was given a wet pack because she was highly excited and threatened to assault another patient.

Wet Pack
September 18, 1954—patient was given a wet pack for being highly excited on September 13.

Wet Pack

September 23, 1954—patient was given a wet pack on 9/12/54 because of being highly excited. She threw a jar at an attendant.

September 27, 1954—from G.B. to Detention.

Wet pack
Oct. 5, 1954—a wet pack was given to patient for being highly excited on Oct. 3, 1954.

Detention Record
Oct. 14, 1954—patient was admitted to Detention on 9/27/54 from G.B. She refused to turn in a note when asked by Mrs. Jerige. Created a disturbance in the dining room by running around. A patrolman had to be called. She was discharged back to G.B. on 10/10/54 when no further benefit could be had from detention.
October 14, 1954—from Detention to G.B.

October 14, 1954
Social Services
See note on Loretta's continued notes dated October 14, 1954 on worker's visit to the home of the mother, Mrs. Harrison Culver, and aunt Mrs. Scanlon.

Wet Pack—Excited
November 5, 1954—patient was given a wet pack on October 28, 1954, because she was highly excited and was inciting others to misbehave. She also threatened to smash the television set. Wet pack ordered by Dr. Semshyn.

Ruth had a health scare over the last two weeks, not for her but for Little Foot. It seemed she had one of her girlfriends watch Little Foot while her granddaughter was visiting for a few days. While she was taking Little Foot over to her girlfriend's house, he had a seizure—rolled over and urinated in the car. The episode scared Ruth half to death. She was very fearful that Little Foot was seriously sick and may even die. His death would devastate her. Ruth was more frightened, I think, of his death than of her own. She felt very bad for him. It made her recollect the period of her life when her then three-year-old daughter was sick, having seizures, and, for a period of time, in a coma. Poor woman had struggled her entire life and continued to do so.

Yet, as she told Little Foot, "I survived. I will survive this too."

On November 17, 1954, Ruth was placed in Geddes St. Colony.

> 12/14/54
> Social Service Summary
> Ruth has apparently accepted Geddes Colony and is making a real effort to get along with the supervisors and with the girls. About 2 weeks after her placement, worker had occasion to talk with Ruth alone. At this time, she stated that when she first went to the Colony, Mrs. Riddell had said to her: "Let's let bygones be bygones. If you want to get ahead in this colony, I want to help you. If you'll go your half the way, I'll go mine." Very emphatically and with a great deal of pride, Ruth said to the worker: "I'm going my halfway." As is her usual pattern, Ruth has adjusted very rapidly to her day employment homes and has an excellent reputation as a good worker. What seems to be more important is her attitude of cooperation and good-naturedness in the Colony. Mrs. Riddell has been allowing her to assume responsibilities in an effort to keep her interests channeled in a constructive vein.

She recognizes that Ruth is already a leader in the group and hopeful that by establishing her leadership in a positive way, she can prevent Ruth from getting into difficulties herself and also disrupting the other girls.

Hospitalization—Vacation Return

December 28, 1954—patient was admitted to the hospital as a vacation return on 12/26/54. Inasmuch as the physical examination did not reveal any signs of contagious disease, patient was discharged on 12/27/54.

3/7/55
Social Services Summary

Ruth continues to be doing well in the Colony placement. Worker has seen her on several occasions when it has been necessary to bring her into the hospital for medical treatment. Ruth made the statement to the worker that she at last had something to be proud of. She had always been a devil, and she knew it, but now she was getting along well, and Mrs. Riddell had told her so, so that she knew it was true. She feels that the time will come when no one will be able to say that Ruth Raymond is the bad girl at the Syracuse State School.

Mrs. Riddell has talked frequently to the worker about Ruth's adjustment. Ruth needs consistent encouragement and needs to know at all times that what she is doing is satisfactory and that people do approve of her. She has responded to this exceedingly well. When the Colony was very short of girls, it was necessary for a time for Ruth to work with Alberta—the two girls are almost sworn enemies, but Ruth did not manage this after she had been told that both she and Alberta were excellent workers and were the only two who could be trusted to carry out the kitchen job efficiently without too much supervision. Ruth made the statement to Mrs. Riddell that at first, she didn't talk to Alberta because you couldn't pick a fight if you didn't talk, but then they got along so well that it seemed pleasanter to have conversation. Ruth has shown a great deal of growth in this respect.

Ruth was allowed to visit her mother on Easter afternoon on April 5, 1955.

On April 7, 1955, she was interviewed by the Colony supervisor. The supervisor reported that she was restless and needed a lot of supervision. It was her opinion that the restlessness stemmed from the fact that she had not heard from her mother, and Ruth presumed that her mother was in the hospital again for treatment of cancer. Ruth had received a letter from her mother on March 5, 1955, stating she has been ill and was recuperating, but Ruth continued to worry about her. During the interview, Ruth was very forthcoming about the fact that she had been smoking in the employment homes, had used the telephone to call other girls, and walked some distances out of her way to meet Rosemarie and would accompany her back to the Colony. She also stated she walked to other employment homes on her way back to the Colony, often going out of her way. Supervisor informed Ruth that these were violations of the Colony rules, that she would have to discontinue these practices if she wanted to stay in the Colony. Ruth had no comment.

At first, the supervisor believed much of the information was fabricated to gain attention. A phone call was received from a man whose wife employed Ruth stating that he was unable to permit her to come in when she called due to the fact that it was an inconvenient time for the family, and he didn't want to offend her. In addition, Ruth had received a card from a previously discharged patient on which was written, "I will see you soon." On April 11, 1955, a worker intended to interview Ruth about the card but was unable to complete the interview because Ruth was working. The theory was that Ruth may be contemplating running away and "might have been discussing in an effort to get some protection." Quickly Ruth was returned to the Syracuse State School from the Geddes Street Colony because "she might be anticipating an elopement."

"Bullshit, if Betty had helped me, I would have run away," was the quick response.

> 4/11/55
> Social Service Interview with Assistant Colony Matron
> Mrs. O'Neil stated that Ruth was returned to the school on Saturday because she was making unusual requests for money, was easily upset, cried frequently, and was unreasonable at these times. It was felt, for her own protection, she should be returned.

Oddly, Ruth remembered nothing pertaining to Mrs. O'Neil's observation but did remember Mrs. O'Neil always singing opera-like songs while working around in the Geddes Street Colony, even while listening to opera on the radio.

> 4/11/55
> Social Service Interview with Ruth
> Ruth was anxious to talk with the worker about her problem at the Colony. She has been in detention since her return to the school but was permitted to visit with her mother on Sunday and even to leave the school with her mother and sister. She looked upon this as an act of good faith on the part of the school since in the past, there were times when visits were denied on the basis of her behavior, and she fully expected to have this visit denied as well. She expressed some relief in finding her mother well enough to make the visit to Syracuse. She has accepted the responsibility

for being returned to the school herself but does not seem overly self-blaming. She feels that the time in detention has been valuable in that she has been able to think through what happened just prior to her return. She admitted breaking colony rules and said she felt extremely guilty about having done so and felt the need to discuss it. She recognized that Mrs. Riddell interpreted some of her behavior to mean that she might run away. While she did not say so, worker feels that Ruth is glad that she was protected from doing so. She said she felt her requests were perfectly logical but that she did not explain herself well in making the requests and, when they were misinterpreted, found herself at a loss to do so and became very angry and upset. She feels now that she has calmed down, that she could quite easily explain her viewpoint without getting angry, and is anxious for an opportunity to do so.

She would like to return to Geddes Colony as soon as possible. She said she felt that she could get a fresh start and progress from where she had been. Worker feels Ruth has handled this return to school much more maturely than any in the past. She recognized her need for protection, accepted it willingly, and has thought through at least some of her problems in connection with the Colony placement. She no longer has the need to seem a tough, completely self-sufficient individual, nor does she need to threaten misbehavior in order to gain her own ends. Worker agreed to take the matter of her return up at the next star meeting, and Ruth was accepting of the need to wait until a decision could be reached.

As the old saying goes, "Even a worm will turn." As quickly as Ruth herself demonstrated behavior problems and allegedly incited others to misbehave, she quickly became cooperative, understood why she was in detention, and would make a constructive concentrated effort to get out. In full contrast to all her previous behavior.

"Even a worm will turn." Again.

> Detention Record
> April 22, 1955—patient was admitted to Detention from Geddes Colony on 4/9/55 in order to prevent her escape. She was discharged back to G.B. when no further benefit could be had from detention.

We had to miss a week last week due to a death of a mutual friend. Ruth wanted to attend a private viewing, so we had to let last week go. The mutual friend was a nice old guy named Francis but was always known by the nickname Chant. In true Ruth fashion, as Chant got older, Ruth would walk to his house, not far from hers, and help him get going in the morning. She would make him coffee, bring the newspaper, and visit with him for a while just to make sure he was good. I also knew Chant since I was a child in that he would do electrical work for my dad in his house. I had an uncle Al, my dad's brother, that was a plumber and the Water Department supervisor for the village of Herkimer. Chant was an electrician and an employee of Verizon. My uncle Al and Chant would work together on jobs all the time in their off-work hours. If Chant did an electrical job and the job required some plumbing also, he would call my uncle. If my uncle did a plumbing job and it required some electrical, he would call Chant. They worked together like this for years, and it proved very lucrative for both of them. Unfortunately, both had the bad habit of smoking and at times drinking too much. Those habits took a terrible toll on my uncle in that he died at about forty. Chant lived to be ninety-four, about fifty years longer than my uncle. Both of them fine, hardworking, honorable men. That left this world with a little bit of a hole.

In the week we missed, I also bumped into another guy I have known for about seven years that also has an incredible story to tell. About twenty-nine years ago, he was tried and convicted of murdering a young sixteen-year-old woman here in Whitesboro with at best flimsy evidence. Steve did about twenty years in prison for the crime and was eventually released due to DNA testing that did not exist at the time of his conviction. Steve was in my brother-in-law's class at St. Paul's when he was in sixth grade. I first met him at school while he was working for Oneida County soon after his release. Steve's story is the next one to be told after Ruth's. When I see him, I'll remind him that he is next on my list and that he needs to read two books. One is called *In the Belly of the Beast* and the other is named *Prisoner without a Name, Cell without a Number*. Both books true accounts of long-term imprisonment. One a correctly convicted criminal and the other about a political prisoner. Great reads for a guy in Steve's position. Steve was eventually freed by way of something called the Innocence Project, whose purpose is to locate and try to free people wrongly convicted. It was started by an attorney named Barry Streck, famous for being one of O. J. Simpson's attorneys that got OJ acquitted of the double murder of OJ's wife and date. Steve's story, as with Ruth's, begs to be told.

Having discussed the possibility of Steve's story as the next project, there was one more on my radar. One I had been thinking about for forty years and, if I live long enough, will hopefully write too. It will be sort of a loose autobiography named *The King of Orchard Street* and will reflect the lives of all the Iocovozzis and Palmieris we can put together. Only time will tell, but it is a possibility.

So, after all that, we picked up with *Ruthie Deeply* on April 14, 1955, with an incident she had told us about before:

> Social Service Interview with Ruth
> Worker informed Ruth that her request had been discussed in staff meeting and that approval had been given for her to return to Geddes Colony. This however will not take place until the supervisor returns from her pass time.

Ruth was accepting of this but did request to be removed from detention as soon as possible. She seemed very upset and described to the worker her feelings about having to assist in giving a wet pack to another patient. It brought back to her very acutely the times when she had been given wet packs. She described with a great deal of intensity the physical reaction an individual has to such a pack and intense pain that he undergoes when the pack is removed. She was almost begging the worker to intercede so that she would not be required to help remove the pack. Worker said she would try if possible, but it might not be to Ruth's advantage for her to interfere in what is commonly accepted practice. She encouraged Ruth to think positively about removing a person from a pack in the hope that it might alleviate some of her feeling. Worker feels very strongly that this girl should not be subjected to this kind of experience.

Whose feeling? Ruth's or the girl's in the wet pack? Ruth guessed that it probably worked out to about one wet pack per month for her. So that totaled twelve a year; over a ten-year period, it's about 120 wet packs when she was asked to remove the wet pack from another person. As Ruth remembered, she had been asked to remove wet packs before but refused to do it. On this occasion, for the first time, it was documented, and Ruth obviously had strong firsthand knowledge of the experience. She understood the frustration of being bound hand and foot for anywhere from at least three hours or until you surrender the information they are looking for. Ruth knew that at times when the sheets came off, you were so weak that you'd pass out. Ruth understood that from the wet pack, you might go to a cell where you then go on bread and milk. After the cell, and if your behavior has improved, you might go back to your ward—regular food and regular day. If your behavior had not improved, you might find yourself in a cell for a week. While in the cell, you would get bread and milk for three days; and if your behavior improved, you might get back to regular food.

Ruth had a vivid recollection of this incident on April 14, 1955.

She recalled, "I refused, so I probably went back into detention because that's what happened when you didn't do what they want. I remember the situation but not the girl who they wanted me to assist them with. It wasn't my job. They didn't give you the choice to refuse, so chances are they put me back in detention. I was probably very upset and crying and pretty angry. I was placed in detention to think about it and then back to the ward. It's just crazy. They expect a young adult to do a job they were being paid to do. I wasn't going to do it even if they paid me. It was horrible, and I knew firsthand what the girl was going through. They thought they were going to convince me to do something terrible. I just refused. The matrons probably removed the sheets themselves. I would never do it. I was so stubborn and so bold that I wasn't going to do it. It wasn't my problem, it was their problem. They put the sheets on, it was their job to take them off. I was miserable about the whole thing. It was not going to happen—not with me anyway."

Seven days later, on April 21, Ruth was allowed to return to the Geddes Colony. Before she returned, she went into a counselor's office and showed her a shawl she had been making. She was very proud of it and had done an excellent job making it. The social worker felt that if Ruth was given this type of handiwork, she could burn off energy and make better adjustments to different situations. When Ruth left the office, she discovered her good coat was missing. Ruth became very upset and cried. Even though she wanted to return to the Geddes Colony, she stayed at the school to look for her coat. She asked if she could go to the Colony and then return to the state school. She was brought to the Colony in an attempt to cheer her up and remain in the Colony to look for the coat. Ruth then decided to return to the state school and found her coat. According to the worker, "She very quickly lost all her anxiety and became very 'cheerful.'" The next day, on April 22, "She has apparently become more mature and has better insight into her behavior than she had had previously."

About ten days later, on May 22, 1955, things got bad again.

> 5/2/55
> Social Service
> Return from Colony Because of Plan to Elope
> It had been rumored for about a week that Ruth Raymond and Amoline planned to run away sometime after the 1st of May. On Sunday, 5/1/55, the Colony supervisor learned that the girls planned to go the following day. Believing that Ruth was the instigator, she did not permit her to go to work this morning but did allow Amoline to do. She discovered that Ruth was wearing dungarees and two t-shirts under her work dress and was planning to meet Amoline instead of going to work. Amoline returned to the Colony about 20 minutes after she left and told the plans to the Colony supervisor. The two girls had intended to go to Denver, Colorado, where Ruth's aunt, Mrs. Ruth Guilfoyle, lives. They had about 60 cents in 3-cent stamps, 2 pennies, and a razor with which to protect themselves in case of any difficulty with hitchhiking. Amoline was very skeptical of the success of the plan and for this reason returned to the Colony.
> Ruth was extremely tense and very much self-contained when the worker saw her at the Colony. She returned willingly to the school. Her only explanation for the plan to run away was that she felt she had to be free and on her own. She has been very restless for the past several months. She had very little concept of the fact that with meager planning, her plan had very little chance of success. It seemed apparent that

Ruth might become very upset once her control broke. This happened almost immediately upon return to the school.

Ruth was now a full-grown adult aged twenty-one years old. She was bouncing back and forth from the House of the Good Shepherd to boarding homes to her mother's home from birth until age twelve or thirteen. From age thirteen to age twenty-one, she had struggled at the Syracuse State School to the colonies to detention to myriad wet packs to bread and milk to sick needles, and so on and so on for over seven years.

Ruth said, "When I think about it, I wonder how I survived. At that point, they could have killed me, and it wouldn't have made any difference. I went right up to Jackson's face one day and told her, 'If it makes you happy, kill me.' How depressing is that? It was really bad. Horrible. I think if Jackson could have killed me and gotten away with it, she would."

Carol added, "What hurt you then, Ruth, is what has allowed you to survive until now."

As my son Michael's kindergarten teacher told Carol and me about him, "His strength is his weakness."

Ruth fit in those same molds.

And the frustration was about to get worse.

The discussion of this particular incident sparked Ruth's memory of the first "elopement" of which she was the motivator. Betty's escape a year previous.

She told us, "When Betty ran, I helped her get over the fence. She went to one of the matrons at the state school's house and hid under the porch until she felt no one was looking for her. The matron knew Betty was there and kept telling her to leave. Betty then went into downtown Syracuse. She met up with Norris's brother, who she had contact with through the fence while in the state school. Betty went and stayed at his house before she went to New Jersey to meet his brother Norris. She later married Norris and had two children. They were married for twelve years until he passed away. She remarried a few years later and had three more children, one of which died at a very young age."

We met again on Labor Day 2018 to begin our fifth year of this project, and we were making good progress. Ruth bought a new car and was very happy about it. She had to be admired for her drive and stamina at eighty-four years old but the same level as when she was nineteen, I'll bet, and certainly the same level when we first met in about 1960. Amazing. Truly amazing. After all this. Amazing. Truly amazing.

So, we start with an equally frightening situation, as the ferocity of her drive and stamina, on May 2, 1955, over sixty-three years ago.

Ruth got a big laugh out of the whole idea of running away to Denver with some stamps, three pennies, and a razor. At least she had a plan, which she got no credit for.

When she returned to the Syracuse State School, the report stated she was highly excited, breaking lights in detention. Dr. Naples Sarno immediately ordered a wet pack. This was the same doctor that stated numerous times that the wet packs were not working.

Ruth's recollection of the situation was that when she returned back from the Geddes Colony, it was at night, and it was too late to apply wet packs. She recalled all of the other residents that were in detention being asleep or in their cots or cells. Ruth was directed to be quiet, which she refused to do and began breaking the lights with her shoe. She recollected she was given a sick needle to thwart her behavior. In order to end Ruth's behavior, she was given a sick needle, with the wet pack to be applied the next day, when the full staff was back to work. The sick needle was processed in the infirmary then brought back to the Girls Building and administered to the resident. Whoever was given the needle would become violently ill and incapacitated to the point they might pass out or be so sick that all deemed inappropriate behavior would cease immediately. This harsh punishment was the precursor to an equally harsh punishment that would be applied the next day.

Ruth had no idea what was in the sick needle serum nor the color of it. Betty remembered the color and all.

This constant cycle of detention, sick needle, wet pack, etc. had been going on for ten years to the point of obviously being ineffective. Yet no one put a stop to it or look for any alternatives to minimize Ruth's inappropriate behavior and maximize her potential. Ruth being over twenty years old, she was constantly crying, frustrated, angry, and acting out.

After being physically and emotionally abused over a twenty-four-hour period, a drained but not broken Ruthie was interviewed by a social worker for the hundredth time in order to evaluate her mental and physical state after such a horrible experience. Likely hundredth horrible experience too.

>5/3/55
>Social Service Interview Ruth
>
>Worker interviewed Ruth in detention on this date. Ruth was amazed at the worker's visit and wondered why she had taken the time to make a visit on "a bad girl." She then launched a long and extremely detailed account of her actions on the preceding day and of the wet pack which was administered to her in the afternoon. Ruth was restless and agitated during the interview and paced the floor in her room. She said she had absolutely no control of herself the preceding day, did not know exactly why she wanted to run away except that she felt her situation was intolerable. She did not feel that any specific incident or occurrences prompted her to want to run away. It was rather a general overall restlessness and feeling of despondency which left her unable to do anything but flee. She said in her period of agitation she realized that if "God Almighty" had come into the room, she would have thrown a shoe at him. She did not feel the same way at the time of the interview and stated she often won-

dered what might be wrong with her that made her lose control of herself in the way that she did.

Worker attempted to give Ruth support by stating that most people from time to time get to the point where they feel they do not know what they will do next and that her behavior was understandable in terms of the way she felt. However, it was not acceptable and that perhaps there might be other ways of working out some of the same feelings should they recur again. Ruth was interested in exploring this and asked the worker if there was any way that she might find out something more about what made her the way she was. Worker suggested a further interview in the worker's office on 5/9/55. Ruth eagerly accepted this.

I would think an "overall restlessness and feeling of dependency" after twenty-one years of figurative/literal torture both emotionally and physically would be a minimization of her life in the NYS foster care system.

How smug? How demeaning? How dare them?

A "misplaced entry" from May 9, 1955 read:

Social Service Interview with Ruth

Ruth kept her appointment with worker without any reminder on the worker's part. She immediately asked the worker if she had heard about Geraldine? Worker said she had not, and Ruth started to tell about Geraldine's attempt to run away. Suddenly she stopped in the middle of this and said, "What am I talking about Geraldine for? I came down to talk about me." She then began to talk about her own feelings in regard to Geraldine's attempted escape and her own involvement in it. She was giving a verbal description of the incidents when she saw the worker's house key lying on the desk. She picked it up, looked at the worker, and said, "You can trust me. I am not going to take this key and go anyplace." She then began to act out the episode in which another girl, Geraldine, took keys from an attendant and attempted to leave the G.B. She first took Geraldine's part and then played her own role in thwarting Geraldine's running away and assisting the attendant. Worker took no part in this acting out except to follow Ruth's directions of what she should do. Ruth insisted on very exact details from the worker and carried the thing through to a stranglehold in which she had the worker's arm pinned behind her back. After it was all over, Ruth said she felt better for having told the worker what her part in the incident was. Ruth had at first assisted Geraldine in making plans, and then at the last minute had been unable to see the attendant placed in a precarious situation and had gone to her rescue. Workers suggested that this might have put Ruth in a very difficult spot and wondered how she felt about being first on one side and then on the other. Ruth said that this was a thing she did not understand. She always took the side of the underdog. She then launched into a very verbal discussion of the number of times in which she felt herself the underdog in a situation. She said she knew these feelings always preceded her periods of agitation. She then described how it felt to be unable to control her actions and wondered again what might be done about it. Worker acknowledged the fact that Ruth could not control herself and that her feelings about frustration were the same as those that others had, but the difference lay in how she worked them off. She wondered if Ruth had ever taken stock of things just before an outburst and if there might be some way she could handle it other than losing control. There was some discussion about physical activity as an outlet. Ruth said she wished that the moment she had been put in detention she had been given a hard job, but there was none since the floors were washed white, and there is no point in scrubbing an already clean floor. This led to a discussion of activity while in detention. There is apparently very little, and Ruth was willing to accept this fact but recognized that she was very nervous if she had nothing to do.

She talked about a quilt she planned to make when she went into the G.B. and asked the worker if it were possible to secure supplies. Ruth will get in touch with the worker when she gets out of detention so that a plan can be made to get the materials for her. Ruth stated that she chose to quilt because it was a big job, and she needed something to work at long and hard in order to keep herself from getting into further difficulties.

This case was later discussed with the supervisor in an effort to work out some plan for giving Ruth some individual help. Ruth has some insight and can probably benefit by some exploration into motivations. It might seem, in view of her need to act out, that some modified form of play therapy would be of help. She is tremendously aggressive—toward herself probably more than toward others, although the acting out takes place in reference to others. She is a sympathetic person, but at this point she overidentifies with others. She appears to lack sufficient identification with her own sex and will need some help in this area.

After ten years of wet packs, seclusion, bread/milk, numerous incidences of statements that the aforementioned protocols didn't work, and the rest of the gamut that Ruth endured, finally someone suggested an alternative. A "modified form of play therapy"? For a twenty-year-old?

How smug again? How demeaning again? How dare them again?

We all agreed enough for today.

Two weeks went by quickly, and we picked up again on September 15, 2018.

Oddly the next entry in the journal that we saw was exactly what stopped us the last time. On June 7, 8, and 10, 1955, Ruth went back and forth from the Girls Building to the detention building for "high pitch of excitement." When she was finally discharged, Dr. Minna Maler again stated, "Had no further benefit can be had from longer detention."

That must be the tenth time that statement had been made, and still no one found an alternative.

Ruth was allowed to go on a vacation sometime in mid-July 1955, and when she returned on July 16, 1955, she was admitted to the hospital as returning from vacation. There was no evidence of contagious diseases and no signs infection contact. She was discharged on July 17, 1955. The admission to the hospital was probably a protocol used to prevent illnesses from spreading into the school.

Ruth didn't feel that way though.

When I read that statement to her, almost instantaneously she said, "That's nonsense, why do they have to put you in the hospital every time you come back? What the hell are they doing? Every time you go on vacation, you have to go to the hospital?"

A report dated August 1, 1955, "Social Services Colony Adjustment" showed clearly the up-and-down emotions of Ruth's daily life. At times it went very well; at other times, it was terrible.

> When Ruth was returned from her vacation, it was decided that she should go to the camp with the other colony girls as it would otherwise mean her having to remain in the Girls Building. Ruth seems to be adjusting at the Colony quite well, and

Mrs. Wynes states that she gets very good reports from all the employers who have Ruth. This of course is not surprising as Ruth has always been known as a very good worker. Worker has talked with Ruth whenever she has been at the Colony and feels that this colony has been a good choice for her. Many times Ruth states that she is only staying at the Colony for six month, and then she will be placed in a private home, but worker points out to her that she, like all the other girls, must work her way out of the Colony and that it may perhaps take more than six months but that she should not be discouraged by the time element. Mrs. Wynes and Mrs. Keller both say that Ruth is also a very great help about the Colony and that she sees work without being told where it is. She is always one of the first ones to volunteer for even jobs that involve drudgery. Ruth has asked the worker for permission to have a talk with Dr. Watts. When she was home on vacation, she wrote a letter asking to be allowed to stay home with her mother. At this time, Ruth was contacted by telephone and told that she had to return from her vacation. The mother has not written asking that she be home at this time. Worker has advised Ruth that she would try to make an appointment for her so she could see Dr. Watts. Worker feels that she wants to ask him about the possibility of being placed at home with her mother. Ruth has told the worker that she needs dental care and also that she has been having trouble with her back. Worker has told Ruth to remind Mrs. Wynes of these things during the daytime and that she will arrange for her to see the dentist and that also to see the physician so that she can examine her back to see if there is any injury. Worker feels that the Colony atmosphere is very beneficial to Ruth. She also feels that Mrs. Wynes's kindness coupled with firmness is something that Ruth probably has not had much of an opportunity to experience and which is beneficial to her. Ruth seems to have a very winning way about her, and it is difficult for people not to make exceptions in her case and to give her, her way. When she was placed into the Colony, she told the worker if she did not like it, she was going to a telephone and going to contact the doctor immediately to have her removed and returned to the school. Worker explained to her that this was not the method that she was to use because the Colony girls are not allowed to use the telephone and that if she wanted to return to the school, she would have to ask Mrs. Wynes to call the school. Worker feels Ruth is doing well in the Colony.

Since we started working on *Ruthie Deeply*, Ruth had always complained about her back. Sure enough, she was hospitalized on September 13, 1955, complaining about back pain, and was diagnosed with sacral myalgia. Ruth told Dr. Lohaza that she hurt her back carrying a box of dishes. Dr. Lohaza examined her and prescribed APC for pain and a hot-water bottle. After these treatments, her complaints disappeared, and she was released from the hospital.

Ruth continued to make good adjustments in the Colony. One employee reported that Ruth was getting restless. An explanation was made to her that like the other girls, she had to prove that she could make a good adjustment once she was released. Ruth explained that she liked her employers, especially Mrs. Wynes. Ruth would like to be placed in convalescent care, and the worker determined that the placement would be inappropriate because there were teenage boys in the home. The worker interviewing Ruth found out from Mrs. Wynes Ruth was reporting what the other girls were doing and saying. The worker explained to Ruth that it was not a praiseworthy trait and told Mrs. Wynes to discourage this behavior.

In an interview conducted on January 26, 1956, Ruth continued to complain about her back. The worker told her that she would arrange for Ruth to visit a doctor. Ruth also stated she needed some dental care and would rather go home than to a private home. Ruth stated that it was senseless to go to a private home, "When she has a good home to which she could go."

"The worm turns." Again.

After all the terrible circumstances in her home for over twenty years, Ruth was so determined, so fed up with the foster care system that she was willing to tell them all most anything to get out of this tragic environment she had been exposed to since she was abandoned at four months old in December of 1934.

Ruth couldn't believe it. Neither could I. Twenty years of her life was, she felt, "pure hell."

The social worker felt that if she was to go home, she could make a good adjustment and will discuss the issue with the supervising psychiatrist. The wheels were slowly turning for Ruth's release. On March 20, 1956, Dr. Maria Naples Sarno recommended Ruth be released for convalescent care. It was recommended that she be placed in the home of Mrs. Louis Farchione. Ruth's wage would be $8.05 per week and $2.50 a week.

On April 2, 1956, a home visit was made, and sometime between then and July 17, 1956, Ruth went on vacation; and on return, she was admitted to the hospital. Showing no infectious disease, she was released.

From May 20, 1956, through August 10, 1956, while at the Farchione residence, Ruth was visited frequently by Social Services. Mrs. Farchione felt Ruth was an outstanding worker and had difficulty convincing Ruth to leave some of the work behind because she couldn't get it all done in a normal workday. Ruth was up between 5:00 and 6:00 a.m. and was ready to work. Mrs. Farchione told Ruth that there was no need to get up any earlier before 7:00 a.m. The social worker didn't believe that Ruth was maintaining this schedule. She also believed Ruth was having difficulty making emotional adjustments and would call on Ruth and Mrs. Farchione in the near future.

The Social Service report of November 13, 1956, showed the placement taking a turn for the worse.

> Patient Returned to School from C.C.
>
> On this date, Ruth called the worker three times in the A.M. consulting with her about the possibility of her attending Beautician School and the educational requirements for admission for this training. When it was learned that Ruth would have to have a minimum of a 10th grade education and that she only had formal academic classes to the 3-2 grade, worker advised her to place her energy in another sphere as too much preliminary training would be necessary before she could start the courses she wanted. Ruth seemed to accept this without too much disappointment.
>
> Worker left the office at 2:40, and when she returned at 3:50, she found Ruth sobbing on the telephone talking to another worker. It seemed that Ruth had called Rose Dakein, being very much upset and that Rose, not knowing how to calm her, called Mrs. Jackson. Mrs. Jackson, feeling it was not her job, notified Dr. Sarno, who referred the call to Miss Nave. Worker arrived at this point, and Ruth was so upset that she called on her at her home immediately. Ruth was crying and speaking incoherently trying to tell the worker that she didn't know what the trouble was but that she was confused and upset. She was most worried because she stated that she didn't know the reason for her upset. While returning her to the school, she cried spasmodically in the car. She was placed in Girls Building as she refused to go into the hospital. The following two days, Ruth was interviewed by worker and also Dr. Sarno. No satisfactory explanation for her

behavior could be obtained. Ruth decided she would take Thursday afternoon off and return from her time off to her employment home. Some question had arisen about the amount of work required of Ruth. Her major complaints were that she has to wash dishes in the morning after her employer had late evening guests, had to wash diapers every evening in the automatic washer and dryer, and had to lug trash. Worker discussed these factors with Mrs. Farchione, the employer, and she said she would see what she could do to make these things less burdensome. The babysitter complains to Ruth that it makes her nervous to watch Ruth working. Ruth told the babysitter that if it makes her nervous, she should not look at her. Worker has repeatedly offered to change Ruth's home, pointing out to her that it would not count against her as it would be her decision. Ruth refuses to have her home changed at this time. Worker feels that it is not so much the home situation that is bothering Ruth as the actual inner turmoil she is feeling.

Patient Returned to School from C.C. continued from page 45

While the worker was at the CYO, Ruth, who had been waiting for her sister, Loretta, dropped into Dr. Sarno's office, and another emotional outburst occurred. Loretta explained to Dr. Sarno that she felt that Ruth was frustrated and ashamed of her lack of formal education and her inability to pursue the training she desired. Ruth turned abruptly against Loretta and walked out of the office. Ruth related to the worker her feeling that Loretta had said something against her which was very bad. Loretta too is very upset by the whole situation. Dr. Sarno decided that Ruth should remain at the School until Monday.

Ruth is getting near the end of her time with the Syracuse State School. She is given a physical by Dr. Lohaza before being placed in convalescent care. She is found to be healthy, clean and neat, and no complaints with physical health. Her vision and health are normal, and her teeth are in good condition. Her inner organs show no gross pathology. She is 5 foot 2 and weighs 140 pounds. Dr. Lohaza determines she is fit for convalescent placement.

November 26, 1956
Social Service
Returned to C.C.

On this date, Ruth returned to her convalescent care home. She remained in the hospital a week instead of just the weekend because she seemed quite upset. Worker believes that her upset is mainly an attention-getting mechanism and also an opportunity for her to remain at the School so she could visit her friend Mrs. LaGraff, who pointed out to her in a very sensible manner that Ruth must learn to get along without complete dependence on her. Ruth had hoped that she could spend Thanksgiving with Mrs. LaGraff, but Mrs. LaGraff said she was invited out for the day. Ruth made some complaints about overwork, but this too, worker feels, is of Ruth's own making.

The report of November 26, 1956, was an indication of how strongly Ruth felt about Mary LaGraff then, and does to this day.

She told us, "She saved my life from a lot of things. She snuck things in for me to eat like candy. She brought soap and odd things we didn't have there that made me feel good about myself. When she worked, I was happy as an angel. As soon as she left on vacation or off for the day, I went flying off the handle into detention or wherever. Wherever she went, I went. Just to be nasty, they would have Mary LaGraff come up to the Girls Building to help them give me the sheets because they knew I liked her. They did nasty stuff like that to a lot of the kids. She had to do it, or she would lose her job, but I'm sure she didn't like it. They waited until the employees that came in at one o'clock signed in, and they would call them to the Girls Building for help with discipline. More than likely they were made to help with giving the child the sheets to make them feel bad also. Anybody that befriended you, they would put in to give you the sheets and embarrass you even more. They would do anything possible to make you feel out of place. But it didn't bother me one bit. They tried to make me feel worthless, but it didn't work. If anything, I felt bad for the workers that were put in that position of doing something they didn't want to do or lose their jobs. What a horrible position to put your employees in. In a way, it's no wonder some of the employees were as miserable as they were. The whole thing was completely inappropriate right to the end."

Ruth insisted, "Anytime you got close to someone that would help you, they immediately tried to cut it off."

On December 17, 1956, the Syracuse State School contacted the Herkimer County Welfare Department to begin a convalescent care investigation, apparently as a precursor to Ruth's full release to her mother's home. After twenty-five years, her nightmare seemed to be coming to an end; but as has happened a thousand times before, nothing was guaranteed.

> Letter to Herkimer County
> On this date, a letter was sent to Herkimer County Welfare Department requesting a brief convalescent care investigation. The balance of this letter was to be dictated by the other worker who carries Ruth's sister, Loretta, and to be sent on. Ruth is very anxious about the whole situation and has been calling the worker about it

quite constantly. She will probably be relieved when she knows the result of the welfare investigation and is presented at staff. She states, however, that if necessary and if she knows she is going home, she could hold out for a couple or three more months.

Ruth's employer has advised the worker that she is planning a varicose vein operation the middle of January. Worker feels that if conditions make it impossible for Ruth to remain at the Farchione home and she is placed on C.C. before this time, the employer should be given ample notice so that she can make other preparations as she has five children, four of whom are of preschool age. Since worker is leaving, she is temporarily transferring the case to Mrs. Jean Warren, and both the employer and Ruth have been advised of this transfer.

February 14, 1957—Social Service
Report Received

A report was received from Herkimer County Department of Public Welfare giving report on Ruth and Loretta Raymond.

Worker visited Mrs. Harrison Culver, mother, and Mrs. Lawrence Scanlon, Aunt. For the most part, report was favorable. For details, see report in folder.

Carol asked Ruth, "Do you remember them discussing the possibility of a full release to your mother's home?"

Ruth replied, "They don't ask you anything. They just have a conversation with your family while you are not present and make plans for your release. They didn't mention anything to me. It would be hard for them to tell anyone anything because I would be so excited to get out, I probably wouldn't stop jumping for joy. Then when they do tell you, they sit you in a room with a group of doctors, social workers, etc., discussing if you were ready to be released. No one knows until the last minute. Then they tell you right then and there to get your things, and you are released. My theory is they don't tell you anything until the last minute because they are afraid that it would upset the other girls who are not being released. A lot of the girls there were not really bad. I was the worse there, at least they led me to think I was. Your mother, Rose, was the one who, when I got out, helped me learn how to bake. She knew I liked lemon pie, so she taught me how to make one. In return, I started her car one day when it wouldn't start. How would I ever know how to do this stuff being in an institution my whole life? All they taught me was how to peel potatoes if you worked in the kitchen. I enjoyed canning, which was hard and heavy work, but I liked it."

Again, it seemed the release was falling into place. Yet, that could fall apart again, depending on many factors, like Ruth's behavior, conditions in Ruth's mother's home, and the possibility of her success once released.

Ruth said, "I couldn't wait to get rid of them, and they couldn't wait to get rid of me."

> February 21, 1957
> Social Service
> Since transfer of case to new worker in December, worker has had several telephone conversations with Ruth and Mrs. Farchione and has seen them both in the home.
> Ruth's work continues to be very good. Mrs. Farchione further states Ruth is excellent with the children, and she does not know how she will get along if Ruth is allowed to go home. Mrs. Farchione feels Ruth has tried very hard to do well and is deserving of going home. However, she believes Ruth will continue to require supervision and guidance and hopes her mother will be capable of providing it.

Summary of Contacts—cont'd from page 47

Ruth calls worker daily. She is anxious to have information whether or not she can go home and desires attention and reassurance. She was put on restriction by Dr. Sarno for 3 weeks in January as she had given matches to a girl in the Girls Building, and later on a fire resulted. Ruth, we believe, had no part in this and was very upset over it.

Ruth occasionally has been moody and depressed. She has felt Mrs. Farchione has not always been appreciative of her efforts. Mrs. Farchione does not want her to call worker without knowing about it. She told worker she does not get out on Sunday until 2:45 or 3 and so does not bother to go out at all. Mrs. Farchione told worker Ruth doesn't go out on Sundays, indicating Ruth doesn't care to. Ruth said when she does go out on Thursdays or Sundays, Mrs. Farchione leave all the dishes for her. As Ruth is hopeful of going home, she asked worker not to discuss this with Mrs. Farchione unless she finds she cannot go home.

On the whole, Ruth has done very well in the Farchione home.

On February 27, 1957, after twenty-three years and two months, in Ruth's exact words: "I couldn't wait to get out of there. Good riddance to bad rubbish. The whole thing was a nightmare. The worst part was not being treated like a human being. The best part was Mrs. LaGraff. If it wasn't for her, I probably would have been dead. She kept me on my toes while she was there, and soon as she left, I started trouble."

Carol's opinion was, "For the most part, Ruth wasn't causing trouble but pointing out what the workers were doing to her and others that was not fair. She often questioned why they would be treating people that way."

Ruth's opinion in comparison to Carol's was, "They robbed me of an education. I would rather have gone to school than pull threads, wax floors, and waste time. They weren't just mean to me but to a lot of people. I have scars because of them."

I wondered if Mary LaGraff would have any idea that she literally saved Ruth's life with just little acts of kindness.

Ruth felt she would. What powerful testament to the strength of small human interactions that most people may not even realize has occurred. What an impact something as simple as candy and soap can have on a person.

Is it the candy and soap? Or is it the kindness? Or is it both?

The soap and candy eventually end.

In Ruth's autograph book from approximately 1954:

Dear Ruth,

May you always be healthy, happy and fat.

Your best friend Mrs. LaGraff

and

Our dear Ruthie has a heart of gold, it's too darn bad she is so bold. When girls were busy sprouting wings, Ruth had ideas about other things. Now that she is going out in my mind, there is no doubt she can be good, and I'm sure she will, 'cause underneath it all, she is not a bad pill.

Your friend Mrs. LaGraff

Ruth had both statements memorized.

And the kindness continued to be alive right through today, October 6, 2018.

That was probably the largest lesson of Ruth's whole experience as "children at the hands of adults."

Finally,

Director's Approval

February 27, 1957—the staff's recommendation that this girl be placed on convalescent care with her mother is approved.

Lloyd E. Watts, M.D.
Acting Director

On March 6, 1957, Social Services sent a letter to Ruth's mother, Mrs. Harrison Culver, advising her that Ruth may go home to live with her. The letter asked when Mrs. Culver could come and pick her up. The letter further explained that once Ruth was released to her mother, if that works out, Loretta could be released at a later date. Ruth was anxious for her mother to pick her up on March 16. On March 16, Mrs. Culver came to the school and picked her up. Mrs. Culver signed a convalescent care agreement.

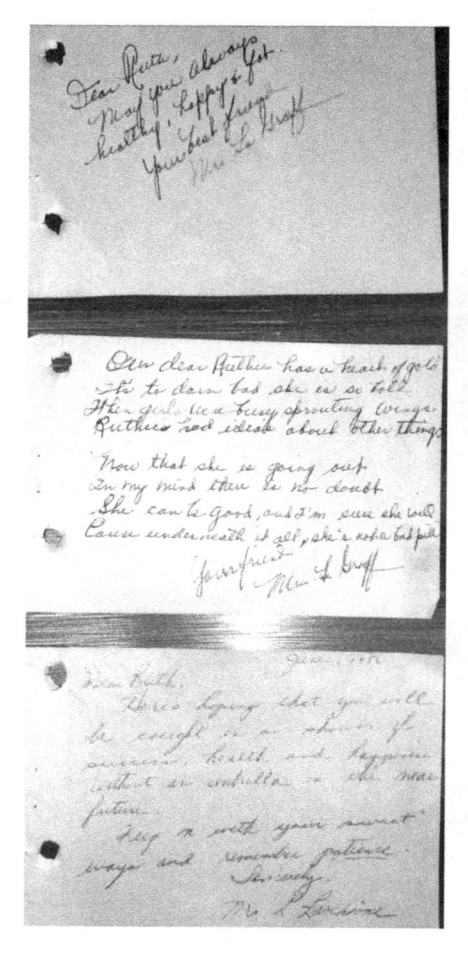

April 20, 1957
Social Services
Report Received

A card was received from Ruth early in April to Dr. Sarno stating that she was working in a laundry and liked it and was on her best behavior.

On April 11, a report was received from the Department of Public Welfare stating that she was working at the Prine Cleaners in Ilion, New York, as a presser. Mrs. Culver, Ruth's mother, told the welfare worker that Ruth was very happy to be at home and that they were getting along fine. The Welfare worker will continue to attempt to contact Mrs. Scanlon, who will help with some supervision of Ruth.

Worker has talked with Loretta, Ruth's sister, and feels that Ruth is very happy to be home. Ruth writes her regularly and has been in Syracuse once to see Loretta at the time Loretta was confirmed.

Prior to Ruth's leaving, she said that she was going to have her mother write in for Loretta this summer and told worker that she was going to make good at home so Loretta would be allowed to come home. Loretta had told worker that she might prefer to stay at Mrs. Cook's, although the worker was not certain whether this was because she really wanted to or she was saying it as a defense because Ruth was going home at this time and to cover her disappointment in not going home.

While on convalescent care, which is basically a trial run in order to determine how an eventual permanent placement might work out, Ruth got numerous visits from Social Services that all tended to show a situation that was functioning pretty well.

The October 1, December 30, and January 6, 1957, Social Services reports all painted a picture of Ruth succeeding outside of the Syracuse State School. A report even came in from Loretta that Ruth was doing good. Ruth requested in June permission from Dr. Sarno to go roller-skating with a boy. Dr. Sarno granted the request on July 12. January 6 report, "Mrs. Culver states that Ruth is doing well. She works at Prine's Cleaners and does some babysitting. Ruth goes to a dance once in a while and to church every Sunday."

Herkimer County Department of Social Service filed a glowing report on February 3, 1958:

> Social Service
> Letter Received
>
> A letter was received from the Herkimer County Department of Public Welfare stating that they had called at Ruth's aunt, Mrs. L. Scanlon, and learned that Ruth is making a fine adjustment and is still working at Prine's Cleaners as a presser. They had been unable to contact Mrs. Culver, Ruth's mother. The aunt

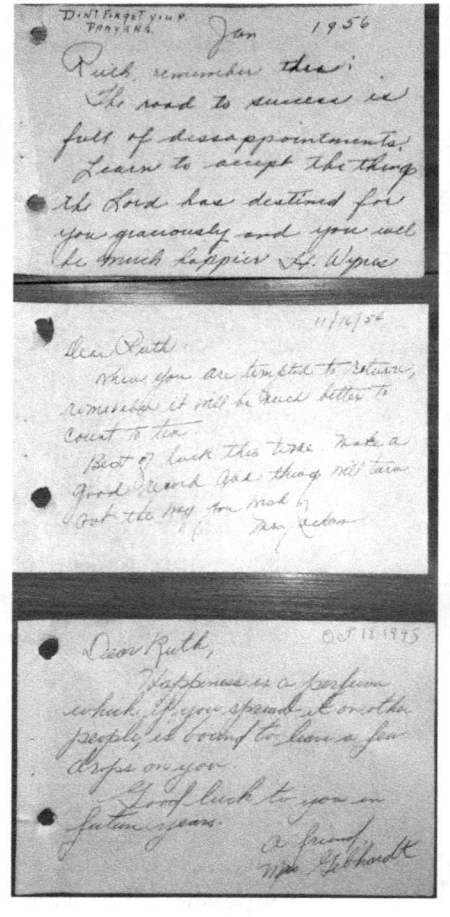

reports that one of the first purchases that Ruth had made was a bicycle that she rides back and forth to work.

Ruth is now living at the home of her aunt and uncle, Mr. and Mrs. Wallace Richardson, North Ilion. Ruth takes care of the Richardson's baby on evenings as Mrs. Richardson works at Little Joe's Dairy in Herkimer from 4 until 11 pm. Mrs. Scanlon added that Ruth is taking a very active part in Church work and that she seldom goes out evenings mostly because she does not seem to want to. Mrs. Scanlon said that she has had fears for Ruth before she went to Syracuse but has none now.

Good news continued with the Social Service progress notes from February 26, 1958.

A social worker says Ruth, on February 15 and 17, went to Syracuse to see her sister, Loretta, and other friends. Ruth is very happy living in her aunt's home, and the reason she moved there was because it was closer to her job. Ruth is working at Prine Cleaner from 7 am to 4 pm, but during the summer, she might work until 9 pm. She earns $32.00 a week and has been able to save $300.00. Ruth enjoys living with her Aunt Margie and takes care of her 5 children, ranging from ages 5 to 12. The social worker discusses with Ruth that she should not be overworking, but it seems to be an area that Ruth always wants—to do more than her share. Also discussed is Ruth's dating situation and that she had written at one time if she could go out on a few dates. Ruth states that she has gone out with a few boys but does not care for them and that some of them like to get "fresh." Ruth asked when she will be permanently discharged—soon as she is making better-than-anticipated adjustments into the community.

July 10, 1958
Social Services
Progress Note

Ruth has been in town on two occasions when she has come to the School and talked with worker. About three months she came with an automobile salesman from home wanting money out of her account in order to buy a car. The salesman did not realize she was from the state school, and she had told him that she had money in a bank in Syracuse, and so he offered to drive her to Syracuse. Worker talked with Ruth and explained why it would be impossible for her to obtain a car. For one thing, she could not have a license till after her discharge and, secondly, felt it unwise to spend that money out of her account as the running of it would be very expensive. She felt that she and her aunt could use a car, and even though she couldn't drive, her aunt could drive as her uncle uses the car in his business. Apparently, there is some difficulty between the aunt and uncle, and Ruth told the worker that of her approximately $500.00, she had loaned her uncle $400.00, but he plans to repay her. Ruth was at first very upset but finally realized it would be better if she did not purchase this car. She thought it was an excellent buy—apparently was. The automobile salesman was very nice and said he had not met Ruth until today, but her aunt had been looking at cars and then called him and said her niece would be interested. He said as he was driving her to Syracuse: he realized there was something peculiar about the story, but he felt that he might as well follow through as he did not want to hurt Ruth. He was very understanding and was not one who would become involved with an outpatient. He said that this was a lesson and a joke on him. If the man at the office heard about it he would probably have to tell him about it and he would get quite a kidding.

Progress Note—continued from page 51

This month, Ruth came to Syracuse to do a little shopping. She said she had been let go from the laundry a couple of months ago because she could not stand the heat, and she fainted occasionally. She said that when she first went there, she was near the door, but recently they moved her to another job, and she could not take it. She then obtained another job at another laundry but lost it about two weeks ago for the same reason. She said she wanted to tell us about it as she did not want us to hear it from someone else or feel that she had done anything wrong. She expects to find work shortly and said she is helping her aunt out with the children, so her aunt would not mind if she could not pay room and board for a while. However, she did not have some money saved ahead and says she has about $100 in her bank account but does not want to spend this. Her uncle has not repaid the money, but it is away in his own office so that he could give it to her all at one time. Ruth says she is happy and has no desire to return to Syracuse. Now that Loretta is living with her family in Frankfort, she sees her occasionally and said that she is getting along very well.

VINCENT PALMIERI

A Social Services home visit from October 9, 1958, indicated that visit to be the last one since approximately one month later, November 6, 1958, unbeknownst to Ruth, she would be finally discharged. The report read:

> Home Visit
> On this date, worker interviewed patient and her aunt, Mrs. Wallace Richardson, at Mrs. Richardson's home on Orchard Street, Frankfort, New York. Patient was seen in relation to her request for discharge. Worker was interested in determining patient's job status and financial situation. After attending a week's trial course at a Beauty School in Utica, patient bought several textbooks from which she has been studying at night. However, she decided to wait before enrolling full time. Her reason for the postponement was to earn some money so that she would have some reserve after paying beauty school tuition, which she estimates at $350–$400. She has $150 in her personal bank account, and her uncle, Wallace Richardson, has $350 of her savings in his account. Mrs. Richardson said that the money is not for use but for evidence of financial stability when Mr. Richardson needs to borrow money. They intend to open a restaurant in the front of their home, which was once a restaurant. Patient said she could have the money any time but didn't need it now and was perfectly willing to maintain this arrangement until withdrawing the money to use for tuition.
> Patient appeared very happy in the Richardson home where she receives free room and board and spending money. She is presently working for the family babysitting from 8:30–4:00 P.M. and has her name in at the local A&P

for a job. Both patient and her aunt feel there are many job opportunities for patients in the area of Frankfort, Ilion, Mohawk, and Herkimer.

Home Visit—continued

A visit was made to Mrs. Lawrence Scanlon, Mohawk, NY, to determine her feelings about discharge of the patient, but Mrs. Scanlon was not at home.

Patient appears to be adjusting satisfactorily on her convalescent care status and has a family, the Richardsons, who are interested in her welfare.

This patient appears suitable for discharge.

Alas, on October 30, 1958:

Social Services
Discussed for Discharge—Approved
This case was discussed for discharge consideration at the Departmental Staff meeting. The case was reviewed, and the patient was recommended for discharge.

Alas! At last!

Discharge Note
Date of Discharge: November 6, 1958
To Whom Discharged Aunt and Uncle, Mr. and Mrs. Wallace Richardson,
Orchard Street, Frankfort, New York
Condition on Discharge Improved, capable of self-support

In the words of Dr. Martin Luther King, "Free at last, free at last, thank God Almighty, free at last."

Thus, finally Ruth stepped as a free person into the tumultuous world of 1958. A lot remained to be seen as to how it would all play out for Ruth right through to today, October 13, 2018. On this October morning we all know that it did turn out well.

That discussion would begin with our next session.

Chapter 8

The Responsibility of Newfound Freedom in 1958, Much Better Than the Syracuse State School but Often Pretty Bad Too

Ruth and Little Foot came today a little wet from a cold rainy wind. She had her lime-green Honda, of which she was very proud.

All of 1958 was a dramatic year in retrospect. The average yearly wage was $4,600, with a new house costing approximately $12,750. The Space Race began with the creation of NASA and the launch of the Explorer 1 satellite. Russia launched the Sputnik satellites, putting the United States far behind in the race to control space. The legendary Hope Diamond was officially donated to the Smithsonian Institute by jeweler Harry Winston. Probably never realizing what they had developed, the microchip was invented by Jack Kilby of Texas Instruments and Robert Noyce of Fairfield Semiconductors and marketed in the United States by Intel. Huge event—the inventors likely never were aware of the significance over the past sixty years.

Popular culture brought to life the famous Hula-Hoop, which every kid in America had to have. *The Bridge on the River Kwai* and *King Creole*, starring Elvis Presley, were the biggest movie hits in

America. Hugely popular television programs like *The Ed Sullivan Show* and *Candid Camera* lit up every living room in America with the infamous "blue haze."

Then, Ruth came finally stepping out into the light of full freedom.

We started discussing the day she was released from the Syracuse State School. Being in early November, the weather, as Ruth could best recollect, was sunny and clear but quite cold. Ruth also thought that shortly after Betty escaped from the school, there was a lot of turmoil, and a number of employees got reprimanded and even fired for the incident. Ruth also remembered hearing the state school closed, at least in the form that it existed while Ruth was there, soon after she was released.

Ruth said that they wouldn't allow you to leave unless you had a ride to wherever you were released. As best she recalls, she was picked up in Syracuse by her mother and Harry Culver, who owned a yellow car. They departed to her mother's apartment on North Washington Street in Mohawk. Betty, Ruth's mother, never owned a home. As Ruth put it, "She only lived in dives." The apartment had three bedrooms of which Ruth got one. Ruth felt that her mother tried to keep the apartment up but wasn't very successful. Even when Betty was married to Culver, as Ruth put it again, "She liked to run." She would take a bus to Utica to meet someone named Bob. Ironically, when she returned, she would have money. Harry, her husband, either didn't know about it or didn't care. Ruth felt he knew exactly what was happening. Betty would go once or twice a week by bus to meet with Bob.

Ruth's aunt Thelma, who lived across the street from her on North Washington Street, was always very good to her. Ruth told us numerous times that she really loved her aunt, and had she known, she would have gone to live with her aunt Thelma before her uncle Wally on Orchard Street in Frankfort. But then if that had happened, I may have never come in contact with her, and we wouldn't be sitting here writing *Ruthie Deeply*. When the situation would get bad in Ruth's own home, she would go to spend time with her aunt Thelma in a much more serene, controlled environment. Ruth was now in a much better situation than she was in the Syracuse State School yet still a very erratic environment. Ruth only lived in her mother's apartment for a very short period of time. Betty was all over town while being married to Harry, and still with Bob in the picture. For the short period that Ruth lived with her mother she hadn't found a job yet. Still, her mother wanted money from her. During that time, Ruth bought a bike at Dick's Bike Shop in Herkimer so she could have transportation to look for a job. Ruth did eventually find a job at Prine's Cleaners in Ilion. Ruth worked at Prine's for about six months until she began passing out from the heat that the pressers created. Prine's changed her job from the Ilion store to the Herkimer store, but it had the same effect on her. Ironically, Ruth's job was then changed from working on the pressers to working on the sheet rollers. The sheets reappeared in her life, but this time for a different purpose. At least we hoped. While working, Ruth recalled almost getting her hand and arm caught in one of the rollers that ended her employment at Prine's Cleaners. Also, while working at Prine's Cleaners during the day, Ruth would then go work at night at the Supreme Dairy. Ruth's job was washing the equipment used to pasteurize milk. Looking back, Ruth felt the main purpose for doing all this work was to keep away from her mother.

When Ruth refused to give her mother any money, Betty told her she had to leave. Betty took the few possessions that Ruth had and abruptly put them on the front porch for Ruth to come and get at some point. Those few possessions sat on the porch for probably a few days until Ruth's aunt, Marge Richardson, and Ruth came and got them.

With her newfound freedom, Ruth was starting to enjoy her life to some degree. Freedom is an amazing advantage that often is overlooked by us all. Although Ruth is very busy caring for six children and young adults, she still found some time for relaxation. She went roller-skating a few times at a rink in Herkimer, which she cannot remember the exact location of and, once in a while, to the movies in Frankfort.

In fall of 1961, Ruth went to a newsstand in Ilion named Power's to buy a watch for work. With a smile, Ruth remembered

George being in Power's News and recalled George being related to the owner. George introduced himself to Ruth and asked her if she would like to go bowling at the State Bowling Center, which still is in business today. Ruth thought George was still wearing his Air Force uniform when she met him. Air Force told him he was too skinny and needed to eat bananas. It seemed he ate bananas all day and never gained any weight. That same day, George walked to Ruth's aunt's house to pick her up for bowling. After bowling, Ruth kept in touch with George mostly by phone. For a while, George lived in Ilion then moved to Frankfort and rented a room from Ruth's uncle Wally on Orchard Street across the street from my grandmother's house.

Ruth vividly remembers a story concerning George's room at Wally's house. She said with a chuckle, "George was working in the kitchen at the rest area on the New York State Thruway in Schuyler. When he came home from work about five, and he took his shirt off to lie down on the bed, and apparently one of Wally's cats had pooped on his bed. George wasn't happy about lying in the cat poop. When George found the cat, he picked him up and threw it outside. I didn't say anything because George had a mean streak. The cat was a big tabby cat named Mr. Grey. I'm not sure if the cat ever came back. George could be mean, even to his kids at times."

Ruth laughed about it now, but there were times in her marriage when it got ugly. Even at that, Ruth always stood up for herself and her kids when she knew in her gut that something was wrong.

Ruth and George dated for one and a half years while they both resided separately at her uncle Wally's house. There being about ten bedrooms in Wally's house, which some were rented out to strangers. Ruth always kept her door locked. After dating for a year and half, Ruth and George were married at the Methodist Church in Ilion, across from the Ilion Public Library, which both are still open today. Ruth was very close with my mother. My mother did Ruth's hair for her wedding day and departed for the church in her sister Loretta's gown from my house. After the ceremony, Wally and Marjorie hosted a small reception for the newlyweds at their house. With someone's car, maybe Ruth's, maybe Wally's, Ruth isn't sure, the couple left for their honeymoon in Washington DC. They stayed in a hotel and went to the usual tourist sites. Ruth recalled there being a lot of people, especially by the White House. George and Ruth went out to dinner a few times and stopped in shops to purchase souvenirs. The weather was hot, and she recalled it being a lot of fun.

Upon returning from their honeymoon, Ruth and George continued to live on Orchard Street with Wally and Aunt Marge. While living there, George got a job at Remington Arms Company. Either George or Ruth saw an ad for a house for rent with an option to buy. The house was about three blocks from Remington, which was perfect so George could walk to work, and Ruth hoped to eventually get a job at Remington also. Ruth and George purchased the house with $800 down, which was Ruth's money, and a mortgage payment of $65 a month for thirteen years, payable to a bank that has been long been absorbed called Marine Midland Bank, which is now a part of huge international bank named Hong Kong Shanghai Bank Corp. (HSBC). The $65 a month included taxes. While George worked at Remington, Ruth was doing cleaning in various locations to make extra money. After moving into her house in June of 1964, Mary Christine Ruth's first child was born in September of 1964. Mary was born in St. Luke's Hospital on September 21, 1964, at noon, after three days of labor. She weighed about eight pounds and was twenty-one inches long, and the delivering doctor gave her a clean bill of health. We did not know that Ruth proudly named Mary after Mary LaGraff of the Syracuse State School, the only person in the entire system that treated Ruth with any decency. The delivering doctor also gave Ruth a dozen roses for all that time in labor and delivery.

After the delivery and at least a three-day stay, Ruth was released with the baby to go home. A neighbor named Beverly gave Ruth a crib and set up a nursery as best they could for Mary. Not owning a washing machine, Ruth washed all their laundry by hand on her washboard. The house contained very little furnishings and was sparsely decorated. Even at that, it was a lot better than the Syracuse State School, and it belonged to her. Not owning a refrigerator either, they used an ice chest on the back porch to store items that had to be kept chilled. While George worked, Ruth had a neighbor who had six boys who would also babysit Mary for free while Ruth worked housecleaning to a small degree. The women wanted a little girl so bad that she was always ready to babysit Mary. All this time, the purpose was to save money to purchase things they needed for their home. During this time, George was being responsible, going to work every day, coming home at night to take care of his family, and attending what as best we can guess was the beginning of Herkimer County Community College, in a space that they rented from Remington Arms. He attended classes for two years and then transferred to Oneonta State University by way of the GI Bill. George intended to be a history teacher someday.

Everything was progressing well. George, Ruth, and Mary were happy and healthy.

Three years later in July 15, 1967, Ruth had her second child—this time a boy named Shawn Michael. She named him Shawn as a name she liked. Shawn was also born at St. Luke's Hospital at eight pounds and eight ounces and twenty-three inches long and delivered by the same doctor. The labor was not as long as Mary's, they and went home from the hospital faster the second time around. Shawn used the same as crib as Mary. Now that three years had passed since Mary's birth and George was working at Remington, there were funds saved to purchase items for Shawn's nursery, more furniture for their house, and a wringer washer they purchased shortly after Mary's birth.

In an interview published for the Foster Grandma Program published by Mohawk Valley Community Action, published at best guess fifteen to twenty years ago, Ruth was quoted, "In the 1960s, I had three beautiful children—nine, six, and three. I had no car. I would take my children to get groceries with the youngest in the cart and the older kids helping to push the cart up the hill. I now walk for enjoyment and exercise. I did not own a washing machine. I washed all the clothing and bedding on a washboard by hand. Eventually I became the proud owner of an old wash/wringer machine."

Still in 1967, after four years of marriage, their lives very busy raising a family, all was progressing well, especially using that washing machine.

George continued to work at Remington, and Ruth worked whenever possible doing housecleaning. Everything was still on track. Everyone had their own room, and the days and months kept going by. Ruth's marriage was strong; the home she never had was now in pretty good shape, considering how the Syracuse State School felt that she could never support herself.

"The joke is on them," Ruth said with a chuckle.

Three years later, on August 2, 1970, Ruth and George had their third child and named her Colleen Marie. Colleen weighed eight pounds and was twenty-one inches long—the last member of their family. Again, birthed at St. Luke's Hospital.

After, the good progression of everything in Ruth's life, marriage, and family for about eight years, issues began to arise in the family. Ruth recalled being in the hospital right after Colleen's birth, and a nurse, for some unknown reason, was asking her if she wanted to surrender her baby. We discussed how maybe someone had knowledge of her past history in the Syracuse State School, or perhaps after meeting George, they wondered about the family status, or perhaps for some other unknown reason that Ruth still had no idea of right up to this day. Ruth still wondered if the hospital saw the status of Colleen's early health and felt that Ruth and George couldn't handle the responsibility of raising another child.

After that question, Ruth's quick reply was, "Are you crazy?"

At least Ruth turned them down and took her newborn home without any hesitation. Ruth's mother on the other hand just left her in a boarding home with a "lodger," goodness only knows who that might be, and here was Ruth some thirty-six years later absolutely refusing to give up her child. She obviously learned somewhere to take responsibility for her children. Certainly not from her mother.

After Ruth and the baby were released from the hospital, from the time Colleen was taken home, she cried constantly and pulled her legs and arms up in to a little ball as if she was in pain. Ruth had friends and neighbors in her house all day long trying to help with Colleen. Meanwhile, George would work at Remington Arms at night and attended college classes that were offered at Remington Arms through the newly begun Herkimer County Community College. Ruth didn't see much of George since he was attending classes and working at the same time. This went on for probably three years until at about the age of three, Colleen, in Ruth's opinion, fell into a coma. For those first three years, Ruth took her to various doctors, and no one could make a diagnosis. She was told by one that she was spoiled; another did brain scans, but it showed nothing.

At some point during the winter of 1973, Ruth went in Colleen's room in the morning to see if she was awake.

Ruth described her as being in a "coma." Her description of what happened next was vivid.

She described it, "I went into Colleen's room and found her pale, stone-cold, and wet. So, I brought her in to the kitchen and sat her up in the high chair to see if I could get her color back. I called her doctor right away, and he told me to bring her right in. I bundled her up and walked to the doctor's office in her carriage about fifteen blocks from home. He thought from examining her that she had epilepsy. He prescribed phenobarbital and Dilantin. She was medicated so much that she would just fall backwards and hit her head. So, I just slowly reduced the medication until I finally stopped it. So, from ages three to five, her health is pretty good, but nothing is ever diagnosed. At five she starts kindergarten, and her pediatrician requests the Ilion School District to transport her by bus due to her health issues. I think the other kids were teasing her about taking the bus, so she tried to walk, but she had to stop and rest every block to catch her breath. The block up the hill to my house was terrible for her. She would come in the house so out of breath, she would lie on down on the couch and gasp for air. That really scared me. This played out over a three- or four-year period. To this day, Colleen is still often out of breath and tired."

While all this was taking place, with Colleen being sick, Ruth decided she had had enough and forcibly had George escorted out of the house. George had been consistently abusive to Shawn. At one point when Shawn was about five years old, George struck him so hard that he literally moved six feet across the kitchen and hit the refrigerator. Ruth recalled an incident when she thought George had tried to set the house on fire. After coming home from work, although she didn't see anything, when she went upstairs to her bedroom, she could smell that something had been burning. Her opinion was that George had tried to set the house on fire. She had no evidence to prove that, but it was her gut feeling. Yet, biggest reason for having him removed was because of a horrible incident involving Mary in which he was abusive and tried to take advantage of her. Ruth finally was able to get a decent car that George then proceeded to drive into the garage door while intoxicated. No matter how long Ruth persisted and kept focused, there was always someone or something that dragged her back into chaos. The whole marriage was getting real ugly real fast.

Ruth's recollection of the incident with Mary when George was removed is vivid.

She recalled, "George was in the tub, and Mary came to me in the bedroom. She told me it was about her father, and she started to cry. I went into the bathroom and told him to get out of the tub. Once he was dressed and came into Mary's bedroom, I told Mary to tell me in front of her father what he did to her. I told her that nothing was going to happen to her. She repeated the same thing she told me earlier. George's face turned beet red, and I told him to get out of the house. His face said it all. He went out and got drunk and, later that night, came back. Mary was downstairs getting a diaper for Colleen, and she noticed the Princess phone downstairs was off the hook. When Mary came upstairs with the diaper, George was threatening me with a knife. I called the police. I told Mary that she had saved her father's life by putting that phone on the hook. Otherwise, I would have thrown him out the out of the second-floor window rather than call the police. When the police came, they escorted him out of the house. The police kept George in jail overnight, and we both appeared in court the next morning. The judge asked me what was going on. I was hysterically crying, and all I could say was 'What about my children?' The judge then told the police to take him back home and gave him fifteen minutes to get his belongings out of the house. Then to escort him wherever he wanted to go. The judge ordered him to stay at least a block away from my house, and if he came any closer, for me to call the police. While leaving the courthouse, George said to me, 'You almost hung me.' I replied, 'I didn't hang you enough.'"

George left the house and went to live with his brother in Utica. He then made all sorts of trouble there. At some point, George punched one of his nephews and gave him a black eye. Sometime later her was found in bed with his other nephew. Ruth's sister-in-law called her and wanted to know why she had thrown George out.

When Ruth told her what had happened, she said, "That son of a bitch isn't living in this house."

As best Ruth knew, George then moved to California. About three years later, she received divorce papers but never received a penny in alimony or child support for any of her children. Apparently, George died at about seventy years old, because Ruth began to receive a larger Social Security payment than hers originally was. Indicating he was deceased, in that Social Security pays to the surviving spouse the larger of the couple's benefit.

Ruth was now by herself again with three growing children to support. She worked constantly doing housecleaning for a number of different families in order to keep her household going. Once Mary and Shawn were off to school, she took Colleen and went to work. Ruth told her employers that she had to bring Colleen with her in that she was afraid to leave her alone. Colleen's health was not that strong, and Ruth worried about her constantly. Even with the lack of money, Ruth was able to scrape together enough money to send her kids to a YMCA day camp where they stayed overnight once a week. She surprised herself because she allowed Colleen to stay there, and she is shocked to this day that she allowed it due to how worried she was about her.

As if Ruth didn't have enough issues out of the blue, she developed migraines. At times the pain became overwhelming to the point she was unable to make breakfast, lunch, etc. for her children and had to depend on Mary to make whatever she could for her brother and sister to eat. With Mary being about ten years old, it was an obvious stretch for her to provide dinner for her seven- and four-year-old brother and sister. Yet, Ruth was very proud of Mary in that she was able to pull it together and did a fine job for her brother and sister and even Ruth at such a young age. She beamed with pride when she talked about it on this cold wintry day in December 2018.

When she felt good, she continued to clean houses whenever she could to make money to keep her family intact. All three of her kids were spending their days at a YMCA day camp mostly so she could to continue to work.

Again, as if Ruth didn't have enough to deal with, a seemingly ugly incident arose between Shawn and Colleen. As best Ruth could remember, Shawn was continually experiencing behavior problems both inside and outside of the family. In this particular case, Shawn behaved in a very irresponsible manner toward his sister. At another time, he endangered the safety of the whole family in the sense of their house. His actions had the potential to make the entire family homeless. Ruth, after all her experiences, saw the possibility of long-term problems for him and was able to obtain counseling services through a county-based family services program. The effect was minimal. Shawn continued to have problems over the next few years to the extent he eventually ended up in foster care for approximately one year. At eighteen, Shawn was released from foster care and joined the National Guard. He did six months of basic training and was placed in a local National Guard unit. He experienced some issues with the National Guard to the extent that they showed up at Ruth's house asking all sorts of questions and wanting to search his room. To this day, Ruth had no idea of what the issue was and really didn't want to find out. Finally, the National Guard, for a variety of reasons unknown to this day, released him from duty.

He returned home to live with Ruth and Colleen while Colleen was attending Ilion High School. The same type of problem that Shawn previously had with his sister bubbled to the surface again. In this case, he got involved with the legal system, and there was not much Ruth could do for him. The situation led to serious criminal charges to which Shawn pled guilty and served a long penalty.

Ruth recalled, "I remember being called to the Herkimer County Jail to see my son and crying the entire time. The Sheriff Officer was telling my son, 'Look what you are doing to your mother.' He was then sent to a state prison for six years and released with four years of parole. I used to go see him once a week at the county jail while his case was making its way through the courts. I didn't know what to think. It is so hard when it is your child, and you can't do anything about it. I still don't know what to make of it. People that I worked for at the time felt so bad for me. But there was nothing they or I could do. It was pretty bad for me. No one can understand what it is like until they go through it. He was so far away in different prisons all over New York State. He didn't make it easy on himself or any of us. Colleen was in high school, and all her friends knew. They felt so bad for her. It was in the newspaper, and everyone knew about it. I believe his first wife knew about his problems, but the second one, I'm not sure. That is between the two of them."

Shawn has resided in Sylvan Beach, New York, for a number of years now, and Ruth hears from him on occasion. In previous years, once in a while, he would contact Ruth and take her out to dinner. This year he sent her a birthday card and a Christmas card for the first time in a long time.

With all the bad experiences Ruth has had in her life up to this point, starting with being abandoned at four months old, right through the tragedy of the Syracuse State School, her marriage gone bad, and struggling to keep her family provided for—with all that, she amazingly has done very well for herself.

As she so aptly put with a chuckle, "I still have my mind."

And she is 100 percent correct.

And her story was still not finished.

After about six weeks and a long vacation to Lahaina, Maui, then to Pleasanton and San Francisco, California, home for about five days to get Michael and Alaina back to college, then Carol and I were off again to Tybee Island, Georgia, and Savannah to a few days in Charlestown, South Carolina—we picked up on *Ruthie Deeply* again.

Mary being the oldest was now at Mohawk High School, not Ilion High School, due to the fact that she refused to attend school every day and was court-ordered to foster care in a home by the Mohawk School District. Being about sixteen years old at the time and living about two miles away, Ruth went to see her every day, and on some occasions, the foster family would invite Ruth to stay for dinner, which she would do. That placement was the second one for Mary. The first placement for Mary was terrible. As Ruth recalled, the home was located in somewhere southern Herkimer County towards West Winfield. The family was German and didn't speak English a great deal. Mary did not like the situation in that the host family had two, possibly three, children of their own plus two or three more foster children. In Ruth's opinion, no child should ever have been placed there. The home was pretty much in turmoil all the time. Mary only lasted about two weeks, and she ran away back home to Ruth. The second placement in Mohawk was a much better environment for Mary. The foster family was very good to her, and then maybe two other children in their care. Ruth could see her every day, which made both of them happier at least. While Mary was in Mohawk, a guy named Henry spotted her walking to school and started following her all over town. Being about ten years older than Mary, married with four kids, Henry would host beer parties for mostly underage kids in the neighborhood while his wife was working. Mary being one of those neighborhood kids would attend, opening up a big opportunity for Henry to get close to Mary. As sure as the day is long, Mary got pregnant and gave birth to a daughter who she named Adrienne. At some point, Henry's wife left the household, and Mary attempted to set up a new household with Henry. Again, as best Ruth could recollect, the couple with the new baby moved to the New York City area, and Ruth could not be sure what happened to the other children. While in residing in New York City, there was an incident of violent domestic abuse that left Mary with no option but to move back to Ilion without her daughter. He didn't last long in New York and was soon back in Ilion and again attempting to set up a household. That didn't work for the second or third time, and Mary was finally no longer a minor. In the meantime, Ruth saw what was happening and tried to get custody of her granddaughter Adrienne. That didn't work, and Henry was awarded custody of the child. Ruth again went to court to obtain custody and lost, with some recollection of Henry specifically lying while under oath. Ruth was still wanting custody of Adrienne, and Henry decided to move back to New York City. Ruth and Mary made several trips to New York City to see Adrienne but could never seem to locate Henry and Adrienne. This went on for six months to a year, then finally Mary and Ruth gave up trying to locate Henry and Adrienne. At some point after this time period, Mary decided to move to Virginia. While there, Ruth has no idea for how long, Mary met and married Ed. The couple was married for a short time and then had a son named Emmitt. After the birth of Emmitt in June of 1996, Mary was again pregnant—this time with twin boys. Ruth's best recollection was that they were stillborn on March 19, 1997. On that sad news, Ruth flew to Virginia but didn't have the heart to go to the hospital to see her two deceased grandchildren. Ruth did attend their funeral while in Virginia, obviously under great stress. Not long after the passing of the twins, Mary's husband, Ed, died on September 13, 1997, when Emmitt was a little over a year old. Ruth was not sure of the cause of Ed's death; she remembered possibly an overdose or congestive heart failure. Mary never remarried and until this day lives in Virginia. Ruth still occasionally talks with Mary on the phone but not to any great extent. When Mary came to visit, perhaps once a year, it usually ended up as a problem for Ruth and Mary. The mother-daughter relationship was there, but not as strong as Ruth, or maybe even Mary, would like it to be. There are many emotional scars that never seem to heal but rather keep reopening after all these years.

While all the heartbreak for Ruth was occurring, Shawn during this time was residing in Sylvan Beach and did attend his brother-in-law Ed's funeral but not his twin nephews' funeral. Colleen continued to do well in high school and was elected class secretary. She was also involved in sports and did well particularly in track and field.

Ruth was continuing to work through all of it, mostly for the Masons and other friends of theirs that belonged to the local temple.

She worked at least five days a week, many weeks six, in order to feed and maintain her family. Ruth waited until her kids all got off to school so that she could go to work. She repeatedly stressed how good and fair the Masons were to her, and continue to be to this day. They helped and supported through the sixty-five years she has known them. Without all the aid that people like the Masons and even my own father and mother gave her, she will readily admit she doesn't know she would have survived this long.

As Shawn and Mary continued to get older and were at least not living at home, although problems persisted with them, Colleen was getting ready to graduate from Ilion High and wanted to apply at Elizabeth's School of Nursing to study to be a registered nurse. She applied, was accepted, but first attended Herkimer County BOCES and enrolled in the LPN program. After a short period of time at BOCES, she then enrolled at St. Elizabeth's. As best Ruth can remember, Colleen was enrolled at St. Elizabeth's for possibly a year but never graduated. She then decided to change schools and enrolled at Morrisville State College to continue with studying nursing. Ruth cannot be certain if she ever graduated from Morrisville or not, but as she remembers, when she went to do an internship with a local MD in Little Falls, she changed her mind completely about nursing and decided nursing was not for her. She got a job working at a local McDonalds temporarily but did gain some medical experience while at BOCES, St. Elizabeth's, and Morrisville State College, which led her to a job at an agency in Utica first then Albany selling health care insurance within the same company. She did pretty well in that job and, along the way the way, met her future husband, Rob, whom she married in 1993, and they had their first child in 1995.

In about 1998, while working on remodeling her bathroom, Ruth needed to buy materials to do the job. She saw an advertisement in the newspaper by a local person selling surplus materials. Not having access to a lot of money, Ruth was looking to save a few dollars any way she could, so she contacted the seller. Turned out to be someone named Walt, a retired employee of a mobile home company; as a retirement business, he bought and sold surplus materials from a variety of sources. Walt at the time was living with his daughter in that he was losing his sight and was not able to live alone any longer. Walt was finding it difficult to live with his daughter because she treated him terribly. Walt then called Ruth from his daughter's and asked Ruth if she could live with her. He was literally destitute, having liquidated all his assets and given the proceeds to his daughter as a payment for living with her to the end of his life. That arrangement was not working out to even a minimal degree, so it seemed he found a friendly ear with Ruth and pursued it. Sure enough, Ruth, having such a good heart, understood his plight and allowed Walt to move into her house with her. As best Ruth could recall, she was living in her house alone when Walt moved in.

"We helped each other while he lived at my house. Walt drove for a short time after he moved in. We would drive to my daughter's house in Albany. On occasion, we would go to Richfield Springs to visit Walt's daughter. It was helpful to have Walt drive and pick up groceries with me or run other errands because I didn't have any other transportation. Since Walt was getting older, it was hard for him to help around the house. He was having a hard time getting up and down the stairs into the house. Plus, his sight was failing more and more each day."

Ruth slept in her room upstairs, and Walt slept downstairs in the living room on the couch, or Ruth may have bought a daybed for him to sleep on. The best recollection Ruth has of the time was that he may have lived with Ruth for at least ten years and, in the end, passed away in her house. Walt was about twelve to fifteen years older than Ruth, and while he lived there, he helped support the household. He would buy groceries, pay for repairs, and at times pay for an occasion's dinner out. Walt was always willing to pitch in money to make the household expenses meet should Ruth be unable to pay all her bills. Walt often bought gifts and necessities for Ruth's kids. Probably the largest benefit was that at times, he provided a vehicle when Ruth may have not had one. There was a possibility that Walt might have helped Colleen pay for some minor updates and repairs to her first house so they could get a better price for selling it. He wasn't wealthy, but he did have access to some money. He also enjoyed buying New York State lottery "scratch-off tickets."

On the negative side, Ruth remembers there would be times when he was quite mean. "He was pretty sick, losing his sight, etc. and all that can manifest in the form of anger. Colleen overall wasn't really fond of him and often stated, 'He's a grumpy old man.'"

Overall, it worked out pretty well for him and Ruth. He helped her when she needed it, and she helped him when he needed it for over ten years. Walt was married for many years prior to meeting Ruth, served his country probably in World War II, and worked every day for many years.

The 1990s began with Ruth having two cats and Walt keeping her company in her house. Everything seemed settled down, but there were still some unresolved issues with Ruth's granddaughter Adrienne. Ruth still was looking to gain custody of the child while Mary was not really sure what to do. Her former husband, Henry, was portraying Mary to the courts as having a drinking issue and not being able to care for the child properly. Ruth had the child evaluated by Bassett Hospital Child Care and Herkimer County Family Services, both of which agreed that the child would be better off being in Ruth's custody and reported that opinion to the Herkimer County Family Court.

Ruth's attorney strongly fought the case for placement with Ruth in the court, only to have the decision to fall to the child's husband. Ruth was livid with the decision, and still is. She feels the child was profoundly damaged by the decision and probably was having issues right to this day. Although she has no way of knowing for certain in that she hasn't seen the Adrienne since she was about two to five years old. Adrienne herself, to the best of Ruth's knowledge, has only two children of her own.

After being married in 1993, Colleen and Rob welcomed their first child, Evan, in 1995. Evan was born at about four pounds and remained in the hospital until he weighed five pounds. Colleen and Rob were required by the hospital for one of them to stay overnight in the hospital with Evan in order for them to learn the necessary skills to use were Evan to get sick at home once he was released. Evan was not born early, just very underweight.

WEDDINGS

Mr. and Mrs. Robert Goodspeed

Once Evan was released from the hospital, everything started to fall in place. At that time, Ruth wasn't working much, and Colleen wanted to return to work. Ruth offered to come and live with Colleen and her husband and son so Colleen could return to work. As best Ruth can remember, she lived on and off with Colleen for about a year while Colleen and her husband were working. After about a year, Evan had a normal weight for a child his age and was deemed by his doctor to be healthy. Ruth had a baby shower for Colleen at the Mohawk Station, a local restaurant that was Colleen's favorite. Along with the baby shower, Evan was also baptized by Father Greene of the Episcopal Church in Ilion. Ruth was working for the owner of the restaurant cleaning his house and the building across the street from the restaurant, which was housing college students. She had the party at the Mohawk Station, and the owner, since Ruth worked for him, even gave Ruth a small discount. The shower was a small family gathering attended by Ruth's daughter Mary and her two children, Adrienne and Emmitt. Along with Roger Hall, Ruth's nephew, who also attended. Ruth also went and invited a few of Colleen's local friends from high school. The food provided was a Sunday buffet that the restaurant offered every Sunday. Colleen and her husband purchased a house in Schenectady that they intended to modernize and resell at a profit. The proposition worked out well. The young couple was able to sell the house at a good profit. Colleen was not crazy about her children attending the Schenectady City Schools due to the school district's weak reputation. They purchased another fixer-upper in Duanesburg again with the intention of modernizing it and reselling at a profit. While living in Duanesburg, Colleen and Rob welcomed three more children to their family—Cameron, Luke, and Faith. The family resided in Duanesburg for about ten years until an incident in the school district with Faith and a teacher while in first grade. With the earlier intention of selling their house at a profit, now that ten years had gone by, Colleen and Rob decided to sell their house and move to Glenville, New York. For about two years, Colleen, Rob, and their children rented a house in Glenville while they searched for a house to buy. The main purpose of the move being the strong reputation the Glenville Schools had and a house to reside in for possibly the rest of their lives.

Throughout that ten-to-twelve-year period, Ruth continued to help Colleen and her family in any way possible. She continued to go back and forth to babysit when necessary. If any or all of the children were sick, Ruth would go stay with them while the parents worked.

An incident occurred when Faith was in preschool that Ruth remembered vividly. It seemed that Faith had a health scare of unknown origin that frightened Ruth. While in preschool, Faith possibly fell into a seizure. The preschool called 911, and the EMS (emergency medical service) brought Faith to the emergency room. The doctors examined her, gave her a brain scan, and decided to keep her at the hospital for a few hours for observation purposes. In the end, there was no diagnosis of any problem, and Faith was released. Yet, in the long run, Ruth's scare with Faith proved prophetic in that

Faith being twelve years old now did receive some services from the school district she attended to help her succeed in school. After all those years in the New York State foster care system, obviously Ruth learned a lot more than they ever taught her. Certainly Ruth learned well beyond her self-taught ability to read and write, which the New York State foster care system never took the time to teach her to do. Very sad but very evident.

The move to Glenville was working out for the family. All the children were enrolled in the Glenville Schools and doing pretty well. Ruth does recall another situation that developed early after the move, but in the long run, it was not a problem. As with any student, especially a high school student that has a group of established friends at the high school they attend, when Evan moved to the Glenville Schools, there was a period of adjustment. He had lost his network of friends from Duanesburg and now had to establish a new set of friends. That is a common challenge anytime a young or old person moves from one area to another. Naturally, there was a period of adjustment. After some time when Evan established a set of new friends, everything fell into place. Ruth does recall a situation where Colleen wondered if she had done the right thing for her whole family and questioned herself as to whether or not she was only looking out for Faith's best interest and maybe not her entire family's.

During this process, Ruth's contact with Shawn and Mary was minimal. She would hear from Shawn on occasion, usually at Christmastime, which most times ended with a confrontation. As was the case right to the present, the contact was practically nonexistent and generally strained. Mary, on the other hand, still maintained the same relationship she had with her mother also up to this day. Ruth would hear from her more than she heard from Shawn, but it was nowhere near the relationship she has with Colleen.

As we got ready to break for lunch, Carol started telling Ruth about the pickled onions she made for the tacos dinner last night. That rang a bell for Ruth.

She said, "When I first got out of the foster care, or maybe even when I was living with my mother at times, before my release, there was little or any food in the house. When you have nothing to eat, you'll eat just about anything. I never remember my mother cooking anything. Whatever there was available to eat, I just ate it, and most times there was nothing. Never remember any fruit or vegetables in the house. There is really not much that I remember because I was so young and constantly moving from place to place. Good thing I liked onions because I ate plenty of onion sandwiches. I am not sure where the idea of the onion sandwiches came from, but at least it was something to eat, which is always better than nothing. Bread and milk were better than having nothing."

All that memory flowed from talking about pickled onions.

Part 3

Chapter 9

Give Back

The century turned as Ruth turned sixty-six. As she always said, "The first hundred years are the hardest." and "You can't kill cast iron."

Ruth began a job at the Foster Grandparents Program part of Head Start, funded by Mohawk Valley Community Action in 2001. The program was intended to aid preschool children in development of school-ready skills in reading and math. Students arrived at 8:30 a.m. and departed at 2:30 p.m. The program was housed in Herkimer, in a building separate from a low-income housing project. Students were typically from the local school districts that were identified as being "possibly at a higher risk to not succeed in kindergarten and the primary grades." Most students were aged three to five years old. Ruth's day started at 8:00 a.m. and ran through to 1:30 p.m. Although it is a volunteer position, Ruth got paid $2.65 per hour. Every two weeks, Ruth netted a pay of $140. It's not a lot of money, but it helped her pay the bills and have a little extra.

Typically, after the students got off the bus, they would store their belongings, wash their hands, and the school day began. The class had eighteen students with very small needs to large needs. The first assignment was for everyone to practice writing their name. Usually in September, everyone needed practice; but as the school year progressed, it got down to maybe five or six that still needed it. Next, students would sit in a circle and would play board games with each other or look at books or just visit. Soon after that, being a Head Start program, everyone was served breakfast. The program was intended to be an all-inclusive day grounded in education but still meant to serve nutritional and family needs. After breakfast was served and cleaned up for approximately two hours, students engaged in academics such as addition/subtraction, basic reading skills such as sight words, and practice with letters/writing simple sentences. Much of the day was also devoted to social skills, sharing and being respectful to yourself and others. By this time, lunch was ready. After lunch, everyone washed their hands and got a cot for a nap. The nap was set up for about an hour, followed by washing their hands again, having a snack, and getting ready to go home. Ruth felt that for many of the children that came to the class, when they reached public school, they were often classified with handicap conditions. She had a few deaf students over the years. She spent a lot of her day working hand in hand with psychologists, social workers, and speech therapists.

That certainly made me wonder what those coworkers would think of Ruth if they knew her life story.

I bet they would be pretty impressed.

Ruth recalled when she first started, the student population seemed much worse. She had students that would throw chairs, fight, swear, and destroy property. Ruth saw some of those students now and then, and they seemed to have done pretty good. Some she saw were not so good. Still to this day, in the class, a student such as the old ones would present similar issues in the class, but she doesn't see as many these days. There was an incident when she first started out where a girl accused Ruth of hitting her. The program spent a lot of time emphasizing personal hygiene. Ruth was helping this young girl brush her teeth after having breakfast. After she was finished brushing, the girl reported to the teacher that Ruth had hit her. When the teacher questioned Ruth about it, naturally Ruth had denied having done it. Simply because she didn't. Ruth requested that the teacher view the security video to determine what the truth was. Sure enough, Ruth never put a hand on the girl other than to help her brush her teeth. The entire incident was categorically dismissed because it had never happened. As with everything else in this world, there has to be a lot of preventive measures taken to stop bad situations from occurring. It is a shame, but it is a fact of life. Now when a student goes in the bathroom, they have to be accompanied by two adults to prevent any situations from occurring where someone might get hurt. Three people in the bathroom at the same time to prevent any unforeseen harm occurring or questionable behavior from happening is overkill, but it is sadly a necessity. Ruth told us this was never necessary when she first started volunteering at the Foster Grandparents. Even though she was paid that minimal amount, she was still considered a volunteer. Some of Ruth's duties, along with the other employees', were to take the class to the grocery store, fire department, and library to get these young people exposed to everyday life in a small community. Life skills are important no matter where you live, no matter what your age or socioeconomic background. Never having been there myself, knowing Ruth as well as I do, I bet she is the first person to pitch in. No matter what the need. She does all of this gladly for $2.65 per hour. "Give back" has been the name of the game for almost twenty years. After all the long- and short-term stresses of her life, she was still proud to help others.

Recently, a student came into the class by the name of Elijah. Ruth felt that chances were he had a number of disabilities affecting him. She felt over all he was a nice little boy but had a lot of problems at home, emotionally and even some physical issues. When the class went to a playground, Elias immediately started screaming and running as best he could around the playground. A teacher's aide with the class tried to get his behavior under control, but he would have none of it. The aide, not knowing what to do, brought him back inside. When Ruth saw what was happening, she urged the teacher and teacher's aide to have patience. She felt he didn't know how to react on a playground because he had probably never been there before. Much like Ruth told us when she was first placed in Farchione's house in Syracuse in her early twenties, and the Farchiones had a birthday party for Ruth, she didn't know how to react. No one had ever been that nice to her. No one had ever had a birthday party plus made a cake for her and gave her a gift. The Farchiones even went as far as inviting Mrs. LaGraff to come. Ruth didn't know what to do. She had never been put in a situation like that before.

Ruth immediately saw the similarity between her situation at the Farchiones' in 1957 and Elijah's situation in 2019. Maybe that's why she's the one that urged patience with Elijah. She lived through this type of experience. Although it was a long time ago, she readily admitted she didn't know how to be nice to people since no one had been nice to her. Elijah didn't know how to react on a playground because he had never been on one. I had a similar experience in the fall of 2018 on Long Sand Beach in Maine. While I was out taking a walk, a young man about twenty-five years was walking his six-month-old puppy on the beach. The dog ran over to me and wanted to be played with. The dog's owner explained to me that he wouldn't bite, and it was his first time on a beach. The surf, the sun, the sand, and all the stimuli of the beach flooded this dog's senses. His senses were overwhelmed.

As were Ruth's at her first ever birthday party at the Farchiones' in 1957, the dog's in November of 2018 while on the beach for the first time, and Elijah's first time stepping on a playground.

Ruth also saw the changes that had taken place over all these years in that Elijah and his family now at least have a place where they can get some help. Ruth didn't have anything. It was completely directionless. Everything was a "fly by the seat of your pants" situation. She knew way back in the Syracuse State School that she was being inappropriate, but she didn't care. She knew it was wrong to be nose-to-nose with Mrs. Jackson telling her, "Kill me if that's what makes you happy, go for it." Ruth was her own worst enemy, and she didn't care. At least that's what they told her, and that's what she believed. Ruth strongly felt that often they made you out to be worse than you were. But being a young inexperienced woman in a volatile situation, she bought it.

In some ways, that hurt her.

Yet, in other ways, it helped her. It is what allowed her to survive all these years, in often terrible situations, and live to give back.

Fittingly, Ruth's nickname in the class was Gramma Ruth.

How fitting for a woman that has endured a life such as hers, has her own grandchildren, and has had strangers' children calling her Gramma Ruth for over eighteen years.

Carol and I took a few hours this week to contact three book publishers to get some initial information about publishing *Ruthie Deeply*. It seemed that there were a number of ways to go about it. Self-publishing seems to be the way many writers go these days, but only time will tell. The publishers I spoke to this week all had different conditions to publish, with all of them seeming to have a variety of ins and outs, so to speak. Again, only time will tell what the correct path is.

Spring seemed to have finally arrived in Upstate New York when Ruth showed up with Little Foot. She came in very short of breath. It must have taken her twenty minutes of rest to catch her breath. Poor woman.

Ruth told us, "I wouldn't wish this on anybody."

I asked, "Would you wish it on Jackson at the state school in light of the mean things she did to you for all those years?"

In typical Ruth fashion, she replied, "No, I couldn't even wish it on her."

Pure, simple, down-to-earth Ruth.

> All of us profit from being corrected, if we are corrected in a positive way. There is no better way to keep someone doing the right things the right way than by letting them know how much you appreciate their performance. If you do that one simple thing, then human nature will take it from there. (Sam Walton, founder of Walmart)

For the first time in Ruth's entire life, beginning about the year 2000, her children have all grown up, and she was in a position of being a grandmother. Her marriage has been long dissolved, and Ruth was free to pursue the rest of her life with few, if any, negative restraints. Although life being what it is, there is always the possibility of more harm being done.

> ## Kid of the Week
>
> ### Cameron Goodspeed of Duanesburg
>
> I would like to nominate my nephew, 6-year-old Cameron Goodspeed of Duanesburg, as the Kid of the Week. Last Saturday, Cameron handled a very couragous task for someone the age of only 6 while his grandmother was babysitting him. While on a ladder attempting to hang curtains, his grandmother fell from the ladder and suffered compound fractures to her leg and was bleeding profusely. Because they could not locate the phone and the grandmother could not move, the grandmother instructed Cameron to go to the neighbor's house to ask them to call 911. The house was a 1/4 mile away. This little boy did as he was told and in turn according to the police trooper saved his grandmother's life. If he had not done this, his grandmother would have bled to death. We think that this was quite amazing considering his age, and feel he should be recognized for his efforts to help his grandmother and to have saved her life.
>
> submitted by Marie and Mike Goodspeed

In the spring of 2008, Ruth's daughter Colleen asked Ruth to come to Duanesburg to watch her two grandchildren while Colleen and her husband went to New York City for a swim meet that Colleen's team, Colleen's son Evan being a member of the team, were competing in. While Ruth was on a ladder attempting to hang curtains, Cameron at about six years old and Luke about three were milling around the house playing with their toys and watching television. As fate would have it, Ruth fell off the ladder, suffering compound fractures on her left leg all the while bleeding profusely. With the fractures, Ruth was unable to move, and Cameron couldn't locate the telephone. She told Cameron to run to a neighbor's house about a quarter of a mile away and ask them to call 911. The then six-year-old Cameron did exactly as his grandmother asked him, and for his efforts, he was proclaimed Kid of the Week in the local newspaper. Within five minutes, a New York State trooper arrived with an ambulance a few minutes behind. Ruth was transported to Albany Medical Center, where surgery was performed to repair the fractures. Being about seventy-two years old at the time, the doctors at the hospital stabilized her but waited for her daughter to come from the swim meet in New York City. In the meantime, the State trooper that responded waited with Cameron and Luke until Cameron or Colleen were able to locate someone to stay with the children so the officer could leave. Altogether, probably about six or seven hours elapsed until Colleen arrived from New York City. After a lengthy surgery, Ruth spent about ten days in the hospital then to Sunny View Rehabilitation Center for another ten days. While in the hospital, as if she didn't have enough going on, something happened on the second day of her ten-day stay. Ruth was reaching for the cell phone that Colleen had let her borrow, which was ringing with a call from Colleen. Ruth was sitting in a wheelchair, and when she reached for the phone, she lost her balance and fractured her wrist. Ruth doesn't remember if it was the same doctor who did the surgery on her leg, but when the doctor did come to visit her, he told her, "You've got to stop breaking bones." Ruth was accepted in the Sunny View Rehab only with a guarantee from her that she could do approximately nine hours a day of rehab. If the patient wasn't able to do it, they would be released from that facility. The therapist that agreed to work with Ruth on her rehab accepted her as her patient because, "She had sense enough to try to get better." Ruth made a strong impression on the entire rehab facility with her efforts. Literally everyone she came in contact with told her that she was doing as well as anyone they had ever had in the facility, and she inspired many of them.

Ruth remembered some quirky encounters in the hospital.

When Colleen finally arrived and was discussing the situation with the doctors who were to do the surgery, she commented to the older of the two doctors how young the assisting doctor was. The older of the two told Colleen, "Don't worry, I'll keep my eyes on him."

When it was all finished, the elder doctor of the two told Ruth, "You're one helluva tough person to have waited that long for that complicated of a surgery."

Isn't that what allowed her to survive—all of the negatives she had experienced up to approximately seventy-two at that time and eighty-four on this Saturday, April 27, 2019?

After her release from Sunny View, Ruth stayed with Colleen for about a month and continued outpatient therapy. Ruth staying at Colleen's house, she paid her neighbor $25 a week to take care of her cats, clean the litter box, etc. Ruth came home from Colleen's to find that her neighbor had done a terrible job. Rob, Colleen, and Ruth in a wheelchair cleaned the entire house from scrubbing floors to cleaning the litter box to vacuuming the entire house. For a few days, she had a visiting nurse to come and check on her. She had a home health aide to vacuum, mop, make her bed, and run a few errands. The visiting health aide tried to do all the work, but Ruth was fussy about it and at times locked her wheelchair and vacuumed/mopped from the wheelchair. To keep herself busy, Leah, a teacher at Head Start, would pick Ruth up so she could go to Head Start to visit with the kids. Ruth also continued to attend the board meetings of Community Action, where she was on the board, by connecting rides with other people from Ilion that were also on the board, while she was still on crutches recovering from her leg surgery.

As unlikely as it could get, Ruth was laid up recuperating for about a year. Since she was unable to drive, she spent most of her time at home. Herkimer County provided home health care services in the form of grocery shopping, light housework, etc. Just as likely as unlikely, Ruth continued to wash her own laundry and hung it out to dry, with her bad leg resting on the wheelchair. After that slow recovery, when she felt better, she began again to attend her grandchildren's swim meets, graduations, birthday parties, etc. Numerous friends would bring her meals and help her in a variety of ways. Slowly she began to drive again and regain her independence. As soon as she was able, she went back to work at Head Start and the Foster Grandparents program. Even though the injury slowed her down, she still was active and maintained her independent lifestyle. Overall, her life finally started to become a very familiar routine and was not constantly flooded with controversy. In true form, she did even more volunteer work at Mohawk Valley Community Action. When Ruth attended her first board meeting after the accident, the other members were all happy to see her and warmly welcomed her back. She accepted a term on the Human Resources Committee of the board and was integral in developing and evolving policies for employees. Ruth also worked on programs for individuals to aid them in their home and community lives in order to support good citizenship and community involvement.

Head Start Volunteer Award

This Certificate is Awarded to:
Foster Grandparent Volunteer
Ruth Morgan
for outstanding volunteer service to the
Head Start Program during the past year.

When Ruth returned to work at Head Start, she spent most of her day working one-on-one with a specific student. She attended meetings on programing for her students and was always welcome to express an opinion concerning her students. Ruth had now been involved with Head Start for eighteen years and continued to be an important cog in the structure of the program. In light of the life that Ruth had led, she has full empathy for the students involved, whether it's her one-on-one student or any student in Head Start. Ruth had no intention of leaving the job until she couldn't do it anymore. On graduation day 2019, Ruth was thrilled that two of the teachers gave her gifts of blouses in front of all the students, parents, and staff. She giggled about it as she explained it to Carol and me today.

In May of 2014, the Utica *Observer-Dispatch* published an article citing Ruth as a Mohawk Valley Community Action "Community Achiever" for overcoming poverty. That was the article that I read in the newspaper that started this five-year process of *Ruthie Deeply*. That award was truly indicative of the life Ruth led. The award was presented to Ruth by Amy Turner, executive director of Mohawk Valley Community Action. Ruth was certainly proud of her achievements.

Life being complicated no matter how much an individual tries to keep it simple, in winter of 2017, Mohawk Valley Community Action came to the conclusion that Ruth's position on the board of directors coupled with the fact that she had received minimal services from Community Action put her in a "conflict of interest" situation. Community Action decided that her services on the board of directors were no longer appropriate. Ruth being very proud of the fact that she served on that board went on her own and solicited eleven letters from various individuals as to why she should continue to serve on the board of directors. Mohawk Valley Community Action, much to Ruth's and my dismay, would have no part of it, and she was released. In my opinion, the entire episode was a poorly shaded effort to remove the most qualified individual, having lived the lifestyle Community Action was intending to prevent, from their midst. The board was more interested in gathering information from a study rather than dealing with the individual that lived her entire life in the environment they were attempting to eliminate. Indeed a sad situation that was only exacerbated by the board of directors of Mohawk Valley Community Action.

Yet, as Elvis Presley once said, "Truth is like the sun, you can shut it out for a time, but ain't it goin' away."

In June of 2017, Ann Perry of Head Start, which may receive some funding from Mohawk Valley Community Action, asked Ruth if she would attend with her and two others a conference in Seattle, Washington, dedicated to aiding elderly citizens in controlling their finances and avoiding poverty. It was especially valuable for Ruth in light of the situations she often found herself in while trying to raise three children by herself. Ruth had no education or skill to speak of and was often confronted by poverty. What better "primary source" could there be than walking, talking Ruth Morgan.

To quote Adlai Stevenson, "All progress has resulted from people who took unpopular positions."

To quote Ruth Morgan, "It never goes away. There are times I still cry about it. The first one hundred years are the hardest."

"Thank God things change"
—Ruth 2020

About the Author

This book is a collaborative project by Ruth Morgan, Carol Palmieri, and the author, Vincent Palmieri. The author and collaborators live in Upstate New York and have been friends for sixty years. Without Ruth's memory and knowledge, this book could never have been written. Ruth's version of her life, as opposed to the New York State foster care system's version, can now finally be heard.